CELESTE PARRISH and EDUCATIONAL REFORM in the PROGRESSIVE-ERA SOUTH

CELESTE PARRISH and EDUCATIONAL REFORM in the PROGRESSIVE-ERA SOUTH

Rebecca S. Montgomery

LOUISIANA STATE UNIVERSITY PRESS   BATON ROUGE

Published by Louisiana State University Press
Manufactured in the United States of America
First printing

Designer: Barbara Neely Bourgoyne
Typeface: Whitman
Printer and binder: Sheridan Books

Library of Congress Cataloging-in-Publication Data
Names: Montgomery, Rebecca S., author.
Title: Celeste Parrish and educational reform in the progressive-era South /
    Rebecca S. Montgomery.
Description: Baton Rouge : Louisiana State University Press, [2018] | Includes
    bibliographical references and index.
Identifiers: LCCN 2018017797| ISBN 978-0-8071-6978-0 (cloth : alk. paper) |
    ISBN 978-0-8071-7050-2 (pdf) | ISBN 978-0-8071-7051-9 (epub)
Subjects: LCSH: Parrish, C. S. (Celestia Susannah), 1853-1918. | Women teachers—
    Virginia—Biography. | Women teachers—Georgia—Biography. | Education—
    Southern States—History—19th century. | Education—Southern States—History—
    20th century. | Women—Education—Southern States—History. | Sex discrimination
    in education—Southern States—History. | Discrimination in education—Southern
    States—History.
Classification: LCC LA2317.P37 M66 2018 | DDC 371.10092—dc23
LC record available at https://lccn.loc.gov/2018017797

The paper in this book meets the guidelines for permanence and durability of the Committee
on Production Guidelines for Book Longevity of the Council on Library Resources. ♾

For feminist teachers,
our unsung heroes

CONTENTS

Illustrations follow page 70.

ACKNOWLEDGMENTS

I owe many debts of gratitude after more than a decade of research. I am especially grateful to a group of individuals that I have affectionately dubbed the Celeste Parrish fan club. Anne Firor Scott heads the list, as she never gave up hope that someone would eventually tell Parrish's story. She put me in touch with Mary Martin Davis Bowen of Atlanta, who in turn put me in touch with Roger K. Thomas of Athens. I will always have fond memories of the summer weekend that Mary Martin and her husband, Ed, and Roger and his wife, Ann, took turns hosting me in their Rabun County homes. They took me to see Parrish's grave and drove me to the hillside overlooking the town of Clayton where Parrish's cabin once stood. I owe a special debt of thanks to Roger for sharing his research and offering encouraging words during times of duress. As professor and chair of psychology at the University of Georgia, he did his best to keep the memory of Parrish's legacy alive. I also am extremely grateful to Betty Parrish Morehouse, who kindly shared with me her grandfather's stories about Parrish's support of his family after his father died. Betty was a remarkable woman who continued Parrish's feminist tradition through leadership in the National Organization for Women. She helped found the West Chester, Pennsylvania, chapter in the mid-1970s and was instrumental in the establishment of the Rape Crisis Council and two domestic violence shelters. I deeply regret that she did not live to see the book's completion. Ronnie Walker, a descendent of Parrish's mother's family, provided an invaluable service in helping me locate county records documenting the fate of her inheritance. How fortuitous that he happened to glance over and notice that I was using his genealogical sheets to guide my search in the Chatham courthouse.

Acknowledgments

This biography could not have been completed without the generous support of institutions, colleagues, and friends. The Virginia Historical Society awarded two fellowships that helped me establish the context of Parrish's early life in Pittsylvania County. Texas State University provided developmental leave and a research enhancement grant that assisted my research in Virginia, Georgia, North Carolina, and the Library of Congress. When other funding wells ran dry, University Provost Gene Bourgeois helped procure the money to subsidize my work in the University of Chicago archives. I am especially thankful to the History Department's former chair, Mary Brennan, whose compassionate support helped me to survive the worst year of my life. Her willingness to give me the time that I needed to recover from family tragedies and resume writing mean more to me than words can express. I also am grateful to everyone who has read and commented on my work, and particularly Glenda Gilmore, who went above and beyond the call of duty as reader for the press. She saved me from what would have been some very embarrassing oversights, and I have tried to live up to the promise of her recommendations. In addition, Rand Dotson and the entire staff at LSU Press deserve thanks for their enthusiasm and professionalism. Last but certainly not least, I am appreciative that LeeAnn Whites was willing to read yet another account of Parrish's life. I know no one who better exemplifies Celeste Parrish's feminist ideals, and the world would be a better place if the rest of us aspired to those exacting standards.

I must also acknowledge the support of my family. My partner, Gary Gerbstadt, has been incredibly patient as I struggled to finish this project. Who knew that a biography would be so difficult to write and that the project would take over more than one room in the house? My sisters, Sheryl Micyk and Beth LaRose, also were very understanding as I struggled to make up for lost time by spending every spare moment reading, writing, and revising. I promise to make it up to them, right after I clear all those books off the dining-room table.

CELESTE PARRISH and EDUCATIONAL REFORM in the PROGRESSIVE-ERA SOUTH

Introduction

This intellectual biography seeks to explain why Celeste Parrish, the daughter of slave-owning Virginia tobacco farmers, became an outspoken feminist and one of the South's leading advocates of progressive, democratic education. In addition to documenting her career as a teacher and educational reformer, it explores how gender structured women's access to opportunity and shaped their life choices in ways she often found unacceptable. Parrish understood that gender and its connections to race presented a formidable obstacle to southern women who sought to use progressivism as a vehicle for regional change. She believed that the centrality of women's labor to social and economic progress necessitated equality, and she had no patience with men whose attempts to confine women to subordinate roles were motivated by selfish interests. This was especially true when it came to education. Rejecting the southern bias against female intellectualism, Parrish developed a concept of universal personhood to explain the injustice of denying women the right to explore and develop their potential. Looking at the educational reform movement through her eyes reveals the truth of her complaint that discriminatory barriers prevented women from contributing the full measure of their abilities to reform.

Parrish was born November 16, 1852, to Perkins Parrish and his second wife, Lucinda Jane Walker.[1] Although her birth name was Celestia Susannah, friends and family knew her as Celeste. She had four older siblings from her father's first marriage, to Rebecca Stone—William Cephus, Mary Ann Elizabeth (Liza), Sarah Paulina (Sallie), and Frances. Her mother gave birth to three more children, giving her a younger sister, Mentora Jane, and two brothers, Abraham Joseph W. and Thomas (who died in infancy). The first decade of Celeste's life was spent on the family farm near Swansonville, a community in west central Pittsylvania County, located on the North Carolina border in Virginia's southern piedmont. The Parrishes and Walkers had lived in the area for generations and earned most of their income from growing tobacco, which had been the main cash crop in the southern piedmont since the late eighteenth century. Once prices recovered from the crash of 1837, Perkins Parrish steadily added acreage to his 538-acre farm and owned a total of 892 acres at the time of his death in 1863. The county's sandy soil was well suited for tobacco, especially the valuable bright-leaf variety, but was good for little else. Local farmers had no incentive to emulate the older tobacco-growing regions of the state, where depleted soils and fluctuating prices motivated planters to experiment with crop diversification and alternative sources of income. In the 1850s bumper crops and higher prices only strengthened Pittsylvania's reliance on tobacco. By 1860 the county's only city, Danville, had forty businesses devoted to the manufacture of tobacco products and a population of more than thirty-five hundred.[2]

Pittsylvania farmers' continued commitment to tobacco production also represented a commitment to the use of slave labor. Tobacco was a labor-intensive crop, and bright leaf required individualized attention throughout the growing, harvesting, and curing processes to maximize quality. As many tobacco planters to the north and east diversified or turned to industrial and commercial endeavors, the slave population became increasingly concentrated in the southern-piedmont tobacco belt. Between 1850 and 1860 slaves declined as a percentage of the total population in three of the state's four sections—the Trans-Allegheny on what was then Virginia's western border, the Valley that lay between the Allegheny Mountains in the West and the Blue Ridge Mountains in the center of the state, and the Tidewater on the southeastern coastal plain. In contrast, slaves remained a fairly constant proportion of the population in the Piedmont, located between the Blue Ridge Mountains and the Tidewater. In 1860 Pittsylvania was one of six southern-piedmont counties in which slaves made up more than 60 percent of the population, and the characteristics of its slaveholders were typical of the region. Slave ownership was relatively widespread; about 40 percent of the county's white households owned slaves in 1860, as compared to roughly 25 percent of all white southerners.[3]

Three-fourths of tobacco-belt slaveholders had ten or fewer slaves, and for the most part Celeste Parrish's family was no different. Her grandmother, uncles, and cousins residing nearby all owned between four and nine slaves each. Census schedules from 1860 show that Perkins Parrish owned a plantation valued at $5,000 and had eighteen slaves, which put him in the top third of the county's slaveholders, but well below the elite 6 percent that owned thirty or more slaves. He was part of a broad middling class of property owners whose success was testament to the financial rewards of growing tobacco on a modest scale with attention to quality more than quantity. Even many landless whites could achieve a degree of economic security by growing tobacco in leased fields with the help of one or two slaves.[4]

Despite her family's relative prosperity, Celeste Parrish had the same limited access to education faced by all but the wealthiest households in the antebellum rural South. Prior to Reconstruction, southern states either permitted but did not require public funding of free schools, required it but did not enforce it, or did not provide the funds necessary to ensure universal access. Although the national common-school movement of the 1830s stimulated popular support for state-funded education among ordinary southerners, in most cases elite control of government prevented passage of effective legislation. This was true even in Virginia, home to Thomas Jefferson, one of the nation's earliest and most ardent advocates of an informed citizenry. His "Bill for the More General Diffusion of Knowledge," introduced in 1779, created a path of upward mobility for intellectually talented children from less privileged households. It proposed to fund three years of free schooling for all white children, after which the best students would go on to grammar schools. The state would pay tuition for those whose parents could not afford it, and students who excelled after four years of study could attend the College of William and Mary for an additional three years, also at state expense. The legislature never acted on the bill, and Jefferson attributed its defeat to the reluctance of wealthy planters to pay the property taxes needed to subsidize a statewide system.[5]

In the absence of effective funding and regulation, a haphazard system of schooling emerged in which individual households and communities were left to shift for themselves. Celeste first attended a field school, a common hybrid of private and public education in which families with the financial means paid tuition and the county or state covered the expenses of poor children, called pauper or indigent students. Academic standards varied as widely as the teachers' training. Parrish claimed that in most cases the curriculum was "beneath contempt" and described her teacher as poorly educated, one of the many "college men who, by some chance, had strayed from the path of promotion" and had to resort to running a school. She next attended an academy in Callands, a community just north of Swansonville, but it was not much of an improvement over the field school. The woman she considered her best teacher had no knowledge of advanced mathematics and could only evaluate work in simple arithmetic through use of an answer key. Looking back on this education in her later years, Parrish reflected that she "had done nothing of real worth."[6]

Parrish's harsh evaluation of her early instruction reflects the impact of the Civil War, which increased the value of education in ways her parents could not have foreseen. When the war began, Celeste was eight years old and likely destined to be a tobacco farmer's wife, but by its end she was orphaned and facing a lifetime of self-support. Her father died in the fall of 1862, followed by her mother the next spring. She and her younger siblings became the wards of their maternal uncle, William Green Walker, and Celeste went to live with his two unmarried sisters, Matilda and Mariah. The trauma of these events was compounded by the ways in which the loss of slave labor and male heads of household put new pressures on white women and children. Their labor was suddenly more central to the daily operation of homes and farms, and in many instances, it was critical for the long-term financial security of their families as well.[7] The loss of male lives forced women to assume bread-winner roles previously filled by men, but without the attendant privileges. For Parrish this meant becoming a teacher at the age of sixteen to help support her younger siblings, even though the state had no program for female teacher training. It was then that the severe shortcomings of her schooling hit home, launching her on a course of self-improvement and a lifelong quest to raise educational standards in the South.

Parrish's exceptional intellect and ambition drove her to take advantage of every new opportunity as it arose, causing her career to mirror the progress of southern education after the war. When she first began teaching in 1868 she had to solicit pupils for a private school, but Reconstruction soon presented an alternative. An interracial constitutional convention met that same year, and the resulting Underwood Constitution of 1869 included provisions for a statewide educational system. By the time the state's first public school term opened in November 1870, Parrish had secured a position in a Swansonville school near her childhood home. A devout Baptist, she viewed professional development as a sacred obligation and diligently worked to improve her knowledge and skills through self-study. In 1875 the county superintendent acknowledged her efforts by transferring her to a school thirteen miles away in the city of Danville. The move allowed her to attend Roanoke Female

College (previously the Baptist Female Seminary and now Averett University), but it was a college in name only. Female seminaries and academies commonly labeled themselves colleges as a marketing strategy, because there was no required set of standards to meet and no way for prospective students to determine the level of study offered. A Massachusetts educator who surveyed conditions in the postwar South referred to these female colleges as "poorly organized primary and grammar academies." Even though Parrish had to study Latin with twelve-year-old girls (at the age of twenty-three) and received a diploma rather than a degree when she graduated in 1878, the "college" was a significant improvement over her earlier schooling.[8]

Parrish was not the only teacher struggling to compensate for the inadequacies of antebellum education, but the state was slow to respond to women's need for further training. In the 1870s there was only one private female college in Virginia authorized to grant degrees, Hollins College, while men had access to no less than nine private colleges and three public institutions—the University of Virginia, Virginia Military Institute (VMI), and Virginia Polytechnic Institute—all of which excluded women. Even men too poor to pay tuition could apply for one of the state-funded scholarships awarded annually at the University of Virginia and VMI to students who promised to teach in public schools after graduation. The Underwood Constitution instructed the board of education to establish a normal school as quickly as possible, a goal wholeheartedly endorsed by state school superintendent William H. Ruffner, but the legislature refused to make the necessary appropriations. The interracial coalition that produced the 1869 constitution had quickly lost power to Conservative white lawmakers who were more concerned with repaying the state debt than with improving public schools. It was mostly philanthropic donations, not state appropriations, which subsidized the normal institutes that provided workshops for teachers during the summers.[9]

The shared misfortune of state neglect united the political interests of white women and African Americans (who also had no state institution to provide normal training), even though their common ground was not immediately apparent in the aftermath of war. The schools and colleges that freedpeople founded with the assistance of the Freedmen's Bureau, denominational groups, and philanthropic organizations were mostly coeducational, which initially gave black women advantages that less privileged white women lacked. In the early 1870s the main teacher-training programs for African Americans in Virginia admitted both male and female students.

These included the programs at Hampton Normal and Industrial School (later Hampton Institute, and now Hampton University), Colver Institute (now Virginia Union University), and the Richmond Colored Normal School (now Armstrong High School). The greater scope of demand, need to secure rights of citizenship, and a common commitment to racial progress linked the educational advancement of black men and women in ways that sharply contrasted with the white educational system that privileged men at women's expense.[10] Even if acknowledging the reality was difficult for southern white women, emancipation had connected their advancement to that of African Americans by severing antebellum ties of dependency and recasting them as independent economic agents who could make demands of the state.

Nothing better illustrated this connection than the actions of the interracial coalition of Readjusters in creating the first state educational institutions for African Americans and white women. The political coalition rose to power on a groundswell of public anger, after Conservatives gutted educational funds to make payments on the state debt. When Readjusters gained control of the state legislature in the 1881 election, one of their first acts was to allocate $100,000 for the establishment of the coeducational Virginia Normal and Collegiate Institute in Petersburg (now Virginia State University). Three years later, they authorized the founding of the State Female Normal School (SFNS) in Farmville (now Longwood University) and allocated $5,000 in start-up funds. Applicants to both institutions were now eligible for the state teachers' scholarships that previously had been available only to white men. Even though the legislature perpetuated the sex-segregation of white institutions and did not provide the resources necessary for collegiate-level study, the new female school was a godsend for Celeste Parrish and other white women in desperate need of teacher training.[11] She enrolled in the opening session of 1884–85 and resigned her position in Danville schools to join the faculty in her second year as a student, earning her diploma in 1886.

The creation of Virginia's first public educational institution for white women was a pivotal event in Parrish's life, for it was in Farmville that she laid the foundations of a professional career. The normal school provided her with the opportunity to cultivate a specialization in pedagogy in addition to her first field of interest, mathematics. A corresponding shift in her teaching duties and employment as instructor in summer teachers' institutes represented the beginnings of a lifelong dedication to teacher training. Parrish valued the opportunity to help young women who were struggling as she had initially, and derived great satisfaction from knowing she had given hope and courage to "many a soul fainting under heavy burdens." She had an intense desire to earn a college degree, but the exclusion of women from Virginia's public colleges and universities made achieving this goal difficult. Family tragedies also intervened. Two older siblings died in the 1870s and another in 1887, and all left behind several or more young children. To Parrish, "the path of duty was plain," so she shelved plans to attend a university out of state and used the money saved for that purpose to assist her siblings' families. She had to settle for informal study with a professor at a nearby private men's college before finally obtaining a year's leave to attend the University of Michigan in 1891–92.[12]

The obstacles Celeste Parrish faced in trying to meet her familial obligations while also furthering her career encouraged her to think about the personal and social costs of gender discrimination. She knew that the exclusion of women from many southern state colleges and universities severely limited the ability of female teachers to acquire professional training, which lowered the overall level of instruction and reinforced their subordination to male educators. Whether teaching in rural or urban schools, they were almost always supervised by men who had access to advanced training and political authority not available to women. When combined with low pay and a dearth of career alternatives, these obstacles to upward mobility demoralized female teachers and encouraged the public to view them as women "waiting around to get married" rather than as professionals.[13] In 1891, Parrish's determination to address these issues propelled her into a leadership role in a campaign to organize the state's teachers. After helping to establish the Educational Association of Virginia, she joined other female members in creating the Society for the Advancement of the Higher Education of Women to serve as an advocate of coeducation. The society's members elected Parrish their first president and launched a spirited but unsuccessful campaign to open the University of Virginia to women.

Parrish's leadership in institute work and the state teachers' association was rewarded in the spring of 1893 by the offer of a job that was a significant advancement over her position at the normal school. Virginia Methodists were planning the opening of Randolph-Macon Woman's College (RMWC, now Randolph College) in the fall, and the school's president, William Waugh Smith, asked Parrish to head two departments—mathematics, and psychology and pedagogy. Smith was an advocate of female education who previously had recommended allowing local women to enroll in the male Randolph-Macon College. The founders of the new institution believed they could effectively compete with other female schools by opening RMWC as a true college that met or exceeded the quality of male degree-granting institutions. Its admission standards were higher than those of local men's colleges, and it emulated northeastern schools by offering a curriculum with electives that allowed for specialization. Parrish jumped at Smith's offer, and with financial difficulties eased by the higher annual salary ($1,150 as compared to $800 at the normal school), she was able to attend Cornell University in the summer sessions of 1893–95. A semester's leave in the spring of 1896 enabled her to finally earn a bachelor's degree in philosophy at the age of forty-three.[14]

The timing of Parrish's enrollment at Cornell was fortuitous, as it put her in the vanguard of the development of the "new psychology." One of her professors, Edward B. Titchener, had only recently accepted a position at Cornell after completing his doctoral research in Wilhelm Wundt's Institute for Experimental Psychology at the University of Leipzig in Germany. Wundt was a pioneer in modern psychology who used techniques grounded in physiology to develop methods of measuring sensation, perception, and reaction time. This new approach to the study of the mind emphasized the need for scientific research in a controlled laboratory environment. Titchener continued his research at Cornell, intent upon documenting the structure of the elements of consciousness—an approach he called "structuralism." Celeste Parrish worked closely with Titchener to gain the training she needed for her new position at chair of psychology and pedagogy at RMWC, and they became good friends and collaborated in laboratory research. She was attracted to his goal of documenting the structure of a general, universal mind, and his insistence on unbiased observation free of preconceived ideas, both of which might serve to discredit theories of sex difference used to justify gender inequality.[15]

Parrish's study at Cornell was a turning point in her intellectual development that had lasting benefits for southern education. She shared Titchener's enthusiasm for the new psychology and established the first laboratory for experimental psychology in the South at RMWC in 1894. Her inclusion of laboratory work in requirements for advanced psychology courses exceeded the recommendations of the National Education Association for teacher training and contributed to the college's ranking as a "Division A" institution that met national collegiate standards.[16] The increasingly feminist bent of her educational philosophy was also partially attributable to her interest in psychology. The more she studied, the more she became convinced of the universality of the human mind and of the injustice of educational practices that made distinctions of sex. These insights would be included in her later analysis of the inferiority of southern female education and the regional factors underpinning it. Furthermore, Cornell's integration of women earlier in the century proved the feasibility of coeducation, which confirmed her belief that southern men's opposition was based on spurious claims.

The final phase of Celeste Parrish's intellectual development took place during three summers of graduate study at the University of Chicago in 1897–99, where she studied with some of the most prominent progressive scholars in the nation. Just as Titchener had introduced her to the new psychology, John Dewey introduced her to the "new education." After his arrival at the university in 1894, Dewey began formulating a democratic interpretation of the purposes of education that influenced theory and practice around the world. At a time when many educators regarded rote memorization and strict authoritarian rule as ways to inculcate discipline and obedience in students, Dewey claimed such practices imprisoned the intellect of children. He proposed instead a classroom in which learning was an interactive process that provided outlets for children's creativity and engaged them in the creation of knowledge. Dewey argued that lessons should give meaning and usefulness to abstract knowledge by relating it to activities common in everyday life, thereby avoiding an artificial separation between school and society. Using his friend Jane Addams's settlement house as a model, he envisioned schools as social centers that facilitated cooperation and mutual understanding in culturally diverse communities while helping citizens adjust to new conditions.[17]

These ideas resonated with Parrish, who found hope in Dewey's definition of education as a "fundamental method of social progress and reform." She understood the psychological basis of his progressive methods and was convinced that the study of mind had almost infinite potential for human betterment. Her enthusiastic promotion of the child-study movement, in which psychologists enlisted the help of teachers and parents in observing and recording children's behavior, stemmed from this conviction. She argued in 1901 that, if "parents and teachers could understand and intelligently apply the laws of imitation, suggestion, instinct and habit in the training of children, we might reasonably hope for an immense advance in . . . individual happiness and efficiency in one generation." Parrish also was attracted to Dewey's concept of the school as social center. It fit well with her conception of the consecrated teacher as a professional whose social responsibilities extended beyond the classroom, and it appeared a promising remedy for both urban class differences and rural isolation in the South.[18] Unlike progressives who adopted Dewey's methods stripped of their democratic foundations, Parrish consistently championed a cooperative approach to reform throughout her career.

In addition to providing her with a democratic framework for progressive reform, Parrish's summers in Chicago reinforced her feminist goals by connecting her to a broader group of college-educated women with a shared commitment to gender equality. Her immersion in the life of the city included exposure to a vibrant community of female intellectuals with overlapping ties to university departments, settlement houses, and women's clubs. Jane Addams, Florence Kelley, Edith Abbott, and Sophonisba Breckinridge were all Hull House residents and sociologists who were employed by the university at various times and who often lectured on campus, and whose social activism provided a model for Dewey's pragmatist theories. Parrish was fortunate to also meet Marion Talbot while staying in the women's dormitories. Talbot, who became the second dean of women when Alice Freeman Palmer resigned in 1895, actively promoted the interests of female faculty and students on campus. Parrish soon joined the Association of Collegiate Alumnae (ACA), an organization cofounded by Talbot in 1881 to promote the interests of women in higher education and the professions. At the ACA annual business meeting held in conjunction with the Chicago conference in October 1899, Parrish announced that she had founded a Virginia branch of the group. She described the new branch's "special field of work" as "arousing a general sentiment in favor of the education of girls in the South."[19]

Parrish explained why there was a need to build support for female education in a paper presented at the 1899 Chicago conference, outlining issues that she had begun to explore in a series of essays. She described the "distinctly aristocratic" nature of antebellum education, in which only the elite had access to advanced training and female schooling was designed to produce culturally refined southern ladies. These female icons of the "old régime" continued to represent the epitome of womanliness in the South, influencing parents to base their daughters' studies on an outmoded ideal rather than "a college education of the sterner sort." Private female seminaries falsely labeled as colleges catered to parents' preference for instruction in the fine arts while not offering even a college-preparatory course of study. The state normal schools established after the war offered women the equivalent of a good high-school education, but they were severely underfunded. Parrish observed that Virginia had shown more support for the education of African Americans than it had for white women. The state annually appropri-

ated $20,000 for the black state college at Petersburg and another $10,000 for Hampton Institute, as compared to only $10,000 for the state female normal school.[20] What she failed to note was that the two black institutions had to accommodate both men and women.

While Parrish's ACA paper focused on the larger social and structural problems with female education in the South, when speaking to southern audiences she was more pointed in her criticisms of men. Male officials were responsible for discriminatory funding, and male faculty and trustees kept state colleges and universities closed to women. Moreover, male opposition to educational equality discouraged girls from aspiring to higher education, so that many failed to pursue even the limited options available to them. Parrish discussed the reasons for men's behavior in a paper delivered at the Conference for Education in the South (CES) in 1899, and in another presented the following year at the Southern Educational Association meeting. She recounted a litany of selfish motives that ranged from men's desire to limit economic competition to their unwillingness to relinquish a womanhood dedicated to serving male needs. She took her grievances to a national audience in 1901, publishing two articles in *The Independent* that elaborated on the immorality and inhumanity of using sex as the sole determinant of woman's purpose.[21] By then, Parrish had acquired a regional reputation as an outspoken critic of gender discrimination. A common theme that ran throughout her writings was the right of women to universal personhood, their right to exist as an end in themselves.

Parrish's understanding of the regional distinctiveness of problems in the South led her to form an organization specifically to address the educational needs of southern women. The ACA had a far-reaching agenda for improving women's access to education and the professions that made southern women's plight seem all the more critical—at a time when the national group was raising funds for female graduate study abroad, Virginia women lacked access to a single state college or university. Furthermore, in 1903 only 2 of the 140 southern institutions claiming to be women's colleges had a four-year college-level program of study. Parrish, Emilie Watts McVea, and Lillian Wyckoff Johnson cofounded the Southern Association of College Women (SACW) that year, with Parrish as president, and began a publicity campaign to persuade southerners of the need to bring female education into compliance with national standards. One of the organization's most effective strategies involved collecting and disseminating data on the academic programs of female institutions, pressuring them to either meet national standards or label their programs accurately. By 1906, college-educated women in Georgia, Kentucky, Tennessee, and Alabama had formed SACW chapters to carry out the work. In addition to monitoring the quality of local programs, they held "go-to-college" days in high schools to encourage female students to consider going to college and to assist them with the application process.[22]

Parrish's commitment to improving southern educational standards made her a natural ally of the southern movement for educational reform that was just launching its first state campaigns. The movement originated in the first Conference for Education in the South held at Capon Springs, West Virginia, in 1898. A group of white male educators and ministers staged the meeting to provide a forum for northerners and southerners who were concerned about the status of public education in the South. Although discussion of black education dominated the first conference, the focus quickly shifted to whites and the need to remedy the substandard quality of southern schools more generally. Proposed solutions included better teacher training and pay, longer school terms, properly equipped schools and libraries, the introduction of manual and industrial training, and local taxation to provide the funding for reforms. After New York businessman Robert C. Ogden became conference president in 1900, the annual meetings rotated among southern cities to gain the support of local and state officials. In 1901 Ogden presided over the creation of the Southern Education Board (SEB), which provided fact-gathering and publicity services and acted as a liaison with the General Education Board (GEB), the movement's main source of funding.[23]

Although the CES remained completely under the control of male officers and board members until its dismantling in 1914, the organization courted women's support. In 1902 the SEB began forming state committees, usually called educational committees or campaign committees, made up of progressive southern men who held positions in education and politics. Hoping a grassroots approach would overcome political obstructionism by building public pressure for legislative reforms, committee members asked club women to organize their communities for school improvement. Sometimes men laid the groundwork by staging rallies and providing public speakers, and afterwards clubwomen worked with teachers to found school-improvement clubs and build interest and pride in area schools. In other instances women paved the way, creating a welcoming environment for the rallies by sending representatives to communities beforehand to speak with parents, teachers, and civic leaders about the need for better schools. In both cases, women's grassroots organizing was critical to building public support for reforms such as local taxation.²⁴ Celeste Parrish, who attended almost every CES meeting, beginning in 1899, regularly contributed to the campaigns as a speaker and publicity agent.

Parrish's leadership in organizations dedicated to southern educational uplift increased her regional visibility and expanded her professional network, leading to another job opportunity in 1901. In December she left Randolph-Macon Woman's College to become professor of psychology and pedagogy at the Georgia State Normal School (GSNS) in Athens. In another case of fortunate timing, the new position enabled her to escape a contentious work environment at RMWC while also giving her the chance to more thoroughly implement what she had learned in Chicago. Shortly after arriving in Athens, Parrish solicited the funds to establish a "practice school" modeled after John Dewey's University of Chicago Laboratory School. She carefully selected and trained the women who taught at Muscogee Elementary School to ensure that they understood the tenets of the new education. Normal-school students observed Muscogee teachers using progressive methods to instruct local children, and the most talented then practiced those methods through student teaching.²⁵ Parrish's effort to redesign the program of pedagogical instruction was a resounding success; however, her relationship with GSNS president Eugene Cunningham Branson soured after a public controversy arose regarding her support for black education. The root cause of the uproar was racist demagoguery surrounding the state campaign for black disfranchisement, but for Branson the central issue was Parrish's assumption of gender equality.

Celeste Parrish's conflict with Branson illustrates the serious consequences women could face when they insisted on being treated as the equals of their male colleagues. During an investigation into their differences conducted by the normal-school board of trustees, Branson produced letters solicited from male faculty at Randolph-Macon Woman's College attesting to Parrish's quarrelsome nature. Her later statements revealed that the men's disgruntlement was related to her challenge to male governance. In a speech to Richmond clubwomen in 1902, she made a thinly veiled reference to RMWC in which she complained that the female faculty "have no vote, the government of the institution being thus left in the hands of men, a number of whom are young men." Similarly, her conflict with Branson stemmed from his refusal to acknowledge her authority over a program of pedagogical instruction that she had spent a decade of her life constructing. Nonetheless, Branson and his supporters used the lingering resentments of her former colleagues to back up their claim that she was responsible for all discord in the normal school. When the trustees terminated Parrish's employment in May 1911, Branson and the board president again blamed her for being a "disturbing element."[26] To the casual observer it would have appeared as if dissention followed in her wake, providing proof that her firing was justified.

The series of events that led to Celeste Parrish's departure from the Georgia State Normal School also illustrated deeper truths about the connections between gender and race in the construction of southern white manhood. In the southern defense of slavery that emerged in the 1830s, male intellectuals rejected the ideals of the American Revolution, arguing that belief in the innate equality of human beings was not only misguided, but also harmful. Men such as Thomas Roderick Dew of the College of William and Mary laid the foundations for scientific racism with their claims that African Americans lacked the capacity for freedom and self-governance and needed white control to protect them from barbaric and self-destructive tendencies. As the argument evolved over the next two decades, others asserted that the subordination of women also was necessary and desirable. George Frederick Jones of the University of Virginia described the hierarchical relationships of master and slave, husband and wife, and parent and child as the "three great fundamental and instinctive relations [that] constitute the base on which the edifice of society is erected." In the view of proslavery writers, the northern model of universal education was a subversion of the natural order that gave dependents inappropriate aspirations for individual accomplishment. It stripped white women of their femininity and encouraged them to abandon their obligations to family, while deluding slaves and free blacks with its illusion of intellectual equality.[27]

The opposition to equality that Parrish confronted as a professional educator was directly linked to the continued insistence of many white southerners that the antebellum social order was superior to the northern model of individual rights. Their stubborn rejection of the new realities created by military defeat and emancipation maintained the regional differences in attitudes toward female education that historians have often noted.[28] Parrish acknowledged as much in her writings, as the dynamics of inequality were not exactly hidden. University of Virginia faculty openly expressed their belief that coeducation was a threat to the gender and racial hierarchy that defined southern regional distinctiveness. Proslavery arguments had strengthened the association of higher education with the preparation of elite white men for mastery, and they were reluctant to give up exclusive access. Celeste Parrish revealed more than she realized when she accused Eugene Branson of treating her "like a Negro," by which she meant a person in need of paternal guidance and control. Male educational professionals may have needed women's labor as teachers, but even those who were progressive on other issues had difficulty relinquishing antebellum relations of domination and subordination that perpetuated white male privilege.[29]

Parrish was fortunate to have a large social network to draw upon in her search for employment, and she quickly acquired a position in the Georgia Department of Education that proved to be her last job. After clubwomen pressured public leaders to correct the injustice of her firing from the normal school, Governor Hoke Smith hired her to direct a series of rural educational rallies during the summer. When the legislature created the position of rural school supervisor in August, he offered her permanent employment. Her new duties included staging teachers' institutes and organizing communities for school improvement in forty-eight counties across north and northwest Georgia.[30] Although the pay was inadequate and the need for constant travel grueling, Parrish's new position freed her to more widely promote the democratic values that shaped her approach to reform. She made community organizing a central part of her work, because she was convinced that residents of rural communities had to be personally invested in schools and have a say in their operation if change was to be permanent. A passionate commitment to rural uplift drove her to continue working despite worsening illness in the summer of 1918, leading to her death on September 7, about two months before her sixty-sixth birthday. Educators and clubwomen from around the state marked her passing with memorials, tributes, and a monument for her grave emblazoned with the words, "Georgia's Greatest Woman."

As Celeste Parrish's friends discovered in their struggle to find the most fitting memorial to her life of service, it is difficult to encapsulate the significance of someone who was on the leading edge of so many important reforms. She brought a scientific approach to the discipline of teaching and a dedication to national professional standards that was severely lacking in most southern institutions, and her leadership in numerous reform campaigns helped to hasten the pace of progressive change. Her friends found themselves "a little breathless" just reviewing the record of her activities, which while impressive, was not the only basis of their admiration for her. They also respected the Christian humanism that underlay her interest in the needs of rural children and her deep concern for the plight of poor children more generally. She saw in the face of every rural child her past self, that awkward, self-conscious orphan girl in hand-me-down clothes and ill-fitting shoes, a girl who had never seen the world outside her county or had a teacher who could unlock the door to her intellectual potential. This was what was at stake for Parrish, what drove her to have such exacting standards and to make such uncompromising demands of herself and others; she understood and deplored the human costs of inadequate schools and poorly trained teachers. As a friend put it, she was "essentially a fighter" who had "little patience with the selfishness, the stupidity, the indifference, the shortsightedness of those who stood in the way of the things she thought were right and must be done."[31]

The following chapters lay the foundations for a broader understanding of the significance of Parrish's life by placing it within the larger course of events between the Civil War and World War I. Chapter 1 examines the conditions that led white women to become teachers and the role of Reconstruction in restoring a measure of stability to their lives. Despite southern white hostility toward federal intervention, Freedmen's Bureau schools and the fledgling public school systems that followed provided jobs for women who lacked the option of dependency.[32] The inferiority of southern female education left them poorly prepared for their duties, and women continued to suffer from the gendering of opportunity as their access to education slowly improved in the 1870s and 1880s.

As chapter 2 explains, southern women had the misfortune of facing a backlash to women's advancement that had both regional and national dimensions. Parrish had to deal with cultural bias against educational equality and the struggle to restore mastery in the South, while men across the nation were constructing fanciful theories to justify the segregation and exclusion of women in higher education and the professions.[33] Professional segregation usually relegated women to positions with lower status and pay, but in education it also fostered a culture of resistance by creating female networks of support. Schools for women valued pedagogical skills and commitment to mentorship and service, unlike the prioritization of research and publication more typical of universities.[34]

Chapter 3 further explores the origins and significance of Parrish's sense of purpose. Her definition of the consecrated woman was rooted in the antebellum concept of Christian womanhood, but its progressive and feminist aims were strongly shaped by the Social Gospel and her summers at the University of Chicago. University president William Rainey Harper; his sociology, psychology, and philosophy faculty; and the city's settlement-house workers all demonstrated how faith and science combined could solve the problems of modern society.[35] Parrish's consecrated woman evolved into the consecrated teacher, a professional whose contributions to community encompassed all forms of social uplift that improved the quality of life for parents and students. A growing conviction that gender equality was a requisite for social progress gave a sense of urgency to her struggle for coeducation and drove Parrish to become more deeply involved in organizational campaigns for reform.

Her views were not welcomed by all Virginians, but it was not until Parrish accepted a position in Georgia in 1901 that she fully realized the costs of her advocacy for equality. Chapter 4 examines how Parrish's first decade in Georgia was marred by the rise of an extreme version of white supremacy that was incompatible with gender equality and progressive educational reform. The terms "reactionary racism" and "white-supremacist extremism" are used to describe white southerners who revived the arguments of proslavery writers and attempted to imbue them with scientific legitimacy in the 1890s. Rejecting religious and paternalist approaches to race relations, they used evolutionary theories to portray segregation, lynching, and black disfranchisement as logical responses to the regression of African Americans to a condition of savagery. Racist demagogues built political careers on the claim that universal education would transform a docile, black workforce into an army of brutal rapists, using inflammatory rhetoric to depict the southern movement for educational reform as a puppet of northern industrialists whose secret aim was racial equality.[36] In this context, Parrish's classroom expression of support for black education became a threat to the gendered foundations of white supremacy, as it denied her need for protection from the mythical black-beast rapist.

Chapters 4 and 5 investigate additional factors that led to Parrish's dismissal from Georgia State Normal School. Eugene Branson hired her because he valued her experience and training, but her assumption of equality quickly became intolerable to him; there was no place for a feminist in an institution in which the professional hierarchy mirrored the structure of the patriarchal household. Despite her superior abilities, Parrish was disadvantaged in the conflict by her lack of formal political power, which in the eyes of male authorities made her less valuable to the school. On the other hand, as in Virginia, professional segregation facilitated the creation of female networks of support. Female students, teachers, and club women became close friends and allies who sprang to Parrish's defense and pressured public officials to create a new position for her, which ultimately allowed her to return to her roots through work in rural communities. If it were not for their efforts to ensure that her professional accomplishments were publicly acknowledged, Parrish's role in modernizing teacher training in Georgia would have been largely erased from the historical record.[37]

Atlanta women demonstrated the power of Parrish's grassroots, collaborative approach to reform in the weeks and months surrounding her death. Although Atlanta's female educators and club women were engaged in school reform prior to Parrish's arrival in Georgia, the events of 1918 symbolized the value of her life's work. During the summer, women used the city council's investigation into the administration of schools to publicize the need for structural reforms, then successfully spearheaded a campaign to revise the city charter and elect a slate of reform candidates to the city board of education. At the heart of women's grievances was a gendered professional hierarchy that allowed male administrators to abuse their authority over female teachers and principals and ignore community needs. The populist revolt that held them accountable was made possible by the extensive organization of mothers and teachers into women's and school-improvement clubs and parent-teacher association chapters. Just as Parrish intended, these groups united educators and parents in opposition to policies that denied children the right to self-development and crippled social progress. Even though complete equality of access was not achieved, women proved the value and effectiveness of Parrish's democratic approach to reform.

Parrish's life story reveals that her fears regarding the gendered limitations of progressivism were well founded. Her incisive analysis of the connections between the intimate relations of the household and the gendering of opportunity in the public sphere explained why many progressive men opposed equality even though it restricted female contributions to reform. Discrimination could drive women from the positions for which they were best qualified, as it drove Celeste Parrish from the normal school and later drove her former pupil Laura Smith from her position as elementary supervisor for the Atlanta public school system. Smith resigned in protest in 1918, staying only long enough to denounce the behavior of city officials at the school-board investigation hearings, and returned after the war to take a lucrative position training telephone operators. It was not just women's lack of formal political power, but also men's difficulty viewing them as ends in themselves rather than as sexual partners that influenced male reformers to devalue their work. Unfortunately, the latter was not something woman suffrage could resolve. The fact that an educator and progressive reformer as talented and productive as Celeste Parrish has remained largely invisible in the historical record stands as a clear example of the gendered construction of power that she spent her life combating.[38]

CHAPTER ONE

An Uncertain Beginning

Between 1861 and 1885 Celeste Parrish witnessed revolutionary changes in Virginia that launched her career and laid the foundations for the progressive worldview she embraced as a mature adult. When federal intervention in the form of the Freedmen's Bureau began the process of establishing public schools in 1865, the proficiency of its northern-educated teachers highlighted the inadequacies of female education in the South. Even though most southern whites later condemned Reconstruction in the bitterest terms, white women benefited from federal efforts to impose a northern model of progress on the South. The political empowerment of black men, both during Reconstruction and in the Readjuster movement, was critical to the establishment of an educational system that provided white women with their first real opportunities for economic independence. Women of Parrish's generation who found themselves in breadwinner roles had little reason to romanticize the antebellum past. As the youngest generation to experience the war, they had the least stake in the Lost Cause, and as women of limited means they profited from a reconstructed state with new commitments to social welfare.[1]

White Virginians resisted setting this series of events in motion, entering the Civil War only after they felt they had exhausted all peaceful solutions. The state's political leaders convened a conference in Washington in February 1861 to find a resolution to the crisis, and the state's voters overwhelmingly chose Unionists and moderates to represent them at the secessionist convention that met later that month. The collapse of the peace conference, constant agitation by secessionists, and Lincoln's refusal to surrender Fort Sumter dashed hopes that war could be averted. In late April, ratification of

Virginia's secession ordinance finally accomplished what decades of political compromise had attempted to prevent—the loss of the state's northwestern counties. Constitutional reforms implemented ten years earlier provided more democratic representation across the state, but they came too late to avoid the rift. Virginians in the west regarded disunion as simply the latest and most rash act of selfish elites who had little thought for the greater public good. In May, delegates met in Wheeling to form their own Unionist state government, and in November the first constitutional convention of West Virginia convened.[2]

Preparations for war in what was left of Virginia impacted the Parrish and Walker households almost immediately. Like most farmers in the southern piedmont, they had relatively small-scale operations and did not qualify for exemption under the Twenty Negro rule of the 1862 Confederate conscription act. Celeste's oldest brother, William Cephus Parrish, and five cousins all served in Company E of the Sixth Virginia Cavalry Regiment, nicknamed the Pittsylvania Dragoons. The cousins included the three oldest sons of Wilson Parrish, one of whom died in the conflict, and two sons of Thomas Parrish who were in their mid-thirties and married with families of their own. Maternal uncle William Green Walker, also married and with a farm of his own, served in Company B of the Thirty-Eighth Infantry Regiment. The departure of men for military service represented a significant hardship for the women and children who were left to manage farms and slaves on their own. Although Perkins Parrish, Celeste's father, was too old to be conscripted, with his oldest son gone he had only daughters to assist him. Celeste was eight years old, and her sisters Frances, Sallie, and Eliza, were eleven, fourteen, and seventeen years old. Her younger brothers were still babies; Joseph W. was only three, and Thomas was not born until November 1861.[3]

In addition to losing male labor, Pittsylvania County families suffered hardships due to runaway inflation and shortages of food and cash. Salt, necessary for preserving meat, was already in short supply by the fall of 1861, and the days designated for its distribution were important events in local communities. During the winter of 1862–63 the prices of bacon and flour almost tripled, and by the end of 1863 the cost of many staple goods had doubled and tripled again. There was little relief available for soldiers' families until the Danville Town Council established a program for allotment of food in 1863. Severe food shortages and related thievery plagued the countryside, and toward the end of the war even more prosperous farmers were suffering from a severe drought. In neighboring Halifax County, William H. Sims complained in the summer of 1864 that his corn and vegetable crops were destroyed, and he worried that "great suffering must be seen in the country, if not actual starvation," if it did not rain soon.[4]

Celeste Parrish witnessed tremendous loss of life as well as deprivation. Maternal uncle Thomas J. Walker died in 1861, most likely from an illness contracted in military camp, and disease took a heavy toll on civilians dealing with the stresses of war. Pittsylvania County endured a measles outbreak in the spring of 1862, and a deadly scarlet-fever epidemic swept through communities the following winter. In 1862 alone, Celeste lost her father, her last surviving grandparent, and a maternal aunt who was only forty-one years old. The following year her mother died at age thirty-seven, and by that time her youngest brother, Thomas, also was deceased. It is not surprising that she rarely spoke of her wartime experiences, since the trauma of instability and loss must have been overwhelming for a child. One of her friends remarked that she never spoke of "childish joys," most likely because "she was never really a child."[5]

The human costs of war were staggering, leaving families scrambling to reconstitute their fragmented households in communities bereft of resources. In addition to the toll that stress and ill health took on the home front, around 59 percent of all white men of military age in Pittsylvania County either died or had diminished capacity to work due to physical or mental disabilities. Men whose military wages did not cover the cost of supporting their families took out loans and returned home to debts they had no way of repaying. Many of the dead left behind widows and orphans who had limited means of self-support and few places to which they could turn for help. The average Confederate veteran family saw its real property value drop 63 percent between 1860 and 1870. Parrish's family, like others, coped with these new conditions by reconfiguring households to share the burdens of loss. Orphaned when their mother died in 1863, Celeste and her younger sister and brother, Mentora and Abram, became guardians of maternal uncle William Walker. Celeste and Abram went to live with their unmarried aunts, Matilda and Mariah Walker (William's younger sisters), and Mentora lived with her married older sister, Eliza Parrish Payne.[6]

Young women in their teens and early twenties could turn to Confederate nationalism to make sense of sacrifices on the home front and battlefield, but political ideology had little meaning for a child of nine or ten. Harriet Matthews, a Pittsylvania County girl a few years older than Parrish, recalled that she could not bear to hear adults discuss the war and acutely felt their anxiety about the fate of men sent off to battle. She described a community farewell celebration for members of Company I of the Thirty-Eighth Infantry Regiment, locally known as the Chatham Grays, which she found particularly disturbing. Viewing the familiar faces of relatives and neighbors among the soldiers, Matthew was "filled with horror at the tears of their mothers and sisters as they bade them good-bye" and fled the scene as quickly as she could. Pattie Booker Tredway, a girl of similar age, reported being filled with "anxiety and sickening suspense" as she waited with friends to hear if their brothers had survived the latest battle. Both girls were frightened by occasional rumors that a Yankee attack was imminent. Even though the county never experienced Union invasion and occupation as did eastern Virginia and the Shenandoah Valley, the threat appeared real enough at times to send prominent men such as Tredway's father into hiding in nearby woods.[7]

The uncertainty that filled both children and adults with dread was worsened by the obstacles they faced in trying to maintain family ties during the war. Soldiers and their families constantly complained about the difficulty of sending and receiving letters. Men were frustrated when they could not get their military pay to wives, and women worried when they were unable to immediately respond to the needs of their brothers and husbands. When the Virginia governor appealed for donations of clothing, women enthusiastically responded as individuals and as members of soldiers' aid societies. Knowing that men sometimes were without tents and had only wood fires for warmth, they tried their best to equip soldiers with coats during the winter months. In November 1862, Rebecca Tredway of Chatham wrote to her brother Rawley Martin that she was sorry he "had to make that long march almost barefooted," adding that she wished she could "get some material to make clothing for the soldiers." The Ladies Soldiers' Aid Society of Pittsylvania Courthouse (Chatham) sent her brother's company a box of blankets, socks, and other goods in the fall of the following year. Much to his family's distress, Martin had to write his letter of thanks from a prison in Baltimore, where he was detained after being wounded and captured at the Battle of Gettysburg.[8]

The prosperity of the town of Danville, which was only a short ride from the Parrish farm, provided a strange contrast to the sacrifice and suffering occurring in rural communities. Because Pittsylvania County remained behind battle lines, wealthy Virginians from Richmond, Williamsburg, and the Peninsula brought their families to the area for safekeeping, and manufacturers from Lynchburg, Richmond, and Petersburg moved the bases of their operations to Danville. The town became a supply center for the Confederate government, which constructed the Piedmont Railroad to connect it with Greensboro and made local businessman William T. Sutherlin quartermaster of the Confederacy. Confederate officials used the town jail to store gunpowder, turned the county courthouse into a military hospital, and converted tobacco warehouses into supply depots, hospitals, and prisons. The Confederacy also established a small foundry on the banks of the Dan River to make and repair weapons, and local businessmen received government contracts to manufacture arms and cloth for military uniforms. Equally importantly, the war increased demand for bright-leaf tobacco by popularizing smoking tobacco, which was easier to produce than chewing tobacco and was favored by soldiers.[9]

What was good for business was not necessarily good for the greater public, and the presence of large numbers of soldiers and Union prisoners created serious problems for the town's citizens. In addition to the usual problems of drunk and disorderly behavior, towns with military encampments had to endure numerous disease outbreaks. Measles, typhoid, and mumps epidemics spread through the troops stationed in Danville during the summer of 1861. Rural soldiers who had little previous contact with such illnesses were especially susceptible to infection in the close quarters of camp. Even worse, thousands of starving and poorly clothed prisoners were crammed into six tobacco factories that quickly became a breeding ground for disease. The crudely constructed buildings were infested with rodents and parasites, and raw sewage flowed from prison grounds. Townspeople were particularly alarmed by a smallpox epidemic that killed hundreds of prisoners in December 1863. They complained to city leaders about the steady deterioration of sanitary conditions, but local officials were unable to get the Confederate government to locate the prisons elsewhere. Several escape attempts, one of which was successful, underscored the threat to public health and safety posed by the captives. Stripped of able-bodied men, plagued by food shortages, and wracked by disease, by 1865 the city appeared a sad and worn version of its former prosperous self.[10]

The end of the war brought even worse chaos. In April the city briefly served as the "last capital of the Confederacy" when President Jefferson Davis and his cabinet relocated there after fleeing Richmond. Confederate officials quickly scattered when news of General Robert E. Lee's surrender reached them eight days later, and hundreds of soldiers and civilians began streaming into Danville, attracted by rumors of Confederate warehouses full of food and clothing. Mobs of men, women, and children ransacked warehouses and shops, stopping only briefly when looters accidentally ignited loose gunpow-der in the Confederate arsenal, obliterating the building and killing fourteen people. Burning debris rained down from the skies for miles, igniting the dresses of two women who drowned when they jumped into the Dan River to extinguish the flames. Panicked local residents thought the series of ex-plosions were signs of a Union attack and prepared to leave. Hastily formed guard patrols were able to partially restore order, but frustration from years of rural scarcity made Danville's rumored abundance of goods an irresistible lure for hungry families and discharged soldiers. The continuing threat of raids made town officials and businessmen welcome the arrival of federal troops who could end the rampant lawlessness.[11]

The chaotic events of April created an unimaginable amount of stress for families struggling to maintain a semblance of normalcy. Since Danville was only about thirteen miles from her home, twelve-year-old Celeste Parrish would have witnessed the steady stream of men and women converging on the city, heard the explosions, and seen the rising smoke. The aunts with whom she lived after her parents' deaths, Matilda and Mariah Walker, suf-fered from what now would be identified as post-traumatic stress disorder. Parrish described them as "hysterical invalids, much given to 'uneasiness.'" Mariah, the younger of the two sisters, apparently never recovered, as U.S. Census records for 1880 listed her as suffering from "nervous debility." Al-though Parrish's aunts did their best to fulfill their responsibilities to their sister's children, anxiety over the instability of their own lives degraded their relationship with their niece, making her feel unwanted. She claimed they made sarcastic comments about her clumsiness and disapproved of her desire for further education. When she developed her own course in nature study to compensate for the closure of schools during the war, they were upset by her "tom-boyish habits" and ordered her "to be a lady and learn embroidery."[12]

The Walkers' critical comments reflected the struggle of white southerners to comprehend the new realities young women faced because of the war. As in the Parrish household, the Walkers provided all their children with a basic education. Matilda and Mariah were literate, but they had no context for understanding or appreciating Celeste's exceptional talents and drive. There had been no expectation of self-support for the women in their family, and there was no place for intellectual ambition in the antebellum ideal of wom-anhood. A popular advice manual for young women published in Richmond in 1830 condemned the public display of female intellectual ability as vain attention-seeking, and described public attention as degrading for women.

The Walker sisters knew that their brother expected them to provide their niece with domestic training in preparation for marriage, and her passion for learning seemed at odds with that goal. According to family lore, her sister Mentora was "the pretty one," and they could have feared that Parrish's intellectual intensity would further diminish her attractiveness in the eyes of potential suitors.[13]

What Parrish interpreted as disapproval also reflected her aunts' reluctance to part with the money necessary to continue her education. Farmers suffered from poor crop yields throughout the 1860s, and widespread impoverishment is evident in the complaints of county residents that petty theft remained as much of a problem during Reconstruction as during the war. Even though the Walker sisters inherited a share of their father's estate and were living on the family homestead, its assessed value declined from $2,500 in 1850 to $1,000 in 1870, and their personal property was valued at only $200. Moreover, by the end of the war, Matilda and Mariah were in their mid-thirties, and prospects for gaining long-term financial security through marriage looked bleak. They also were caring for Celeste's younger brother, Joseph, who in 1865 was only seven years old and unable to contribute toward his keep. The tensions between the Walker sisters and their niece were replicated across the countryside, as adults and children struggled to adjust expectations rooted in the past with the harsh conditions of the present. Ironically, when her aunts informed Parrish in 1868 that she must work to support herself and her younger brother, one of the few sources of employment open to her was teaching, an occupation for which she desperately needed further education.[14]

Although Parrish's career proved to be more lengthy and prominent than most, she was one of many women who chose to begin teaching when postwar financial insecurity forced them into the position of breadwinner. Southern women in middling and upper-class households rarely sought paid employment until the wartime loss of savings, property, and labor left families dependent upon the cash earnings of female kin. Elite women with resources opened private schools. This option allowed them to appear to remain in the domestic sphere by teaching in their homes, and produce income without compromising their class status and respectability. Maria Louisa Carrington, whose family was from neighboring Campbell County, was a widow when she opened a school in 1868 as a means of supporting herself and her children. She was left almost destitute when the father-in-law with whom she had been living died, and she was determined to avoid lapsing into dependency upon family.[15]

Parrish, who was not part of the antebellum elite and lacked the option of dependency on family, had little choice but to turn to teaching. After receiving her aunts' ultimatum, she canvassed the community to solicit students for a private school and saved what she earned during a three-month term of instruction in hopes of financing further study. According to her account of these years, her first attempt at teaching was a complete failure, but she persevered "with the desperation of a drowning woman." She was painfully aware of being ill prepared due to the haphazard nature of antebellum education. Anyone could open a school, as there were no requirements other than the willingness of parents to pay tuition. Her best teacher had only a rudimentary grasp of arithmetic and taught history, science, and composition solely through rote memorization of textbooks. Since the state had no normal school to provide her with training, Parrish pursued a course of self-study. When she discovered a copy of David Perkins Page's *Theory and Practice of Teaching*, she was so amazed and grateful to find a source of pedagogical instruction that she stayed awake all night to finish reading it. The book by Page, the first principal of New York State Normal School in Albany, was the best-selling textbook in teacher education at that time. Parrish described the experience as "a baptism of the Holy Spirit," a sign of divine guidance that moved her to dedicate herself to lifelong professional improvement.[16]

Although Parrish's early education was a product of the antebellum past, as a teacher she was poised to become part of a very different future. During the previous five years the Freedmen's Bureau had disrupted the status quo by laying the foundations for public school systems across the South. The 1865 law creating the Bureau of Refugees, Freedmen, and Abandoned Lands authorized the agency to oversee all matters concerning freedpeople, without providing it with any federal funding or specifically mentioning education. Despite the lack of direction, bureau commissioner Oliver O. Howard immediately began assisting secular and religious groups already engaged in founding and operating schools for freed slaves. Bureau assistance mainly consisted of providing military protection and supplying funds for school furnishings, textbooks, and the transportation of northern teachers to the South. Howard also centralized the coordination of educational work by appointing a general superintendent of freedmen's schools, John W. Alvord, who supervised bureau superintendents in each southern state. When Congress extended the bureau's life for another two years in 1866, the revised bill approved the educational activities already underway and appropriated money explicitly for school buildings and superintendents' salaries.[17]

As many of its officials intended, the Freedmen's Bureau advanced the cause of public education in Virginia by laying the foundations for a state school system and demonstrating the value of centralized administration. In Alexandria, Hampton, Norfolk, Petersburg, and Richmond, officials organized elementary, secondary, and normal schools that later transitioned to public school systems. Not all schools were for African Americans—the American Union Commission established schools for poor and working-class white children in Richmond, and the bureau's assistant commissioner for Virginia, Orestes Brown, opened similar schools in Petersburg and Fredericksburg. According to General Superintendent Alvord and Virginia State Superintendent R. M. (Ralza Morse) Manly, the high quality of bureau schools made them the standard against which white communities measured the worth of their own educational services. The bureau also improved access to teacher training by acquiescing to local demands for native-born teachers. Hiring southerners was less expensive than transporting teachers from northern states and, officials hoped, would defuse local white hostility toward the schools. Moreover, even though freedpeople had a great deal of affection and appreciation for some of their white teachers, they were very frank about preferring teachers of their own race. Their persistence was an important factor in the founding of normal schools, which were the first training programs of their kind in the South.[18]

The purposeful actions of freedpeople continually pushed forward the work of the bureau in other ways, greatly enhancing the overall impact of its educational division. Their determination to acquire schools and their willingness to sacrifice basic necessities to help fund them were critical given the bureau's limited funding and the South's economic devastation after the war. Black resolve was evident soon after the war began, when African American regiments in southeastern Virginia pooled their resources and labor to build schools for refugee children. When missionary schools established on abandoned land were threatened by the return of Confederate property after the war, black soldiers enabled some to survive by raising the money to purchase locations for permanent institutions. Undeterred by southern white opposition, freed slaves held fundraisers and contributed labor and supplies for the construction of schools, sometimes rushing to build them before there was a promise of teachers and equipment. African Americans in Richmond had founded an astounding forty schools by 1866. Pittsylvania County freedpeople raised $600 to purchase the land on which to build a school in April 1867.

Two black men, one of whom was a freedman, opened private schools when outside assistance was not quick enough in coming. Freedmen also provided physical protection for the white Quakers who operated a school in Danville, standing guard every night after a white man broke into the home of the female teacher with the intention of killing her and burning the school.[19]

Black churches played a central role in organizing communities in support of educational goals, offering moral support and financial assistance in what was often a hostile environment. They helped raise funds, as in 1867 when the Ebenezer Baptist Church held a concert in Richmond to raise funds for a school despite fears that it would be burned by whites when completed. Black churches also provided literacy instruction in Sunday schools, and sometimes held classes during the week as well. The First African Baptist Church opened a school for more than one thousand pupils in Richmond only two weeks after Lee's surrender. A Baptist church in Clover, in Halifax County, and the Union African Church in Appomattox both housed schools during the week. By 1870 such resourcefulness had enabled black Virginians to own more than a hundred schools and contribute to the support of another hundred. African Americans rightfully felt betrayed when Congress prematurely abolished the Freedmen's Bureau, knowing that their herculean efforts had justified its services and expanded the agency's scope of influence well beyond what its inadequate federal funding could have accomplished alone.[20]

Despite widespread hostility toward the Freedmen's Bureau, some southern whites looked to its schools for employment during the hard times following the war. Between 1861 and 1876 almost a quarter of all bureau teachers were white southerners, and by 1870 they outnumbered northern whites. As Celeste Parrish later explained, most southern whites who taught blacks during Reconstruction did so because they desperately needed a source of income. Those who wrote letters to the Freedmen's Bureau mentioned their dire financial straits, and poor white women were especially forthright in stating their need for money. Although bureau officials were mistaken in interpreting an increase in white applicants as evidence that attitudes toward black schools were improving in 1867, Parrish claimed that at least some white teachers had admirable motivations. She argued that the "more thoughtful" sought "to accomplish good in co-operation with the people of the North" by creating "relations of mutual understanding and sympathy." However, they risked ridicule and social ostracism and most reported bitter opposition to their schools, making them reluctant to leave written accounts of this chapter in their lives. As Parrish put it, public disapproval was so strong that "only the bravest philanthropist or a person pressed by great pecuniary need would undertake the task."[21]

White resistance to Reconstruction soon brought federal intervention, providing greater protection and support for the educational ambitions of freedpeople. Virginia was able to avoid radical rule when Lincoln acknowledged the legitimacy of a Unionist state government created in Wheeling in 1861 by opponents of secession. Headed by Governor Francis H. Pierpont, it moved to Alexandria when West Virginia became a state and finally returned to Richmond after the war. When a newly elected legislature convened in December 1865, it was obvious that Conservatives had regained control of state government. They removed a ban on Confederates serving in public office, approved a harsh vagrancy law, and refused to ratify the Fourteenth Amendment. Similar and worse acts of defiance in the former Confederate states convinced Congress to pass the First Reconstruction Act in March 1867. It established martial law in most of the old Confederacy, disfranchised former Confederate officials and banned them from office, enfranchised black men, and required states to hold elections for delegates to state constitutional conventions. These provisions ensured that African American priorities—such as universal education—would have fair consideration in the creation of new state constitutions.[22]

Black delegates were the most passionate advocates of public schools at the Virginia convention and played a prominent role in determining the characteristics of the new system. In the Republican delegation there were twenty-three men from other states, almost all outside the South, and twenty-four black men. Republicans were the first to call for the creation of a public school system, and black delegates introduced numerous resolutions involving all aspects of a modern educational system—administration, funding, training, and compulsory attendance, among others. Conservatives tried unsuccessfully to divide school funds by race and objected to funding provisions they thought would harm the state's credit or unduly burden impoverished Virginians, but the real flashpoint issue was integration. They were unmoved by the sincere appeals of black radicals such as Lewis Lindsey of Richmond, who argued that having one system for all children was a matter of "equal rights and justice to all men." Despite the best efforts of Lindsey and fellow radicals Thomas Bayne and Willis Hodges, proponents of integration lost the battle in the end. Even though Republicans of both races came from modest backgrounds and lacked the Conservative bias against state-funded education, they were split on the issue of mixed schools.[23]

While Republican delegates gained a significant victory in requiring the next legislature to create a public school system, the rhetoric of their opponents plagued advocates of universal education for many decades to come. The Underwood Constitution of 1869 established the office of state superintendent, a state board of education, and a state property tax to supplement the Literary Fund and capitation tax (assessed on voting-age men). Conservative opponents immediately launched an attack on the legitimacy of the constitution, publicizing the northern origins of many radical Republicans. Echoing complaints made against the Freedmen's Bureau, they claimed that advocacy of universal education was motivated by abolitionist bias and a northern desire to punish the white South. Conservatives argued that northerners intended to use education to politically empower blacks and further humiliate whites by forcing former slave owners to pay for the education of persons whose emancipation impoverished them. Virginia bureau superintendent R. M. Manly observed during the convention that whites' opposition to political equality and universal male suffrage made them less likely to support any attempts to improve the status of freedpeople. He witnessed an "unusual hostility" towards black education and a "general dislike of the public school system of the north" during the proceedings. Consequently, although voters ratified the constitution, the provisions for public schools met with an uneven reception among whites.[24]

The significance of the new constitution for single female breadwinners was nothing less than life-changing, as the statewide system of education created a new source of reliable and respectable employment. Celeste Parrish's guardian uncle died in January 1870, and when she went to the county courthouse in Chatham to inquire about her inheritance, what she discovered was truly dismaying. William Walker had used his wards' inheritance as security for a debt and died intestate. Between the suits filed by the administrator of her father's estate and those filed by Walker's debtors, the matter was tied up in the court for years. Parrish had hoped to use her share to finance her education, but after the conflicting claims were settled there was little left to divide with her younger siblings. Fortunately, while she was in Chatham she encountered Dr. George Dame, the first superintendent of schools for Pittsylvania County. He recruited her to take charge of a rural school in the Swansonville community and arranged for her to board in the home of J. W.

Cook Swanson, a family friend who tutored her in mathematics and became her legal guardian. Even though Parrish's monthly salary was less than thirty dollars, it was regular income, a significant improvement over a private fee-based school that relied upon the willingness and ability of parents to pay tuition in any given year.[25]

Celeste Parrish ran the one-room school in Swansonville for five years, building a local reputation that enabled her to acquire a better position. One of her pupils was Claude Augustus Swanson, who served six terms as U.S. representative for Pittsylvania County beginning in 1882 and went on to become governor and U.S. senator. Like her, he began teaching at the age of sixteen and had to earn the money to pay for a college education. Parrish tried to alleviate this burden for her younger sister, using part of her meager salary to pay Mentora's tuition at Roanoke Female College in Danville. She also diligently worked to master the methods described in Page's pedagogical manual and to adapt them to a one-room school with students of all ages. Her success made her school "much noted" in surrounding communities, and in 1875 the county superintendent offered her a position in Danville. This was an important step up for a teacher, as urban schools had more resources than rural ones. Her monthly salary increased by a third, to forty dollars, and equally importantly, relocation to Danville allowed her to enroll in Roanoke Female College.

Married women from modest backgrounds also benefited from the local school systems established during Reconstruction, as teaching positions enabled them to contribute to the support of their families and maintain independence after becoming widowed. In the early 1870s Katherine Graves Moses and her husband depended upon the regular income she brought in through teaching in Pittsylvania County schools to supplement what they could earn on their 165-acre farm. After becoming widowed she continued farming with the help of a nephew while also operating a Danville tobacco warehouse she inherited from her family. Her teaching, which she also continued into the 1880s, provided a steady source of income that served to offset the instability of the agricultural economy. The county school superintendent seemed to recognize that the paid labor of women played an important role in maintaining the solvency of farm and planter households, since he continually supported Katherine's reappointment despite her low scores on qualifying exams. After the death of her husband the superintendent urged Moses to keep teaching and offered to make special arrangements for her to take the teacher exams. Although he may have been desperate for teachers, his sympathy for her plight was obvious in his praise of her good character and dedication to teaching.[26]

The life of Virginia Wilson Hankins further illustrates how teaching positions and access to education were critical to the ability of middling white families to maintain their class status in the aftermath of the Civil War. The fragmentation of households, loss of slave labor, and an unstable agricultural economy made it increasingly difficult to make a living off the land, and education provided a gateway to new sources of support. Hankins's family had been part of the planter elite, but by the time of her father's death in 1870 there was little money left. Her mother had died five years earlier, and as the second oldest of eight children, Virginia was largely responsible for preparing her younger siblings for adulthood. She later claimed that she became a teacher to fulfill a promise made to her dying mother that she would keep her sister and five younger brothers "from sinking by our poverty into ignorance." She used her teacher's salary to support her younger sister Mary and to pay the tuition and living expenses of her brother Louis while he pursued an engineering degree at Auburn University. It is likely that she accepted a teaching position at Montgomery Female College in Alabama to be closer to Louis, since she was eager to return to Virginia when he graduated. In the difficult years of the 1870s Virginia loaned money to another brother who was temporarily incapacitated by illness.[27]

Although Parrish shared some common ground with Hankins and Katherine Moses, generational and class differences made her situation distinct. Moses came from a similar class background as Parrish, but she was more than thirty years old and had a husband and a farm in 1865. Since she and her husband had no children, she had only herself to support after her husband's death. Virginia Hankins, who was only nine years older than Parrish, had wealthy family members able and willing to ease her way in life. She and her younger sister Mary enjoyed lengthy summer visits in the home of a wealthy cousin who took them on vacations and paid their living and traveling expenses. As with Maria Carrington, Virginia's pride and determined independence imposed the only real limit on the financial support she received from extended family. Women such as Parrish—young, single, and lacking family resources—were most heavily dependent on employment in public schools and most in need of higher education. This was especially true if they assumed responsibility for the support of kin, as she did.[28]

Parrish's experiences at Roanoke Female College represented the beginning of a decades-long battle to continue her education against the greatest odds. The only way she could attend classes while continuing to teach in public schools was by boarding at the college, but the main meal there was served during her work hours. She frequently lacked the money and time to eat elsewhere and had to go without dinner. Even though she felt "hungry and faint," she studied into the night to keep up with her classes, plunging her head into cold water to say awake. She later described how she once knelt on the floor instead of sitting in a desperate attempt to keep from falling asleep, only to awaken in pain after she nodded off and her cheek fell onto the kerosene lamp. She received the mathematics medal with her diploma in 1878, but remained "profoundly discouraged." Associating with much younger students who had not experienced her hardship made her profoundly aware of the deprivation she had suffered as a result of the war and her parents' deaths, leaving her "broken-hearted" and "tempted to give up the struggle."[29]

In his efforts to persuade the legislature to provide for their training, the first state superintendent of education, William H. Ruffner, acknowledged how the hardships of war had driven women into teaching. Women comprised little more than a third of all public schoolteachers in the 1870s, but this figure increased to almost half by the mid-1880s, and to two-thirds by the end of the century. In his first annual report, Ruffner explained how the financial difficulties facing white households "were incidentally converted into blessings to the children of the State, by furnishing a large number of accomplished teachers." Ruffner described women as competent and even "superior to males" in elementary-level instruction, echoing the common belief that women's maternal instincts made them especially effective at teaching young children. He went on to note that, even though female teachers exhibited admirable moral character and cultural refinement, hallmarks of the antebellum ideal of womanhood, "no amount of general culture . . . can supply the want of special training in the theory and practice of teaching." Without overtly challenging southern bias against female intellectualism, he implied that the old approach to female education no longer met social needs. After providing state legislators with a basic overview of the content of normal-school curricula, Ruffner made the first of many pitches for the establishment of a state institution for teacher training.[30]

The need to establish uniform professional standards in Virginia's education system required increasing women's access to advanced study, but changes were slow in coming. In the previous two decades the influence of proslavery ideology and rejection of everything northern had caused the South to fall behind the rest of the nation in the education of women. Freedmen's Bureau officials remarked on the superior training of northern women who worked in bureau schools, claiming their pupils were so well educated it was difficult to find native-born southerners qualified to take over their instruction. The obstacles to resolving this problem were poverty and a lack of public colleges open to women. White Virginians established female academies between 1840 and 1860 that catered to the needs of the planter class, but their offerings were mostly at the secondary level. Serving as private high schools for the privileged, they were intended to prepare girls for marriage rather than work. Of the three well-regarded private schools operating in 1870—Hollins Institute (now Hollins University), Augusta Female Seminary (now Mary Baldwin College), and Rawlings Institute—only Hollins briefly offered teacher training between 1865 and 1877, a time when young women who needed an education the most could not have afforded tuition.[31]

The inadequacies of southern female education were in part a result of the proslavery politicization of female dependency and the related assumption that women's influence would be exerted primarily in the domestic sphere. The better schools for girls had a broad curriculum modeled after that of male academies, but differed from boys' schools in objectives. Parents wanted a high-quality education for their daughters as well as for their sons and hoped it would develop the emotional and religious qualities most prized in women. In contrast to northern female academies, which were preparing students to meet the growing need for teachers created by the common-school movement, southern institutions were most concerned with fostering cultural refinement, piety, and filial loyalty. Even as they championed high academic standards, teachers and principals discouraged individualist ambitions that might make girls dissatisfied with the narrowness of their options. In contrast to the expectation that planter sons would leave the academy for college and careers, southern whites fully expected that young women's education would end around the age of sixteen when they returned home to await marriage and motherhood.[32] This assumption was no longer valid after the Civil War, as many women had no homes of their own to return to and no men waiting in the wings to support them.

In the absence of state support, northern philanthropy was crucial in helping female teachers to bridge the gap between past practices and present needs. Southern states scrambling to establish modern school systems used teachers' institutes, usually consisting of several weeks of lectures and course work, as the fastest and most economical way to improve the quality of instruction. The sessions offered an abbreviated version of normal-school curricula, including a review of common school subjects and instruction in methods of organization, administration, and classroom management. However, in Virginia the state constitution prohibited the use of school funds for teacher training, and local governments often lacked the resources to hold institutes. The Peabody Education Fund, established by northern businessman George Peabody in 1867, began donating money for teacher training in the 1870s as part of its mission to improve the quality of southern elementary education. The fund contributed almost $39,000 to Virginia schools in 1874, and while only a small portion of this was earmarked for institutes, fund trustees promised to increase the latter amount if the legislature would establish a state normal school. The appropriations steadily increased throughout the decade, and school officials came to rely upon them so heavily that Virginians often referred to the training sessions as Peabody Institutes.[33]

Even though there was a critical need for state-funded higher education for women, Superintendent Ruffner's campaigns for both a state women's college and a coeducational teachers' college were stymied by complications arising from the restoration of white Conservative control. After the 1869 constitutional convention, moderate white Republicans conspired with moderate Conservatives to end a stalemate with hardline opponents of black suffrage so that Virginia's readmission to the Union could proceed. Their solution was to obtain President Grant's permission to allow voters to approve the new constitution enfranchising black men while voting separately to reject the clauses banning ex-Confederates from public office. Former Confederates endorsed the compromise, and Congress acquiesced to Grant's request to readmit Virginia despite this obvious evasion of Reconstruction policy. "True" Republicans and Conservatives then swept the polls in the 1869 elections, gaining majority control of state government. As Conservatives made further gains in the 1870 and 1871 elections, the split between radicals and moderates led to the marginalization of black men in the Republican Party. The number of African Americans in the state legislature steadily dropped as white Republicans withdrew their support and gerrymandering and suffrage restrictions limited black political clout.[34]

The waning power of radical Republicans had disastrous consequences for public education. With their influence restored in the Conservative Party, eastern elites endorsed fiscal policies that undermined the new system of free schools. Like other southern states, Virginia borrowed heavily to expand canals and railroads in the antebellum era and found repayment difficult after the war. Conservative "funders" refused to endorse the solution adopted in other states—repudiation of most debt—arguing that adhering to their contractual agreements was a matter of honor. In 1871 they passed a bill that funded two-thirds of the state's debt with new interest-bearing bonds and allowed bondholders to use coupons (representing interest owed them) as a substitute for cash when paying their taxes. The Funding Act led to a sharp decline in state revenue and an ever-increasing budget deficit. Unable to push property taxes any higher, Conservatives began taking money earmarked for schools and diverting it to the general fund. Ruffin complained in his reports about a shortfall in state funding, which he estimated to be around $80,000 annually. In 1877–78 the amount of withheld funds ballooned to $250,000, forcing roughly half of the state's schools to remain closed the following fall. African Americans were especially impacted, because even though black children comprised more than 40 percent of the school population, they had access to only 25 percent of public schools.[35]

The statements politicians made in defense of their actions reprised antebellum arguments against public education rooted in concepts of limited government and a natural order. As justification for the diversion of school funds, Governor Frederick Holliday told state legislators that education was a privilege rather than a right, and acquiring it was the responsibility of the individual and not the state. Robert Lewis Dabney, a professor at Union Theological Seminary, agreed that the state had no legitimate authority to compel taxpayers to pay for common schools. Labeling universal education "a false system imposed upon us by our conquerors," he claimed that class and race differences resulted from innate qualities that could not be altered by schools. Education was not appropriate for the "laboring class" of any race, but it was especially dangerous for black youth who had grown up in freedom. Dabney warned that suffrage rights and free schools had given African Americans unrealistic expectations, and educating them to think they were above manual labor would spark race war. The bitter animus flowing from Dabney's pen was partly due to congressional debate over the 1875 civil rights bill, as the version authored by the much-hated Benjamin Butler called for integration of southern public schools and their federal oversight.[36]

Conservatives' race- and class-based arguments did not resonate with the public, and their failure to grasp the extent to which Virginians favored the state school system cost them politically. White opposition came not only from the western counties, but also from farmers active in the Grange and eastern Conservatives who were at odds with elite policies. Public discontent was great enough in 1877 to give Conservative and independent candidates who advocated "readjusting" the state debt a majority of seats in the state legislature. Hindered by a lack of organization, at first Readjusters were reluctant to reach out to African Americans for fear of alienating white voters. In the 1879 elections the split in the white vote enabled radical Republicans to elect twenty-six of their members to the General Assembly, including fourteen blacks. Realizing that African American support would give his party control of both houses of the legislature, Readjuster leader William Mahone won over black lawmakers by pledging to support black education and a reversal of discriminatory policies. The interracial coalition elected Mahone to the U.S. Senate, where he remained until 1886. Funders' white supremacist rhetoric in the 1881 elections could not prevent the Readjusters from maintaining dominance in the state legislature and electing William E. Cameron as governor. The dissent movement was especially attractive to young black men and women who had grown up in freedom and resented the uneven record of white Republicans on civil rights.[37]

It would be difficult to overestimate the importance of the Readjuster victory for white and black teachers from ordinary backgrounds, as it provided them with their first real avenue of upward mobility. When the new legislature met after the election, lawmakers allocated $100,000 for the establishment of the coeducational Virginia Normal and Collegiate Institute in Petersburg, and three years later they passed a bill authorizing the founding of the State Female Normal School in Farmville. The legislature also made provisions for the admission of "state students" who received free tuition in exchange for teaching two years in public schools, a privilege that white men had enjoyed since the 1840s, and which now offered white and black women a way out of poverty. Even though the new schools received only a fraction of the appropriations given annually to the University of Virginia and Virginia Military Institute, their creation was vitally important for young women who aspired to a career in education. They met immediate needs by equipping women to pass teacher examinations, and made attending college a possibility by providing secondary-level instruction that bridged the gap between primary and advanced study.[38]

Celeste Parrish's ability to acquire professional training was almost entirely due to the creation of a state normal school at which women who taught or who planned to teach paid no tuition. She was one of the hundred young women who enrolled in the opening session in October 1884, and she quickly distinguished herself as a talented teacher. Her persistent efforts at self-improvement were obvious when she gave her first practice lesson in the "model school," an elementary school in which normal-school students taught under the supervision of faculty. As Parrish later described it, she "fell easily into the work," and did so well that her supervising teacher insisted that she "had been trained." After she had attended classes for only six weeks, the school principal, former state school superintendent William H. Ruffner, asked her to join the faculty the following year. Even though the state normal school offered only the equivalent of a good high-school education, it represented an important step up for Parrish, who was now academically prepared to pursue college study and could further develop her skills as a teacher.[39]

Just as women of limited means had benefited from black political empowerment during Reconstruction, they found greater stability and opportunity under Readjuster rule. When Conservatives were in control, schoolteachers often had to go without pay for extended periods of time, and many lost their positions when school funds were used to pay interest on the state debt. The Readjusters finally fulfilled a promise made by the 1877 legislature to submit quarterly payments on the amount owed public schools, and used most of the proceeds from sale of the state's railroad investments for school expenses. Between the 1879–80 and 1884–85 terms the number of white schools increased by 1,060 and the number of black schools by 661. Salaries did not appreciably increase during the early 1880s, but they were paid in a timely manner, and communities were more likely to open schools when they could be assured that state contributions would be forthcoming. Readjuster officials also granted black parents' requests for African American teachers and required county officials to give them equal pay. Even though most county and state administrative positions were still held by whites, black local control of education was the greatest it had been since Emancipation.[40]

Black women benefited from the employment opportunities created by the removal of white teachers from black schools, and new positions in schools for both races increasingly went to women. In 1878, women comprised 36 percent of all black teachers and 38 percent of all white teachers. These figures increased to 45 percent of black teachers and more than 50 percent of white teachers in 1885, and then to 61 percent of black teachers and 71 percent of white teachers in 1900. Initially, white men and women monopolized the better-paying positions in Virginia's urban schools, and in 1881 more than 30 percent of black schools, including three out of four in Richmond, had white teachers. This quickly changed as Readjusters gave African Americans greater control of their children's education, but black schools continued to suffer from racial disparities in funding. In 1882 the state superintendent noted that there was one school for every 77 white school-age children in comparison to one for every 158 black school-age children.[41]

Although Readjusters failed to eliminate all forms of discrimination, the balance of power in cities with large African American populations shifted perceptibly. The public visibility and authority of black men increased as Readjuster officials dispensed patronage positions to both races, the legislature abolished the poll tax, and Readjuster judges allowed blacks to serve on juries. In Danville, African American leaders convinced the state legislature to amend the town charter so as to divide the city into three wards, two of which had a black majority. This allowed them to elect four African Americans and four whites to the city council in 1882, giving Readjusters control of municipal government. The city also had two black policemen and a black magistrate of the police court, and shortly after the election city officials removed all white teachers from black schools. Parrish, who was thirty years old and teaching in Danville public schools at the time, personally witnessed these profound changes. She was not displaced by the hiring of black teachers, but she undoubtedly knew white women who were.[42]

Conservatives wasted no time in appealing to white fears that black political empowerment would lead to racial equality. They had a history of playing the race card, but their warnings of Negro dominance did not produce results until interracial politics began to significantly impact the balance of power at the local level. At their 1883 convention in Lynchburg, Conservatives renamed themselves Democrats to distance their party from the "funder" label and then co-opted Readjuster issues by endorsing the state debt settlement (accomplished through the Riddleberger Act in 1882) and free public schools for both races. After thoroughly organizing the state, Democratic speakers in every county and legislative district continually hammered on the threat Readjusters presented for white supremacy. Democratic clubs distributed circulars, and Democratic newspapers published editorials that described a vote for the Readjusters as a vote for integrated schools and interracial marriage. In Danville, where campaigns were especially heated because of its black majority, the Democratic *Times* asserted the need for white unity, telling its readers, "If you want to protect your wives and daughters and keep off bloodshed you must stand up like men for your race and your civilization."[43]

Democrats schemed to use Danville as an example of the dangers of Readjuster rule, creating a climate of intolerance that had disastrous consequences. In October, W. N. Ruffin, a member of the city's Third Ward Democratic Club, helped write the *Danville Circular,* a broadside that described local black officeholders as corrupt, immoral, and dangerous men who were bent on total domination of government. Its litany of white humiliations included the claim that black women were intentionally forcing white women off sidewalks and were insultingly referring to white citizens as men and women while describing black citizens as gentlemen and ladies. A letter to a Lynchburg newspaper editor supposedly written by a Danville merchant decried the "brutality of the black women who flaunt their tawdry, cheap finery about the streets looking for opportunities to insult white women." The circular, also signed by Danville merchants, noted that white property owners were paying most of the taxes that supported African American schools and warned that black political rule would destroy the economy of the state. Distributed only ten days before the election, the statement stoked the racist fires carefully tended by Democratic operatives for months.[44]

The white backlash to black political empowerment hit Danville hard, driving Celeste Parrish out of the public schools. Only three days before the November election, an exchange of insults and a fistfight that occurred after a white man stepped on a black man's foot became further proof that African Americans no longer knew their proper place and must be ushered back to it by force. The mundane street altercation led to a full-blown riot when white men fired into a crowd of black men, women, and children, killing three and fatally wounding another. Although it is unlikely that Virginia Democrats planned the massacre as Readjusters claimed, they deliberately set the stage for confrontation and shamelessly used it afterward to frighten white voters into their camp. Democrats rushed to spread incendiary accounts of the incident, all the while assuring black citizens they would be well treated if they would only stop trying to assert their political rights. Danville resembled an armed encampment on election day, and Democrats threatened more violence if black men attempted to vote. Fearing for their lives, only thirty out of twelve hundred registered black voters cast their ballots. When polling results were tallied, Democrats carried all cities but Norfolk and Petersburg and most counties west of the Blue Ridge. Without directly mentioning the events of 1883, Parrish stated that she "resigned in disgust" that year because of "political complications" in the school system. She taught at Roanoke Female College for a year before enrolling in the State Female Normal School when it opened in 1884, and never returned to public schools as a teacher.[45]

Parrish was thirty-one years of age in 1883, old enough to have a historical context for the Democrats' racist campaign. Claims that integrated classrooms would lead to intermarriage appeared preposterous, as white women had been teaching in African American schools for more than a decade with no corresponding increase in miscegenation. Their role as teachers easily fit the mold of the care-giving duties white slaveholding women performed on farms and plantations before the war, which in Parrish's Baptist household likely included religious instruction. It was socially acceptable exactly because they retained a position of authority over their black pupils and were presumed to exert a positive moral influence. Democratic claims that mixed schools were inevitable also seemed implausible, since white Readjusters made it perfectly clear that this was where they drew the line; they would support black teachers in black schools, and even black men on municipal school boards, but not integrated classrooms. It was a politically necessary position, since support for integration would alienate white voters, but it also reflected the racial biases of white politicians.[46]

Since Celeste Parrish was not the only Virginian with a historical memory, the question remains as to why white men responded to race baiting in 1883 when they had rejected it in 1881. Historian Jane Dailey has convincingly argued that the answer lies in the status of the school as an institution that overlaps public and private. Readjusters wanted white Virginians to believe that they could implement political equality in the public sphere without creating social equality in the private sphere, but schools exposed the artificiality of the division. Governor Cameron unwittingly played into the hands of Democrats when he gave black men direct authority over white female teachers and students by placing them on school boards in Petersburg and Richmond. This seemed to usurp white parents' authority over their children, and it also angered white men who associated the subordination of women to men in the public sphere with women's subordination to men in marriage. Therein lay the logical link in what appeared to be an irrational leap from municipal authority to miscegenation. It did not help that black Readjusters were agitating for the repeal of laws banning interracial marriage, which they regarded as an infringement of individual liberty that codified their inferior legal status.[47]

Scientific racism offered white leaders a rationale for white supremacy that was easier to explain than sexual jealousy. In the late nineteenth century, professors in some of the nation's most prestigious institutions used evolutionary theory to support pseudo-scientific claims of a hierarchy of races. Although race was not a central consideration of sociologist Herbert Spencer when he constructed the intellectual foundations of Social Darwinism, other scholars quickly found racist uses for his concept of social evolution as a corollary of biological evolution. One of the most influential, Harvard professor Nathaniel Southgate Shaler, began arguing in the 1880s that races had evolved differently due to variations in environment. The resulting differences in racial traits had developed over centuries, and if not permanently fixed, could only change through a natural course of evolution over similar periods of time. Scholars who accepted this extrapolation of Spencer's theories agreed that attempts to artificially manipulate the process, such as through education, would be futile. Shaler was particularly insistent in his claim that any semblance of civilization exhibited by freedpeople was a superficial and temporary illusion created by the beneficial influence of white masters under slavery. He repeatedly warned white southerners to guard against the likely regression of African Americans into a state of savagery.[48]

Even progressive-minded men such as state school superintendent William H. Ruffner, who was widely regarded as a champion of black education, were influenced by pseudo-scientific claims that African Americans were innately inferior in morals and self-discipline. On the one hand, Ruffner thought there were no racial differences in the ability of children to learn and grow in intellect and character, and he consistently argued for an equitable division of school funds. On the other hand, he condemned integrated schools in the strongest possible terms, asserting that "moral considerations of the highest obligation" necessitated segregation. These considerations included freedpeople's "notorious laxity in their sexual relations" (as demonstrated by their acceptance of cohabitation and illegitimate births) and a hereditary tendency to duplicity. Educating the races together risked the moral degradation of white children, Ruffin warned, while segregated schools would instill in them the racial pride and segregationist beliefs necessary to prevent amalgamation. R. R. Farr, the Readjuster superintendent who replaced Ruffner in 1882, was equally adamant in his opposition to integration, saying that "white teachers for colored schools is too much mixing for us."[49]

The difficulty of skirting white responsibility for black problems contributed to the convoluted structure of segregationist arguments. In the antebellum South the public and private spheres overlapped on slaveholding farms and plantations; house servants and field workers were members of white households, and their moral education was the responsibility of their masters. The collars of southern white men got a little tighter when they tried to reconcile the purported beneficial influence of slavery with justifications for segregation. They were painfully aware of abolitionist claims that slavery corrupted both white and black southerners, retarding the moral development of slaves while encouraging narcissism and tyranny in masters. Taking a page from the antebellum defense of slavery, they turned to scientific racism to explain how African Americans could be unfit for citizenship and social association with whites after 250 years of intimate contact. White educational leaders seized on industrial education as the answer; just as under slavery, hard work and white supervision would build black character and keep African Americans in their proper place. Virginia's most vocal proponent of this philosophy was Samuel Armstrong, whose Hampton Institute was a regular recipient of state aid.[50]

While Parrish had not yet gained her public voice, her experiences with interracial cooperation produced somewhat different interpretations of the connections between race, education, and the public good. As the daughter, sister, and niece of former slaveholders, she inherited assumptions of white racial superiority and had no reason to identify with the plight of former slaves. However, unlike white men, Parrish did not experience the education and enfranchisement of African Americans as a direct threat to her authority. Her description of the origins of public schools in Reconstruction was sharply critical of Conservative opposition to universal education and praised the founders of Virginia's first school system as "brave." And while she described the Underwood constitution as the product of "negroes, 'carpetbaggers,' and 'scalawags,'" she also insightfully noted that the authors of the "educational provision" represented an "incipient middle class" who were only responding to public needs. Parrish had no reason to view interracial politics or interracial classrooms as dangerous. Reconstruction improved democratic access to education and provided her with a livelihood, and despite Democratic complaints about the corruption of Mahone's regime, for the most part Readjusters were efficient administrators who put public education on sound footing.[51] In her experiences, interracial cooperation was compatible with social progress, and the expansion of state authority could serve the greater good. As she struggled for access to the education and training she needed to rise in her profession, it was white men, not African Americans, who appeared the biggest stumbling block to southerners' adjustment to postbellum conditions.

CHAPTER TWO

The Origins of Activism

I n the 1880s and 1890s, the hurdles she had to overcome in her struggle
for self-improvement and professional advancement only strengthened
Celeste Parrish's commitment to the cause of gender equality. She faced
constant reminders of the handicaps she carried as a member of the last Civil
War generation, and her poverty and awareness of lost opportunities gave her
compassion for the plight of young women of limited means. Parrish knew
that women's exclusion from Virginia's colleges and universities represented
an unjust burden for female teachers, most of whom found it difficult—if
not impossible—to finance an education out of state. In her efforts to bring
current practices into alignment with current needs, Parrish learned valuable lessons about the benefits of forming alliances with men and women
of similar interests. At the same time, her study in northern coeducational
institutions proved the practicality of coeducation and introduced her to a
world of science that held great democratic promise. These experiences laid
the foundations of not only a feminist worldview, but also a sense of purpose
grounded in progressive ideals.

Although the opposition to coeducation that Parrish faced in Virginia had
distinctively southern roots, it had much in common with the larger national
debate about gender roles and intellectual equality of the sexes that increased
in intensity after the Civil War. Disappointed at their exclusion from the Reconstruction amendments, women's rights activists changed their strategy for
attaining full rights of citizenship and launched campaigns in the Northeast
and Midwest to open state colleges and universities to women. The movement gained momentum as the expansion of public school systems created a
need for more teachers, and public pressure soon led to the opening of state

institutions to women in Wisconsin, Kansas, Indiana, and Minnesota. By the 1870s, Cornell University and the state universities of Missouri, Michigan, and California also accepted female students. Despite women's relatively uneventful integration into campus life, many administrators and faculty continued to oppose their presence. Male educators questioned the efficacy of providing men and women with the same education when they were destined for different social roles, and expressed doubts as to the ability of female students to master a course of study designed for the male mind. Opponents of coeducation also drew upon notions of sex difference rooted in evolutionary theory to justify the exclusion of women. In *Sex in Education* (1873) and *The Building of the Brain* (1874), Dr. Edward H. Clarke claimed that rigorous academic study damaged women's reproductive health and masculinized their behavior and appearance. He advised that female fertility could be preserved only by confining young women to bed and strictly limiting their intellectual activity during menstruation.[1]

Such scholarly claims cloaked in the legitimacy of science undermined feminist efforts to convince the public to consider women as individuals and citizens apart from their reproductive role. Theories on sex differences in brain structure had perhaps the most detrimental impact on female education, as they seemed to prove that women's desire for educational equality was unnatural and futile. Numerous scientists noted that women's brains were smaller and lighter on average than men's, which they presumed was either a result of growing sex differentiation (and a part of the progress of civilization) or evidence than women evolved more slowly than men. Although not the first to make such claims, neurologist William A. Hammond popularized the notion that these physiological differences accounted for "diversities of perception, of emotion, of intellect, [and] of will" that made men excel in some areas and women in others. He argued that women were incapable of the abstract thought necessary for intellectual and political leadership and lacked a capacity for higher mathematics. Teaching them subjects that were beyond their abilities was absurd and inefficient; what they needed was teaching methods compatible with their mental traits and a course of study that would "fit them for the duties of their sex."[2]

This argument was similar to white justifications for creating separate institutions and courses of study for African Americans, as both used evolutionary theory to present the struggle for equality as unnatural and misguided. When colleges for women and blacks adopted the curricula of white male institutions to prove equality of intellect and the right to equal participation in public life, their critics trotted out scientific justifications for maintaining the status quo. Sociologists drew upon the concept of a hierarchy of races to assert that African Americans were less evolved and would never equal whites in intellectual development. Male scholars commonly argued in regards to both black people and women that they had innate characteristics that required a segregated education designed to fit them for their rightful (and subordinate) place in the social order. Educating black children to become anything other than artisans and laborers was a waste of resources and only set them up for failure. Refuting claims that black poverty and criminality were the result of unequal opportunity, medical doctors and social scientists argued that the problem was not inferior schools, but inferior students.[3]

In the 1870s and 1880s the cultural authority of evolutionism influenced many educational administrators to agree that female students needed a course of study that fit their particular abilities and the subordinate roles they were to fulfill. Some coeducational colleges, such as Oberlin (which was also interracial) and Knox, created a "Ladies' Course" that partially eliminated requirements of the collegiate course of study to accommodate "differences in mental tendencies between the two sexes." Oberlin's women's course, which omitted Greek and calculus and added classes in French, drawing, and the natural sciences, was fairly typical. Even educators and administrators who believed women had equal capacity for linguistics and higher mathematics accepted other theories of innate intellectual difference. John H. Raymond, president of Vassar College from 1864 to 1878, supported a rigorous course of study that included classic languages, science, and mathematics, but he agreed with male educators who believed that no amount of training could fit a woman to do a man's work. He argued that there was a natural sexual division of labor in the sciences in which men developed theories and the processes of experimentation necessary to prove them, and women assisted in the laboratory and completed the laborious tasks of computation and record-keeping. Apparently, the tasks that best fit women's innate abilities were those that best advanced male careers. As Raymond put it, "Everywhere and always, Eve is Adam's willing, deft, and beautiful 'help-meet.'"[4]

Celeste Parrish was fortunate to have in William H. Ruffner a mentor who did not view women's domestic and reproductive roles as a determinant of their intellectual needs. Educated at Princeton and widely read, Ruffner accepted the basic humanity and autonomy of women as intellectual beings and persons in their own right. First as state school commissioner and then as principal of the State Female Normal School, he was an extraordinary advocate for equality of educational opportunity for women. Giving them access to normal schools was not enough in Ruffner's view; they deserved institutions of "like grade" as those provided for men, a need that private schools could not meet because of their limited resources. In response to state senators' request for advice on female education, Ruffner included in his 1879 report an extended essay on the equal intellectual capacity of women and their equal need for a liberal education. He not only asserted that equality of intellectual development would enrich and uplift marital relations, but also that marriage was "an incidental relation, which should or should not be entered into, according to circumstances." He deplored educational practices that focused on marriage as the end goal, since many women never married and others were soon widowed. Forcefully arguing that, for a woman, "self-culture is her first duty, and self-support her only indispensable purpose," he predicted that equality of opportunity would not be achieved until both men and women regarded a woman as "complete in herself."[5]

At the age of twenty-seven, Parrish finally had a chance to see the world of opportunity denied her as a woman when the University of Virginia temporarily opened its doors to teachers. In 1880, William Ruffner obtained $3,500 dollars from the Peabody Education Fund to pay for two large teachers' institutes—one for black teachers at Lynchburg, and another for white teachers in Charlottesville. The latter event opened the university campus to women for the first time, giving 312 female participants access to dormitories, lecture halls, laboratories, and libraries. Parrish, who stayed for the entire session, described the experience as "another intellectual awakening." The libraries and laboratories were "revelations" to her, and the professors' lectures revealed "great fields of knowledge" about which she had known nothing. Conversations with male university students left her profoundly discouraged, as her education appeared pathetic in comparison to theirs; however, once again, she refused to indulge in feelings of hopelessness. Parrish decided instead to take inspiration from her surroundings. She carefully studied the methods of the "more skillful" instructors and "tried to select all that was good and adapt it" to her public school classroom.[6]

Unfortunately for Parrish, the passionate and erudite essays Ruffner included in his annual reports did little to correct generations of inertia. It was not as if the shortcomings of southern female education were anything new; it was commonly known that antebellum female academies employed northern teachers because of the lack of adequately trained southerners. Virginians attending an education conference in 1841 proposed to remedy this problem by converting "all asylums for female children . . . into institutes for the education of female teachers." The General Assembly declined to take this advice, and when it later passed enabling legislation for the State Female Normal School it allocated a mere $5,000 for initial expenses and $10,000 annually thereafter. The legislature allocated three times as much in annual appropriations for the exclusively male University of Virginia and Virginia Military Institute, as well as regularly providing them with additional funding. Ruffner did not let his appointment as SFNS principal keep him from protesting such blatant discrimination. Observing the liberality with which male politicians doled out money to benefit men, Ruffner implored them to "do justice to the women of Virginia." His discouragement was evident in his simultaneous efforts to influence President Grover Cleveland to appoint him U.S. commissioner of education.

Ruffner's disappointment with the creation of the normal school stemmed not just from its inadequate funding, but also from the fact that he had intended it to be coeducational and not a substitute for a women's university. When state senators asked him for advice on how to address the need for female higher education, he presented three options: coeducation at existing colleges and universities, a separate women's college, or a coeducational teachers' college. His hopes were raised in March 1880 when the General Assembly passed a bill authorizing the establishment of a female university in the Danville area, but legislators failed to appropriate money for that purpose. The ongoing crisis with the Literary Fund probably was to blame, as it would have been difficult for Readjusters to make a case for another university when the common schools were in such desperate circumstances. A growing chorus of voices joined Ruffner in arguing that, if there would be no equivalent institution for women, simple justice and common sense required admitting them to the state university.[7]

Single women who were facing a lifetime of self-support felt the failures of the state most acutely. Parrish's occasional moments of despair came partly from the knowledge that she was well into middle age and still lacked the resources necessary to achieve her professional goals. Even though postbellum reforms increased democratic access to education in the South, public institutions for women rarely matched the quality of those open to men. Like other normal schools, SFNS did not offer college-level work, but rather focused on subjects taught in the public schools and their associated teaching methods. It initially covered only the curricula of primary schools, because it lacked the resources to include high-school subjects. The normal school opened in the old Farmville Female College, which as one teacher described it, had a "small, primitive assembly hall and two shabby classrooms" and a dormitory that consisted of a "series of cubicles." The model school was in an outbuilding, and the library was a "box of books belonging to one of the teachers." State students (who received priority admission) and public school-teachers received free tuition, which made the school heavily dependent on state funding and philanthropic donations for its expenses.[8]

If Ruffner hoped the 1880 summer institute would be an opening wedge for the admission of female students to the University of Virginia, he was disappointed with that outcome as well. The faculty approved plans to hold the institute on campus, but insisted that it remain a separate entity that could not confer university credit for its course of study. Only eight university professors chose to participate, and of those only two—William M. Thornton and Francis H. Smith—proved to be supporters of coeducation. That fall the faculty formed a committee to explore the university's role in the education of teachers, and the conclusions contained it its report seemed promising. Committee members recommended creating a normal department open to women and allowing female students to enroll in other programs of study, providing that an annex with separate residences was established to protect their "womanly modesty and social position." Although a majority of faculty members initially voted to approve the committee report, by the spring they had backed away from its proposals. In their report to the university's board of visitors they stressed that they were merely expressing their opinions and were not suggesting any further action be taken. The issue was not revisited for another decade, and a special course for teachers offered in the fall of 1886 was open only to men.[9]

Southern women's limited access to higher education forced Ruffner to look to the North for instructors with the knowledge and experience necessary to create a teacher-training program that met national standards. He hired two women from the faculty of the Connecticut State Normal School (now Central Connecticut State University), Lillian Lee, and SFNS vice-principal Celeste E. Bush. Music teacher Clara Brimblecom was Boston trained, and Clara W. Miner, a normal-school teacher from New York, took charge of the model school for student teaching. Faculty from the South included Pauline Gash, a graduate of the highly regarded State Normal School at the University of Nashville (later Peabody Normal School and now part of Vanderbilt University) and Richmond teacher Carrie Bartkowska. Parrish became an assistant teacher in her second semester as a student, and her professional competence persuaded Ruffner to hire her to teach mathematics half-time the following year. In his report to the SFNS trustees he explained that she needed the employment to afford the cost of attendance.[10]

Parrish's dedication to her craft was unmistakable, and her duties expanded as Ruffner's estimation of her abilities grew. She had fifteen years of experience as a schoolteacher, and it was obvious that she had worked hard to develop her pedagogical skills. After observing her teaching in the model school, Clara Miner found it difficult to believe that she did not already have normal-school training. Ruffner initially taught the required courses in psychology, ethics, school management, and instructional methods, but as his managerial duties became more demanding he started to assign the courses to Parrish. In the 1885–86 session, her last as a student, she taught the methods class in addition to courses in arithmetic and algebra. When Ruffner had to be absent for an extended period of time in the spring of 1887, he temporarily relieved Parrish of her duties in mathematics so she could teach the rest of his courses in his absence. Ruffner found her "exceedingly thorough and progressive in all she undertook" and persuaded the school's board of trustees to raise her salary to match that of the other full-time instructors, who had been making $800 annually in comparison to her $600.[11]

Parrish's rapid rise in status contributed to tensions that had been building among faculty since the school's opening. Much of the trouble can be traced back to the ways in which living together complicated professional lives. Most of the faculty and staff resided at the school, both for convenience and because it had low rates to make boarding affordable for poor students. Vice-Principal Bush was in charge of the premises when Ruffner was absent and clashed with the woman hired as matron regarding policies governing student conduct. Bush's authority to assign rooms and set rates for faculty boarders was another potential source of friction, as it further blurred the lines between work and home. Living and working in such close quarters exaggerated what otherwise would have been minor differences, causing colleagues to sometimes act more like siblings. The discord that developed between Parrish and the northern teachers apparently was rooted in their belief that Ruffner showed her unwarranted favoritism. He allowed her to attend faculty meetings in her last semester as a student and repeatedly singled her out for praise and promotion. When the relationship between Ruffner and Bush began to deteriorate, the teachers thought Parrish was turning him against the vice-principal.[12]

Matters came to a head in the spring semester of 1887, when the northern teachers closed ranks and tried to force Ruffner and the SFNS Board of Trustees to oust Parrish. At the end of the semester, Ruffner informed Bush of his decision to eliminate the vice-principal position, which would have demoted her to regular faculty status. She responded by declining reappointment for the next year. She told the board that Ruffner had failed to clearly communicate her managerial duties as vice-principal, leaving her uncertain as to exactly when and how to exert her authority. She further claimed that his attitude toward her had degraded to one of suspicion and distrust, making it impossible for her to remain at the school. The other northern teachers— Clara Brimblecom, Clara Miner, and Lillian Lee—wrote to the board, saying that they also would not accept reappointment due to the "course of injustice and misrepresentation pursued by certain members of this faculty." By "certain members" they apparently meant Celeste Parrish, as an investigative committee reported to the board that the teachers most likely would remain if she was refused reappointment. Board members did not appreciate this attempt at manipulation and simply offered to renew the contracts of all the faculty. When Bush and her supporters held firm, the trustees authorized Ruffner to hire replacements and followed his recommendation to abolish the position of vice-principal.[13]

Although professional jealousy no doubt played a role in the controversy, there was more to the conflict than a simple clash of egos. The banding together of the northerners strongly suggests regional differences were involved. Many white southerners were critical of what they regarded as inappropriate northern interference in southern affairs after the Civil War, and they were especially resentful of the teachers who instructed freed slaves. Celeste Bush refused Ruffner's first offer of a position because she feared a Yankee would not be welcome in Virginia, and she might have been overly sensitive to real or imagined slights. The social dynamics of scarcity also could have contributed to the northern teachers' displeasure with Parrish. Historian Carter G. Woodson described how black educators and ministers who had to continually compete for access to scarce resources often began to view one another as rivals rather than as comrades. Professional women faced a similar environment of scarcity in the 1880s, one that was exacerbated in education by the uncertain status of normal schools. Female faculty shared with their institutions an ambiguous professional identity, one that was part academic, part vocational, and located somewhere between a public school and a college. Inadequate state funding, the masculinization of public school administration, and gender discrimination in higher education further undermined their sense of security and constricted their options.[14]

Despite fears that the loss of four instructors would lead to its ruin, the normal school survived the crisis of 1887 and opened under new leadership the next fall. Ruffner retired to pursue his research interests in geology, and Richmond native John Cunningham, a former professor with administrative experience, took his place as principal. The entire Farmville community turned out to bid the departing teachers goodbye as they left on the train together. Remembering the event twenty-two years later, Celeste Bush cryptically concluded, "The four Northern teachers, who had cast in their lots with the school at its start, had never intended a lengthy stay, but they were not permitted to depart without convincing proof that they had done well (for themselves, at least) to come." Of the women hired as their replacements, only one, Virginia Reynolds of Kittaning, Pennsylvania, was from outside the South. Martha Coulling and Madeline Mapp were native Virginians, and Julia Johnson was from Mississippi. There was no further evidence of strife among faculty or between instructors and the principal. Although he paid close attention to every detail of the school's operation, Cunningham also welcomed and respected the teachers' opinions. In his annual reports to the state department of education, he described curricular and policy changes as joint decisions made in consultation with faculty.[15]

The background of one of the new teachers illustrates the difference only fourteen years could make in expanding the options of single women, especially those living in urban areas. Martha Willis Coulling was born in Richmond in 1866 to William D. and Lucy Field Keesee Coulling. She was the second of four children born before her mother died in December 1876. The impact of the Civil War is evident in her household, as three unmarried aunts and a forty-year-old female cousin lived with her family in 1870. Her father's sisters had been in their twenties during the Civil War and were part of the generation of women who had limited opportunities for marriage due to the deaths of so many men. Her father held a clerical position at the First National Bank, and by 1880 her older brother also was working as a clerk and the family was doing well enough to afford a cook. Martha clearly benefited from a stable household and Reconstruction reforms that increased access to education. One aunt was able to obtain a job teaching in the public school system, helping to ease the financial burden of extra household members. After attending Richmond schools, Martha graduated from the State Normal

School in Nashville, which was established in 1875 as one of the South's many postwar educational improvements financed by the Peabody Education Fund.[16]

Although Celeste Parrish frequently noted that younger women had options not available to her generation, she was concerned about those for whom poverty and rural isolation continued to be obstacles to advancement. Even a product of urban schools like Martha Coulling could attend college in Nashville because she was one of the fortunate few to receive a Peabody Education Fund scholarship awarded for that purpose. Most teachers were graduates of the rural schools they taught and could not afford to give up their wages long enough to attend the normal school, much less an out-of-state college, which is why teachers' institutes were so critically necessary. According to the state superintendent, the only resources such teachers had to rely on were "professional reading, *institute work*, and their own experience in their school-room." Parrish could see her younger self in that description, and memories of the angst she suffered due to inadequate preparation motivated her lifetime commitment to teachers' institutes. She graduated from SFNS on June 2, 1886, at the age of thirty-three and, five days later, was teaching 136 teachers gathered in Farmville for one of the four-week institutes financed annually by the Peabody Education Fund. After it was over, she taught another four-week session in Staunton, beginning a pattern that she repeated almost every summer for more than a decade.[17]

Parrish discovered that teachers were still struggling with the same problems she faced in her early years in public schools and was gratified to be able to share her hard-won solutions with them. Her report on the 1886 institutes described the intelligent innovation that underlay her reputation as a skilled teacher. She explained that she had developed her own method for teaching mathematics by integrating the most useful aspects of established methods with what she and other teachers had discovered was most effective through experience. Parrish advised teachers to start with the concrete and move toward the abstract, using as few technical terms and formal definitions as possible. Lessons needed to be appropriate for children's levels of development and relevant to their everyday lives. She emphasized the importance of "having statements developed from the class, instead of having them memorized from a textbook." Knowing that one- and two-room schools with students of mixed ages and skill levels carried their own set of challenges, she provided numerous examples of assignments that could keep one group of students busy while the teacher worked with another. Two years later she published an essay in the state teachers' journal on how to grade a rural one-room school that explained the merits of a graded school and how to convince communities of its value.[18]

Parrish gained benefits from her participation in teachers' institutes that went beyond the satisfaction she derived from mentoring young women. The summer normal sessions served as a professional circuit in which educators could find work to supplement their salaries while exploring educational and employment opportunities. William Ruffner described the position of institute instructor as "the highest career offering to the women of the South, and the most remunerative." In addition to providing her with supplemental income, the institutes helped Parrish develop a larger network of professional acquaintances that included men and women from across the state and nation. For the first five years of sessions, the staff of each institute usually included one or two male lecturers from another state and educators from Virginia's colleges, private academies, and public schools. Beginning in 1891, there was at least one large "Summer School of Methods" that employed a roughly equal number of instructors from inside and outside the state. The institute programs reflected the gendered hierarchy in education, in that virtually all men were listed as professors even if they were public schoolteachers or principals (the latter all male), while women had titles of "Miss" and "Mrs." that indicated marital rather than professional status. However, like normal schools, the institutes offered female educators the chance to teach subjects typically defined as male, such as mathematics and the sciences.[19]

Participation in summer institutes provided Parrish with the opportunity to instruct African American teachers, something rare in the segregated state system. During the 1880s and 1890s institutes for whites and blacks were held in different locations. The sessions for black teachers were staffed by black educators who were mostly from Hampton Institute, Virginia Normal and Collegiate Institute (VNCI), and public schools. In 1899 the black institutes were held in central and eastern Virginia, and the time and expense involved in traveling to Petersburg or Hampton would have prevented many teachers in the western part of the state from attending. Planners of the School of Methods in Roanoke, located between the Blue Ridge and Allegheny mountains in southwestern Virginia, decided to allow local African American teachers to enroll in the white institute. The state superintendent's annual report noted that the sessions were racially segregated. Parrish, who offered instruction in arithmetic and psychology, went to a separate building where the black teachers were gathered to conduct her lessons. Although she had seen white educators instructing black students in Danville, unlike after the Civil War when white economic self-interest had played a major role, in this instance it was part of her professional duties and an extension of the larger campaign to improve the quality of public schools.[20]

Parrish's institute work made her one of the state's best-known and re-spected female educators, putting her in the forefront of Virginia's movement to professionalize teaching. One of the first steps toward establishing a set of uniform standards was the creation of a statewide organization that could provide educators with a unified political voice. While black teachers were organized in the Virginia Teachers Association, white teachers had been with-out representation since the Educational Association of Virginia dissolved in 1882. Taking advantage of the gathering of white teachers at the Lynchburg institute in July 1890, male superintendents invited them to attend a meet-ing at a local hall to discuss forming a state teachers' association. When the meeting was over, Parrish was a member of both the executive committee, which was charged with publicizing the need for a new association, and the program committee for the founding conference to be held the next summer. She understood the significance of including women in the initial stages of organization. The defunct group was male-only when formed in 1863, and a resolution to admit women failed in 1870. When the issue arose again in 1874, members approved it on the condition that female members could not participate in discussion, vote, or hold office.[21]

Parrish's belief in the democratic promise of the new association was clear in her published appeal to educators to support the effort. She claimed the organization would improve the status of female teachers by inspiring them to embrace professional standards and to regard themselves as knowledge-able experts worthy of respect. This, in turn, would convince the public that "teaching is a profession and not a makeshift" form of temporary employment for young men in search of a "more remunerative occupation" and young women desiring "enough money to buy a *trousseau*." Most importantly, the association would provide a democratic forum for the "freest discussion of all subjects connected with the schools," in which female teachers had equal stat-ure with male teachers and administrators. It would enable teachers to take active part in crafting a curriculum that was based on sound pedagogical prin-ciples, yet was "born of our needs and capable of growing with our growth." What Virginia required, Parrish declared, was a system "free from the shackles of sex and class prejudice, yet not wildly radical in its tendencies, which shall place us side by side with our proudest neighbors in intellectual progress."[22]

It was obvious at the 1891 conference in Bedford City that there was no need to fear radical tendencies on the issue of women's higher education. Two of the three presenters on a panel devoted to the topic were Confederate veterans who had little of substance to contribute. The oldest, Superintendent R. C. Saunders of Campbell County, rudely dismissed the issue as irrelevant for public school officials (despite its significance for teacher training) and proceeded to discuss the structure and funding of the school system. He was followed by Brunswick County superintendent and fellow veteran George R. Blick, who acknowledged that women could "learn to think" and waxed poetic on the moral and social value of their education, but closed by suggesting that the needs of primary schools should take priority. The third presenter was a superintendent four years younger than Parrish who expressed opinions more representative of the generation of officials who came of age after the Civil War. In his introductory remarks Gavin Rawls recognized female teachers' need for collegiate training and advocated the policy of separate and equal institutions for women as the best way to meet it. He argued that coeducation was impractical, because public opinion was against it and existing institutions were not equipped to admit female students. Rawls then proceeded to the focus of his talk, which was the importance of educated mothers in the home.[23]

The three superintendents must have been dismayed at the unexpected inclusion of Celeste Parrish as a discussant, for she was unsparing in her criticisms. SFNS instructor Clara Bartkowska was scheduled to comment, but when Rawls finished speaking she asked the session chair to allow her colleague to respond instead. Parrish began by chastising the men for using the panel as a forum to address a variety of topics unrelated to female higher education. Her patience with chivalric flattery worn thin, she complained that women "were growing tired of pretty speeches about their mental equality with men, while by male votes every avenue to higher education was blocked to women." She rejected the notion that the state lacked the resources to accommodate female students in its colleges and universities and promised that the women of Virginia would "actively and energetically fight" for their right to "more than a rudimentary education." She and Bartkowska were members of the committee on the higher education of women that subsequently urged association members "to vigorously agitate the subject [of coeducation] through the coming scholastic year" and to make plans to discuss it again at the next conference.[24]

The conservatism of the male panelists revealed how the new Educational Association of Virginia represented both a challenge and an opportunity for teachers who sought gender equality. When the first year's nominations and elections were over, all offices and committee chairs were held by men, and even those who were supportive of female teachers tended to view them as junior partners. Portsmouth principal Willis A. Jenkins, who attended his mother's private female academy until he was fourteen years old and taught there for several years after college, asserted women's "natural right" to teach while also maintaining there was a "proper division of work between male and female teachers." Like many educational administrators, he believed women's maternal instincts made them superior teachers in the primary grades, a piece of common wisdom that concentrated them in the lowest-paid positions. However, despite male biases, the new association allowed women to vote and serve on panels and committees, providing a space in which they could contest the artificial limits placed on their educational and professional advancement. By uniting hundreds of the state's female teachers in one location, the annual meetings enabled women to gain courage from their numbers and make common cause on issues of justice and equality.[25]

When educators met again in conjunction with the Bedford City School of Methods in the summer of 1892, a group of female participants founded the Society for the Advancement of the Higher Education of Women to press their cause. They elected Celeste Parrish as president and created a committee to ensure that coeducation would be on the state association's program at its next meeting. The women resolved to launch a publicity campaign in the interim by submitting editorials to newspapers and the *Virginia School Journal,* the official organ of the Educational Association of Virginia and the State Department of Public Instruction. They had the whole-hearted support of the state school superintendent, John E. Massey, a former Readjuster who issued a plea to the state legislature for "fairness and justice" in his 1893 report. He noted that self-supporting women had few vocations open to them and would increasingly dominate teaching as men sought more lucrative employment. Observing that Virginia could not afford to establish a separate set of female institutions, Massey argued that there was no "good reason why women should not be admitted to the University of Virginia upon precisely the same terms that men are, and be entitled to all the rights and privileges that men have." Governor Philip McKinney also endorsed the admission of women to the university in his annual address to the legislature that year.[26]

As members of the State Board of Education, Massey and McKinney knew that coeducation was a critical necessity for women who planned careers in teaching but lacked the resources to leave the state. Many young women arrived at the State Female Normal School with marginal academic qualifications and were happy to return to their communities to teach after graduation, expecting to work only until marriage. Others looked to normal-school faculty as role models and developed heightened expectations that were difficult to meet in a state that excluded women from higher education. Men who wanted to teach could get state-supported tuition at the University of Virginia, Virginia Military Institute, and the College of William and Mary, but women—who comprised 65 percent of white teachers and 56 percent of black teachers in 1893—had no such financial aid for college-level study. This is one reason Richmond County superintendent Robert Williamson described the "poor and middling classes" as the strongest advocates of coeducation. They understood that it was the most economical way to provide both men and women with the means of self-support, and liked the convenience of being able to send sons and daughters to the same schools. They were less likely to endorse the exaggerated notions of gender difference used to justify separation of the sexes, since their children went to public schools that, unlike most private academies, educated boys and girls in the same classrooms.[27]

Exclusion from the University of Virginia was a true hardship for single breadwinners like Parrish, whose family obligations prevented them from attending college out of state. Once again the burdens of the Civil War generation came to rest on her shoulders, as depressed land and crop values made it difficult for relatives to absorb shocks to the family labor system that made small-scale agricultural production profitable. Presuming she could help because she had no children of her own, family members repeatedly called upon her to assist them financially when a parent died and there were young mouths to feed. When her oldest brother, William, died in 1879, Parrish helped support his twenty-five-year-old widow and five nieces and nephews. William's youngest son, Joseph Cephus, later told his children and grandchildren how Aunt Celeste had kept his family from starving after his father died. Parrish's sister Frances also died in the 1870s, leaving her husband to support three young children on his income as an agricultural laborer, and sister Sallie Paulina left behind three children when she died in 1887. For years Parrish spent every penny above what she needed for subsistence on the support of her younger sister and brother and her older siblings' children.[28]

In the early 1890s a temporary reprieve from family demands finally enabled Parrish to attend the University of Michigan, where her belief in the practicality of coeducation was fully confirmed. The university's board of regents voted to allow the admission of female students in 1870 after several years of prodding by the state legislature, and President James Angell's enthusiastic support for coeducation helped to ensure that women would be treated with respect. Although there were no female faculty members when Parrish arrived in the spring of 1892, she found a campus where the integration of women had been achieved with little conflict or fanfare. Determined to make the most of her year's leave, she obtained permission to take advanced algebra, analytical geometry, and calculus concurrently. Her successful completion of course work in higher mathematics and astronomy strengthened her resolve to complete her degree, and at year's end Parrish reluctantly returned to Virginia, a state where she was "refused, not only admission to, but even a correspondence course in the university." She had to make special arrangements for independent study while teaching at SFNS in the spring of 1893, driving seven miles every Saturday to meet with a professor at Hampden-Sydney College for men.[29]

That spring, Parrish accepted a new position that required her to again leave the state for college study. The Virginia Conference of the Methodist Episcopal Church, South, which had operated the male Randolph-Macon College in Ashland since 1832, planned to open a women's college in Lynchburg in the fall. The founders of Randolph-Macon Woman's College (RMWC) intended it to be the first institution in the state to offer women a collegiate education equal in quality to the best programs available to men. The first president, William Waugh Smith, chose Parrish to head two departments despite her lack of a college degree—mathematics, based on her formal training, and psychology and pedagogy based on her self-study and practical experience. Parrish lacked Smith's confidence in her ability to teach courses in psychology and spent the summer studying at Cornell University to strengthen her grounding in the field. She found in psychology a social relevance that had been lacking in mathematics. As a close friend later explained her new area of specialization, Parrish was attracted to "a field which more nearly touched the lives of the people." Psychology and pedagogy became the primary focus of her course of study, and after 1898 she gave up her duties in mathematics and made it the focus of her teaching as well.[30]

The intellectual stimulation and purposefulness that Parrish derived from collegiate study enhanced the sense of injustice she shared with members of the Society for the Advancement of the Higher Education of Women (SA-HEW). Their activism was a direct outgrowth of their frustration at the unfair obstacles female teachers faced in trying to develop their scholarly interests. A normal-school colleague, Mary F. Stone, was one of two women whose 1892 petitions to the University of Virginia persuaded the faculty and board of visitors to allow women to stand for examinations. The new policy permitted them to make arrangements with individual professors to complete course work and take exams separately; however, they could not attend lectures or any class activity and earned no university credit. The first woman to complete course work was instructed by a male teaching assistant and took exams at his mother's home near campus. Another SFNS teacher, Fannie Littleton (Kline), completed several summers of work under the supervision of Chemistry Professor John W. Mallet, one of a handful of faculty who actively promoted coeducation. She published three papers based on research conducted in his laboratory, and Cornell University gave her two years of course credit in chemistry for her work with him. Most Virginia faculty opposed even this mild concession to women's needs, and few female students were able to take advantage of the opportunity before it was abolished.[31]

While the new policy seemed to be a step in the right direction, Parrish protested the smallness of the step. In an editorial published in the *Virginia School Journal,* she critically commented, "If I cannot be admitted to the great feast of learning which is spread for men, I will eat of the crumbs that fall from the table rather than not eat at all, but I am looking longingly at the feast proper." She pointed out that professors did not have to grant a woman's request for enrollment, and when they did they were likely to assign her to an assistant rather than perform work for which they would not be compensated. Worse still, women had to pay more than four times as much in course fees as Virginia men (and more than twice the amount charged out-of-state male students) even though they received no university credit. Parrish complained that, if room and board were added to the costs of enrollment, the total expense would "place even the limited privilege[s] offered by the university far beyond the reach of the very women who want them most." The unfairness of such policies either discouraged women from seeking a college degree or forced them to acquire it out of state.[32]

SAHEW members continued to pressure university officials to adopt more inclusive policies throughout 1893. Parrish publicly challenged the claim of the university faculty chair that public sentiment was opposed to coeducation, observing that even the "best families" sent their children to coeducational high schools. She rhetorically asked *Virginia School Journal* readers, "What harm could come from ladies and gentlemen sitting for an hour each day in the same room, especially when they are directly under the eye of an honorable professor?" She observed that the University of Michigan had experienced "twenty years of the fullest and freest co-education" without "one serious scandal." In another editorial she praised the Cornell policy of housing women in a separate building under the "protection and care of a wise matron" while still giving them full access to the university, an arrangement in accordance with "Virginia ideals of social life." She ridiculed the notion that the University of Virginia did not have room for female students, asking why administrators failed to place limits on male enrollment (which was steadily increasing) or to ask the legislature for additional funding if that were the case. At their annual meeting in July, held again in conjunction with the Summer School of Methods and the Educational Association of Virginia conference, members of SAHEW circulated a petition asking the University of Virginia to admit women on equal terms with men, obtaining almost four hundred signatures before sending it to the board of visitors.[33]

Despite the increased pressure from teachers, most university faculty held fast in their opposition, and the board of visitors refused to go against them. After members of the board received the petition, they simply referred the matter back to faculty. The professors responded by creating a committee of five to consider three options—continuing to allow women to stand for exams only, creating a female annex, and implementing coeducation. The university's annual report to state officials for 1893 was a harbinger of what was to come. It described coeducation as contrary to southerners' "settled convictions and rooted prejudices" and arrogantly suggested that wealthy women finance the establishment of a separate female college. When the committee of five completed its investigation the next May, its report agreed with advocates of coeducation that the admission of women on the same terms as men was the best option. The committee's carefully researched and documented conclusions were rejected by two-thirds of faculty members, who voted instead to advise the board of visitors that coeducation "would be unwise and injurious to the best interests of the university." Faculty also moved to discontinue allowing women to stand for examination, beginning in September 1895. Board members endorsed both motions, firmly shutting both the back and the front doors of the state university to women.[34]

The board's decision was strongly influenced by Professor Noah K. Davis, whose separate report outlining the reasons for the faculty's decision included appeals to regional identity. Ignoring the fact that SAHEW was a home-grown organization, Davis attributed its campaign to the "wild schemes of outside agitators." His claim that coeducation would invariably unsex women, making them "familiar, boisterous, bold in manners, often rudely aggressive, and ambitiously competitive with men," was not uniquely southern; however, he argued that crucial aspects of southern identity were at stake. Echoing the antebellum arguments of proslavery writers, Davis insisted that women's social segregation gave them a privileged position in society, one that was the cornerstone of domestic tranquility and stability. He implored the board to consider the larger implications of their decision, claiming that the university was "not acting for ourselves alone, nor for the State of Virginia alone, but for the whole South." Coeducation threatened "the fundamental order of Southern Society," he warned, as it "proposes indirectly, but surely, to remodel our homes." Davis also argued that coeducation would prevent the masculine development of male students and lower academic standards, claims disputed for decades by administrators and faculty of coeducational institutions.[35]

Professor Davis's extended treatise on the dangers of coeducation contained the kind of narrow conception of women's reason for existence that infuriated members of SAHEW and feminists everywhere. His analysis considered female students only as the future sexual partners of men, not as human beings who existed for their own purposes. His main concern was that daily interaction with male students would render young women unfit for matrimony. He worried that female students would lose the modest and beguiling charm that southern men found appealing, and that they might even become sterile from the strain of academic study. Davis repeatedly described the evils that would result from the "comingling of the sexes" in highly sexualized terms, claiming at one point that protecting the virtue of female students would require a "watchful supervision like that over an oriental harem." Strongly suggesting without actually naming seduction and rape as two of the potential evils, Davis asked the board of visitors, "Shall we familiarize our daughters with the thought of such possibilities?"[36]

A speech delivered by one of Davis's colleagues a few days after the faculty decision illustrated how male perspectives were also strongly influenced by the antebellum elite view of equality as a false notion. Professor Charles W. Kent was the only member of the committee of five who openly disagreed with its conclusions, and the issue of gender equality was still on his mind when he addressed female graduates at the Hollins Institute's commencement ceremony. He began by deploring what he regarded as an excess of democracy among the "unwise masses." A spirit of restlessness had infected industrial workers and immigrants, whose constant challenges to traditional leadership were part of a growing social-leveling tendency that would inevitably lead to a "leveling downward." This restlessness had spread to women, influencing them to seek the removal of all distinctions of sex separating them from men. Describing southern whites as conservators of the British aristocratic traits of "knightly bearing and womanly modesty," Kent flatly stated that "man and woman are not equal, similar or the same," and "were not created for the same duties or for similar services." He despaired that any Virginia woman would be willing to throw away her privileged status in pursuit of political and social rights that appropriately belonged to men.[37]

Although Kent's critique of inappropriate aspirations of equality mostly equated gender with class, race also played a part in the university professors' rationale for rejecting coeducation. Noah Davis argued that women could not say that as taxpayers they had a right to attend the university, since "there is another class of inadmissible citizens having this claim." He turned white women's race privilege against them, knowing it would be difficult for them to refute his point if they accepted the legitimacy of excluding black students from the university. Davis concluded that tax-paying citizens merely had the right to an education of equal quality—the separate-but-equal doctrine—deeming it irrelevant that neither women nor blacks had access to a public institution that matched the quality of the university. Moreover, while the state's coeducational black institution, Virginia Normal and Collegiate Institute in Petersburg, at least offered college-level study, the State Female Normal School for white women did not. Male supporters of coeducation were often not far from Davis and Kent in their attitudes toward social roles. Most accepted that sex and race delineated different spheres of influence with distinct personal and social responsibilities, and they even agreed with gender segregation in certain settings. Where they differed was in their willingness to acknowledge that women were not being given equal opportunity to fully explore and prove their potential.[38]

While western Virginians had long criticized the university's elitism, the issue of coeducation exposed for the first time the gendered dimensions of its isolation from ordinary citizens. Charles Kent expressed disapproval of a female friend who had presided over a "promiscuous meeting" of men and women, introduced the male speaker, and sat alone on the platform during his address. He was even more horrified at the thought of a woman delivering a public lecture to a mixed audience. A yawning chasm separated his world from that of SAHEW members who regularly addressed men and women at institutes and conferences. Ignoring Kent's condemnation of societies as "hot-beds of dissention and evil," SAHEW continued to work within the Educational Association of Virginia to build support for coeducation among educators who understood that higher professional standards could not be achieved in public schools unless women had access to collegiate training. The group's influence is evident in EAV proceedings, which included addresses from male professors and officials who advocated opening all state institutions to women, and in the election of a woman to the office of vice-president in 1894. Parrish spoke on "Women as Educators" at the opening session that year before leaving with colleague Kate Hunt for another summer at Cornell. At the conclusion of her presentation, Parrish pointedly observed that she had to go north every year if she wanted to study the "best and latest thoughts and methods."[39]

One of the women in Parrish's audience exemplified the potential connections between coeducation, women's rights, and racial equality that seemed to worry conservative men. Orra Langhorne had served as the state's self-appointed delegate to national suffrage conventions since 1880 and was an outspoken advocate of integrated public schools. Having founded a suffrage organization in Lynchburg the previous year, she was using the summer institutes to recruit new members. She distributed suffrage literature to participants, about three-fourths of whom she estimated to be female, and challenged the male history lecturer to explain why women should not revolt against taxation without representation as the nation's revolutionary leaders had done; he sternly told her the question was inappropriate. Langhorne admired Celeste Parrish for her tenacity, intelligence, and forthrightness, and began citing her in editorials as an example of the potential of educated southern womanhood. She described Parrish as "extremely anxious that Virginia women should have greater advantages than are now offered to them," and optimistically predicted the eventual success of the SAHEW campaign and the realization of Thomas Jefferson's dream of a democratic system of education.[40]

One of female teachers' most prominent male supporters also summoned the image of Thomas Jefferson to shame the university. William A. Fentress was born during the lean years of the 1860s and struggled throughout his shortened life from pain and disability resulting from a childhood bout with polio. After attending public schools, he worked for three years as a telegraph-office clerk to earn the money to study law at the University of Virginia, and continued to work nights after graduation while building his practice. During a two-year term in the House of Delegates he made education his central cause, sponsoring a bill to provide state funding for teachers' institutes and another to eliminate obstacles to local taxation for schools. A speech on the higher education of women he delivered to university alumni (who opposed coeducation) in the spring of 1894 expressed sentiments that sprang from his own experiences with hardship. Fentress described "popular progressive education" as a democratic "diffusion of knowledge" that improves communities and safeguards the state by providing for an intelligent and informed citizenry. Scornfully observing that the men who approved the founding of the State Female Normal School were motivated by a need for teachers rather than by a desire for justice, he asked by what right did men limit women's choices? The university should not blindly hold onto conservative traditions or hide behind public opinion, he argued; it had a duty to provide leadership as Jefferson had done, to be "in the vanguard of this progressive march, not lagging in the rear."[41]

Forced to deal with conditions as they were and not as they should be, Parrish found at Cornell a brief respite from southern conservatism and a model for higher education in which male professors took women's scholarly abilities seriously. To develop an expertise in psychology, she began working with Edward B. Titchener, a British-born experimental psychologist who was only in his mid-twenties when he arrived at Cornell in 1893. Although historians have criticized him for excluding women from his study group, the Experimentalists, Titchener was otherwise supportive of female students. More than a third of the doctorates earned by his students went to women, and one, Margaret Floy Washburn, was the first woman in the United States to receive a PhD in psychology. Parrish took Titchener's introductory course during her first summer in New York and convinced him to continue tutoring her until the fall semester began. She also persuaded him to supervise correspondence work after she returned to Virginia, even though Cornell had no provisions for independent study. Desperate to acquire the knowledge she needed for her new position, Parrish overcame his initial reluctance by pleading that "a man who sits down to the rich feasts which are spread before you has no right to deny a few crumbs to a poor starveling like me." In 1895 she conducted research in his laboratory using three Cornell professors and their spouses (including Titchener and his wife) as subjects, which along with work completed the following year became the basis of two articles published in the *American Journal of Psychology.*[42]

Parrish's research was typical of the new psychology practiced by Titchener and other students of German scholar Wilhelm Wundt, in that it recorded subjects' responses to sensations as a method of exploring the elements of consciousness. Experimental psychology as Titchener practiced it involved the collection of data on the structure of the basic elements—sensations, images, and thought or feelings—in a controlled laboratory environment. The emphasis on experimentation and observation served to establish the scientific credentials of psychology and to distance the study of the mind from its past associations with philosophical speculation and paranormal phenomena. Other prominent psychologists who earned their doctorates with Wundt included the first professor of psychology in the United States, James McKeen Cattell, as well as Frank Angell and G. Stanley Hall. Hall established the first American psychological laboratory at Johns Hopkins University in 1883 and founded the *American Journal of Psychology* four years later to provide a forum for publication of experimental research. Angell founded the laboratory at Cornell and recommended Titchener as his replacement when he left for Stanford University, where he established another laboratory.[43]

Even with Titchener's friendship and support it took a herculean effort for Parrish to complete her undergraduate degree. Cornell's policies were not created for women who took nontraditional paths in their education. She was fortunate that the university was willing to credit her year of work at Michigan and "work done without a teacher" toward degree requirements. To receive credit for the latter she had to take a series of grueling examinations that covered material she had studied informally or under a professor's guidance while in Virginia. In the summer of 1895 she enrolled in twenty-four course hours and took additional examinations so that she could finish her degree the following year, only to discover that she would not meet the residency requirements. She could only get a one-semester leave from RMWC the next spring and Cornell did not count summer sessions toward the one-year minimum residence requirement. Parrish made an appointment to meet with the university president, Jacob G. Schurman, to plead her case. Schurman was sympathetic, but claimed he lacked the authority to make an exception and recommended that she repeat her story to every member of the faculty. Her petition was granted after she followed his advice, but the process was so stressful that it was months before Parrish recovered from the toll it took on her health. Still feeling unwell, she returned to New York in the spring and was awarded a bachelor of philosophy degree in June 1896.[44]

The benefits of women's collegiate study for southern education were evident soon after Parrish began her work with Titchener, when she asked President Smith to fund the establishment of a psychological laboratory at RMWC.

Most midwestern state universities had such laboratories by 1894, but there were none in the South and only one at a woman's college, Wellesley. Smith was like most college administrators in doubting the feasibility of including experimental psychology in the curriculum, especially at the undergraduate level. He told Parrish he could give her only twenty-five dollars, which she spent on basic equipment for use in the fall of 1894. She used her notes from Titchener's course as text until he published a textbook for undergraduate studies in 1896.[45]

Parrish added to the prestige and academic standing of Randolph-Macon Woman's College by implementing a program of study that not only met but actually exceeded professional standards. A report prepared for the U.S. commissioner of education on the "psychological revival" in higher education mentioned RMWC, along with Wellesley and Bryn Mawr, in its discussion of women's colleges offering a course of study in psychology. The introductory and advanced psychology courses taught by Parrish included experimental work in addition to lectures and readings that she chose specifically for students who intended to teach or who already were teachers. In combining experimental psychology with courses in theoretical and practical pedagogy, she went beyond the latest recommendations of the National Educational Association for teacher training. The advanced nature of the program no doubt contributed to the classification of RMWC as a "Division A" institution that met national collegiate standards, making it the only women's college in the South—and one of the smallest in the nation—to receive that designation in 1894. A history of the college credits Parrish's work as being "one of the most important factors in the success of the institution."[46]

Parrish's embrace of the new psychology was based in part on its promise as a tool of educational reform. Educators had great expectations regarding its ability to improve pedagogical practices and raise the professional status of teaching by grounding it in science. They were encouraged by psychologists who valued teachers as partners in child study, a popular branch of the new discipline dedicated to exploring the nature and phases of child development. Advocates of child study promoted a comprehensive program of research consisting primarily of directed observation conducted by psychologists, teachers, and parents. They believed the results would provide a blueprint for coordinating modes and topics of instruction with stages of physiological development. Experimental psychology and child study shared an interest in the central nervous system and its relation to mental processes, although experts in the two branches often were at odds with one another. Evolutionary theory also stimulated psychologists' interest in child development, since children were supposed to recapitulate the evolution of humankind during their first six years of life. G. Stanley Hall, leader of the child-study movement, argued that the growth of infants "epitomizes under our eyes the history of the race, each day sometimes representing perhaps the race-development of centuries."[47]

The democratic structure of the child-study movement held particular appeal for Parrish. While its critics ridiculed the idea of amateurs conducting scientific research, a broad cross-section of educators appreciated the closer connections it formed between the university, the normal school, and the public school. As Hall explained, interest in child study helped "to break down to some extent the partitions between grades of work, so that the kindergartener and university professor can cooperate in the same task." This aspect of the movement was at odds with the prevailing concentration of academic authority in the overwhelmingly male upper echelons of higher education. Child study had democratic qualities at the other end of the educational spectrum as well, prescribing a holistic approach to child welfare that required closer relations between teachers and parents. Middle-class women with college educations were especially drawn to the movement, and in clubs across the nation they turned to child-study literature for insights that might be applied to their own homes and schools. Male psychologists who opposed the cooperative approach to research had legitimate complaints, since it was difficult to simultaneously create a democracy of knowledge and maintain strict scholarly standards; however, in many instances their words betrayed a contempt for the intellectual abilities of female schoolteachers, and perhaps even concern for the feminization of their profession.[48]

In December 1898 Parrish took Harvard psychologist Hugo Münsterberg to task for his arrogant dismissal of the value of the new psychology for educators. Even though he was interested in the practical application of psychological principles, Münsterberg published two articles earlier in the year in which he deplored the fact that "experimenting with children has become the teacher's sport." Expressing sentiments shared by other male psychologists, he argued that training in psychology was likely to ruin a good teacher, since "love and tact and patience and sympathy and interest are more important for the teacher than any psychological observations." In a conference paper that was reprinted in the *Southern Educational Journal,* Parrish expressed her astonishment that Münsterberg would claim that "knowledge of the laws of the mind is not necessary to the teacher whose business is to train the mind." She countered that for "so important a work" as child development, "both mother and teacher need training." Regarding his statement that he loved his children but would never study them, Parrish tartly replied that this attitude may be "fortunate or unfortunate for the juvenile Münsterbergs according to circumstances, but it also indicates a kind of parental neglect which the nineteenth century father of even average enlightenment does not ordinarily boast of."[49]

From Celeste Parrish's perspective, it appeared that the actual conditions of life were changing much more quickly than male attitudes in the last decade of the nineteenth century. Mothers who faced the sudden need for self-sufficiency in the 1860s and 1870s tried to instill a "feeling of independence" in their daughters and looked to teaching as a way to ensure young women would always have a means of self-support. Public officials in dire need of teachers recognized the convenient confluence of needs, but this did not necessarily translate into equal access to professional training and opportunities. As women increasingly sought the credentials necessary for career advancement, elitist tendencies in southern higher education previously defined mostly in class terms acquired a distinctive gendered dimension that ran parallel to exclusion based on race. Antebellum notions of a natural order converged with male fears of economic competition to produce hierarchies of knowledge and power that belied the democratic promise of the evolving sciences. Faced with obstacles on multiple fronts, Parrish honed her organizational skills while earning a reputation in her home state as a brilliant educator and a force to be reckoned with on the issue of gender equality. Not surprisingly, she soon was drawn to the nation's most progressive university for graduate study, where she developed the mature voice necessary to become a regional leader in progressive reform.[50]

Celeste Parrish in about 1905. Courtesy of the Psychology
Department, University of Georgia-Athens.

Parrish (standing, at left) in the Randolph-Macon Woman's College Psychology
Lab that she founded after studying with Edward Titchener at Cornell University.
Courtesy of Randolph College.

The Georgia State Normal School in Athens as it appeared in the 1898–1899 school term. Georgia State Normal School Records, Box 3, Folder 57. Courtesy of the Heritage Room, Athens-Clarke County Library, Athens, Georgia.

A panoramic view of the practice school that Parrish founded at the Georgia State Normal School with donations solicited from philanthropist George Foster Peabody. She used it to showcase the efficacy and value of John Dewey's "new education." Georgia State Normal School Records, Box 4, Folder 98, Courtesy of the Heritage Room, Athens-Clarke County Library, Athens, Georgia.

The officers of the Georgia State Normal School chapter of the Young Women's Christian Association in 1906. Although Parrish was not their faculty sponsor, she regularly participated in YWCA conventions and helped to found college chapters in the South. Courtesy of Hargrett Rare Book and Manuscript Library, University of Georgia Libraries.

C. S. Parrish, Ph.B.,
Chair of Psychology and Pedagogy.

She's the darling of the Seniors, the pride of all the School,
  And "Development" 's the hobby that she rides;
She keeps so very busy giving other folks a rule
  That she hasn't time for anything besides.

Georgia State Normal School students penned this tribute to Parrish, which acknowledged her commitment to progressive reform and public service. They published it in their 1907 yearbook below a photograph taken earlier in her career. Courtesy of Hargrett Rare Book and Manuscript Library, University of Georgia Libraries.

A group of faculty from the Georgia State Normal School, circa 1901. Normal School President Eugene Cunningham Branson is in the front row, far right. Courtesy of Hargrett Rare Book and Manuscript Library, University of Georgia Libraries.

CHAPTER THREE

The Integration of Faith and Science

C eleste Parrish's enrollment in the University of Chicago graduate program ranked second only to the Civil War in its transformational effects
on her life. The three summers she spent in Chicago between 1896 and
1898 exposed her to some of the nation's most talented progressive intellectuals, providing her with a wider context in which to evaluate the problems
and needs of the South. She had the opportunity to study under university
president William Rainey Harper, who was a fellow Baptist and advocate of
the Social Gospel, as well as educational innovator John Dewey and other
faculty who embraced the intellectual's obligation to public service. She also
became acquainted with women such as Marion Talbot who shared her views
on gender equality and female education. One result, membership in the
Association of Collegiate Alumnae, extended Parrish's professional network
to include prominent college-educated women from across the nation who
were active in social reform. As she expanded her activities to include a variety of regional and national organizations, Parrish wrote a series of essays
that incorporated a new synthesis of faith and science in a sweeping analysis
of the need for educational reform that was particularly pointed in its critique
of southern gender relations.

Like many progressive reformers, Parrish had been strongly influenced
by the Social Gospel movement in the decade prior to her enrollment at the
University of Chicago. The movement emerged in the 1880s among ministers and community activists who were concerned about the many problems
resulting from industrialization. They focused on the need for both personal
and social salvation, and advocated reforms they believed would fulfill God's
will by grounding society in the precepts of Christian ethics. These powerful

ideals appealed to many professionals in the social sciences and galvanized ordinary churchgoers across the nation. The Social Gospel's call to service was especially appealing to women, for whom it justified a more public role. After she became president of the Woman's Christian Temperance Union (WCTU) in 1879, Frances Willard developed a concept of womanhood as a powerful force for good in the world. She envisioned an army of strong, self-reliant Christian women dedicated to social uplift and working to create a more egalitarian and democratic society. Among black women, dedication to this goal was fused with a commitment to race uplift, and for many women embrace of Social Gospel ideals led to support for woman suffrage.[1]

While southern white women were less likely to endorse suffragism, they appreciated the opportunity offered by Christian organizations to engage in social reform work without overtly challenging male authority. Urged by their ministers to embrace the Christian duty of service to others, they rejected the notion that feminine selflessness should be defined only in terms of their personal relationships with men. In 1882, an Alabama woman informed members of her Baptist female missionary society that the gospel freed them from a life of menial labor serving men's physical needs, elevating and widening their purpose to include fulfillment of duties to themselves, God, and society. Evangelical women responded to this sense of higher duty by creating social-service committees that tackled a wide range of issues. Many defied their ministers by expanding their activities beyond their own churches and communities, first through missionary work and then through membership in the Woman's Christian Temperance Union. Even though southern chapters of the WCTU tended to be more conservative than was typical of chapters elsewhere in the nation, they helped to ease the transition of women, both white and black, from missionary work to political organization in the 1880s–90s.[2]

As Christian women expanded the scope of their work, they found that there were limits to the autonomy and control that male ministers and congregants were willing to allow them. Baptist women's efforts to create female missionary societies in the 1870s and 1880s met with resistance from both northern and southern men who feared women's separate organization would blur gender roles in the church and challenge male control of the pulpit. Resistance was greatest in the South, and southern ministers were most likely to interpret the Bible as prohibiting a leadership role for women. As a result, the Southern Baptist Convention did not create the (white) Women's Missionary Union until 1888, even though northern Baptists had formed female foreign and home missionary societies more than a decade earlier. Southern black women faced similar resistance when they began forming separate state conventions in 1883. Believing they had a special role to play in advancing the race, they insisted on the right to control their own work despite encountering sharp criticism.[3]

Parrish, who was a member of the WCTU and church missionary societies, played a key role in the separate organization of white Baptist women in Virginia. Autonomous female missionary societies had a long history of conflict with the Baptist General Association of Virginia (the state convention) due to male fears that women's separate organization would produce female preachers and "suffragettes." These concerns prevented Virginia women from joining the new female auxiliary to the Southern Baptist Convention in 1888, even though it was created at a Richmond meeting called by them. In 1897 Celeste Parrish presented a motion at a meeting of the Central Committee of Woman's Missionary Societies—Virginia women's liaison with the general association—recommending the adoption of a more democratic organizational structure that included representatives from every female missionary society and church group in the state. Attendees unanimously approved her plan and appointed her chair of the committee charged with hammering out the details. Over the next three years, Parrish piloted the Baptist women through the structural transformation, helping them to revise their constitution and bylaws and gain the recognition of Baptist men. Her guidance was crucial to the creation of an organization at the state level, the Woman's Missionary Union of Virginia, that was analogous to the regional auxiliary they had been unable to join more than a decade earlier.[4]

Parrish's leadership role in the reorganization of Virginia's female missionary societies illustrated her tendency to define—and justify—female autonomy in terms of religious and social service. Her Baptist faith and Social Gospel ideals provided Parrish with a sense of purpose that defied the notion that women who chose a career over marriage were shirking their duties to family and society. In her understanding of the connection between intellectual and moral development, her responsibilities as an educator were an extension of her wider Christian duties. She regarded teaching as a sacred calling and equated her dedication to professional excellence with dedication to God. Selflessness meant, among other things, putting the educational needs of the South ahead of personal ambition. As she explained it, women imbued with a "spirit of service" who went north for their college education would not remain there to take advantage of superior career opportunities.

Instead, they would "come back to their own people, take the small salary, do the drudgery," and dedicate "the time and energy which they would like to expend in scholarly ways to the work of developing the society of which they were born a part." By following this path of duty, a woman would "consecrate her best self." It was not a matter of individual rights, but of moral obligations, and one of Parrish's main objectives as a teacher was to instill this sense of social responsibility in female students.[5]

Parrish's belief that women had a special role to play in social reform gave her concern for educational equality a particular urgency. She disapproved of students who were more interested in social life than in their studies and had little use for rules that held women to academic standards less rigorous than those applied to men. She would not let normal-school students avoid difficult subjects, in one instance forcing two of them to drop their French class instead of her mathematics course. Her examinations were notoriously difficult, and she sometimes ignored an SFNS rule that students be subjected to only one test per day, which was Ruffner's concession to parents who feared intense study would compromise their daughters' health. Randolph-Macon Woman's College rejected such gender-based distinctions, and one RMWC pupil recalled that Parrish "took pride in marshalling her students before skeptics to show that their health was unimpaired." Some students suspected that she assigned them twice the normal reading load to demonstrate that "girls could do as much work as the boys." Despite the rewards of teaching in a more progressive institution, Parrish remained frustrated with the social pressure exerted on her students to prioritize marriage over intellectual development and the duty of social service.[6]

Parrish's inclination to view the duties of a teacher through a Christian lens was reinforced by the prominence of religion in southern education. Churches played a key role in founding schools for girls and women prior to the establishment of a public school system, and they continued to provide critical support after the Civil War. Roanoke Female College, where Parrish received a diploma in 1878, was previously the Baptist Female Seminary and had a long history of patronage by Danville churches and the Roanoke Baptist Association. Although established more recently, Randolph-Macon Woman's College was part of an extensive system of academies and colleges operated by the Methodist Episcopal Church, South. Even secular public institutions were frequently headed by ministers and included religious worship in their daily activities. At the State Female Normal School, students met for a short devotional service every weekday morning and on Sundays attended Bible school at their church of choice. Parrish taught Bible classes as well as occasionally leading chapel services on campus. One SFNS student described the entire faculty as Christians who "taught in Sunday School and tried in every way to influence us for good."[7]

Parrish led by example in her attempts to encourage students to adopt a higher sense of purpose. Gillie Larew, a colleague at Randolph-Macon Woman's College, described the wide range of activities that characterized Parrish's life in Virginia: "Through the whole fabric of her busy life runs, too, an unending sequence of services to others—relatives helped with time and money and interest; girls who needed money or sympathy or advice finding them all in her; neighborhood groups to be led—a group of young mothers studying child-psychology, a group of young teachers learning how to teach, a Sunday School class fired with her enthusiasm and spiritual devotion, an informal gathering of college girls coming Sunday after Sunday to discuss the questions of conduct and faith and ideals that college girls should be discussing. Some way she found time for all of this."[8]

Students and colleagues were impressed by the exacting standards to which Parrish held herself. Fannie Littleton Kline, a normal-school student who became her colleague, was deeply moved by Parrish's reverence for truth and thoughtful consideration of the needs of others. Kline admitted that Parrish could become impatient with students who did not "live up to her standard," but enthused that "it was just because this standard was so rare and high, and so perfectly embodied in her life that it became to many of us a thing alive, vital, and self-perpetuating." Nellie Virginia Powell, a student who assisted Parrish in the psychological laboratory at Randolph-Macon Woman's College, also remarked on her unqualified honesty, generosity, and selflessness. After relating Parrish's "conviction that intelligent service could aid in revitalizing Christianity," Powell added, "With Miss Parrish, action crowded on the heels of conviction."[9]

As a Baptist institution hospitable to Social Gospel ideals, the University of Chicago held obvious appeal for Parrish. William Rainey Harper, who was a professor of Hebrew at the Baptist Theological Union before becoming the university's first president, was a proponent of the new theology dedicated to upholding the relevance of religion in an age of science. He supported the university founders' decision to ban the use of religion as a factor in the hiring of faculty and staff, confident that, since "Searching for the truth is searching for God," there was nothing to fear from academic freedom. He contended that a collaborative process of free inquiry preserved religious freedom by encouraging appreciation for diverse perspectives. Harper shared with other nationally prominent educators, such as Nicholas Murray Butler, a corresponding belief that education was a bulwark of democracy. Their reasoning echoed Thomas Jefferson's concern for maintaining an educated citizenry imbued with public virtue, or public-mindedness, a civic form of selflessness now threatened by political bossism and the spoils system. Harper envisioned the university as the "guide of the people" in this endeavor, an "ally of humanity in its struggle for advancement."[10]

To this end, Harper tried to integrate the university into the community life of the city and to make it a force for civic improvement. He created a University Extension Division with public lectures, evening classes, and correspondence work that took the classroom to the people, and encouraged professors to engage in community affairs. The early faculty in the departments of sociology and philosophy were especially responsive to the call. Sociology chair Albion Small was the son of a Baptist preacher who had trained for the ministry before pursuing graduate study abroad. He maintained close ties with the city's social settlements (once offering Jane Addams a half-time graduate faculty position that she turned down) and was a member of the Civic Federation of Chicago. His colleague, Charles R. Henderson, was a Baptist minister who was attracted to sociology primarily for its practical applications to social problems. Both Small and Henderson regarded "applied sociology" as especially appropriate for women who wished to use the discipline as a tool of reform. Philosophers John Dewey, George Herbert Mead, and James H. Tufts also were actively involved in issues of social and economic justice and served on the board of Hull House. Like Small, Mead and Tufts were sons of ministers.[11]

Many women associated with the university demonstrated an even deeper commitment to service by living the ideals of democratic community in social settlements. As sociologist Mary Jo Deegan has meticulously documented in her research on the women of Chicago, the city's female reform networks closely linked campus and community and played a major role in the development of both sociology and pragmatism. Hull House residents Jane Addams, Julia Lathrop, and Florence Kelley conducted sociological research on problems impacting working-class families and frequently spoke on campus, either as extension faculty or at club meetings and other events. A former member of Hull House, Mary E. McDowell, became head resident of the University of Chicago Settlement when it opened in 1894 and remained there for most of her life. She was outspoken in her opposition to xenophobia and racism, and

Chicagoans dubbed her the "angel of the stockyards" for her fierce advocacy of workers' rights. Two women who were graduate students at the same time as Celeste Parrish, Sophonisba Breckinridge and Annie Marion MacLean, later joined the faculty and contributed to Hull House research projects.[12]

As the careers of Breckinridge and MacLean illustrate, the Chicago faculty was more welcoming of female graduate students than was typical of most coeducational universities. The university's charter was unequivocal in stating that it would "provide, impart, and furnish opportunities for all departments of higher education to persons of both sexes on equal terms." Although institutional support for gender equality was uneven at best, the university quickly became a national leader in the award of doctoral degrees to women. Female graduate students benefited from the opportunity to work with young professors who had gone to coeducational institutions, married educated women, and were comfortable interacting with them as intellectual equals. This category included the professors of philosophy and psychology— James R. Angell, Dewey, Mead, and Tufts—with whom Parrish took most of her courses. Equally important for the creation of a hospitable environment was the University of Chicago's unique status in having nine female faculty members when it opened in 1892. In contrast, Cornell University did not hire a woman for an instructional position until the late 1890s, and it did not have a female professor of any rank in its College of Arts and Sciences until 1947.[13]

A final characteristic of the university that drew Parrish to Chicago was its innovative plan of year-round study. In most colleges and universities the summer sessions were of shorter duration and had fewer offerings than the fall and spring semesters, because they were not a regular part of the academic year. Harper favored the quarter system because it made more efficient use of university facilities. It also gave faculty and students greater flexibility, since professors could teach any three quarters in a year and students could complete their degrees earlier if they wished. At first professors were skeptical of the system, but the seriousness and diversity of the summer-quarter students soon overcame their resistance. Most summer students were faculty and administrators from secondary schools and colleges, and the opportunity to teach teachers appealed to professors committed to public service; they liked to imagine their students returning to institutions across the nation freshly motivated and better prepared to offer high-quality instruction. Traditional students remarked on the presence of the "middle-aged woman" whose predominance in classrooms during the summer quarter changed the tenor of discussion. In August 1898 the university's student publication humorously lamented the departure of the "spectacled high-school teacher" who distracted professors from the inadequacies of less-prepared classmates by taking determined stands and attempting "to show to the learned professor that she knew what she was talking about."[14]

The students who flocked to the university during the summer quarters changed the climate of campus social life as well as the classroom environment. Registration numbers steadily increased as female teachers eagerly took advantage of the unprecedented access to higher education, and the women's quadrangle virtually hummed with activity. Parrish stayed in the women's dormitories, whose residents took turns hosting events for students, faculty, and President Harper and his wife. When not studying or entertaining guests, groups of women went on bicycle rides down Chicago boulevards and enjoyed private gatherings in their individual halls. In Parrish's second summer of enrollment, Jane Addams made one of her many appearances on the women's quadrangle to speak on Hull House and invite students to visit the settlement. Female students also staged a function for women only in which they formed groups according to state of origin and staged presentations that expressed something about their home cultures. Southern women regaled the participants with a rendition of "Dixie," and representatives of Georgia formed their own club and staged a reception for all the female halls.[15]

The spirit of camaraderie that permeated the women's quadrangle was carefully cultivated by the dean of women, Marion Talbot. She understood the awkward position of college women who did not fit easily into either male-dominated professions or traditional female social circles. The feeling of alienation she experienced as a young woman led her to found a national organization for college-educated women while working on a master's degree at Boston University. At the urging of her mother, Emily Talbot, she called together a group of women that included Alice Freeman Palmer, then president of Wellesley College and later Talbot's predecessor as dean of women at Chicago, and Ellen H. Richards of the Massachusetts Institute of Technology. The first meeting, in November 1881, laid the groundwork for the creation of the Association of Collegiate Alumnae the following January. The ACA provided a social and professional network for college-educated women and tried to improve their access to advanced training and careers through fundraising and research. Talbot worked to produce a similar pattern of cooperation on campus by encouraging the founding of women's organizations and using the residence halls to create female community. She believed intensive social interaction and collaboration prepared female students for leadership roles by inculcating feelings of "mutual understanding, sympathy, generosity, and thoughtfulness."[16]

The female community extended beyond the campus to include numerous organizations with overlapping memberships and a shared commitment to social reform. University faculty were members of Chicago women's clubs, such as the Woman's City Club, and settlement workers were members of the Association of Collegiate Alumnae. Students volunteered at Hull House, university graduates went on to become residents, and numerous professors were current or former residents of the settlement. The University Settlement, located in the stockyards neighborhood near campus, was entirely staffed by faculty and students when it opened in January 1894. It served as an extension of municipal government, housing a branch of the public library, a public school for deaf children, and a resident juvenile-court probation officer. It coordinated charitable services with the Southside Women's Club and received financial support from the University of Chicago Settlement League, a group of female graduate students, faculty, and wives of faculty who joined forces to promote its work. The league regularly invited prominent settlement workers to speak on campus, including Graham Taylor of Chicago Commons and Addams and Kelley of Hull House.[17]

Just as with men, for many women there was a direct link between commitment to public service and concern for the continued relevance of Christianity as a moral force in society. Fearing that the corrupt bargain between government and business had stripped society of its moral compass, they regarded reformers whose motives were grounded in faith as best equipped to stay the course. Jane Addams argued that Christian college women had a special role to play in adjusting Christianity to current needs, as they had the scientific skills and sense of selflessness necessary for informed, cooperative change. She described a revival of Christianity rooted in humanitarianism as one of the main motives for the founding of social settlements. Mary McDowell of the University Settlement similarly claimed that a "new conception of the teachings of Christ has awakened a social conscience which today demands social deeds." Settlement workers responded to the call by raising the standards of civic duty and proving that social democracy and unity could exist among diverse groups. McDowell described her own dedication to social service as a "consecration" and defined settlement work as "objective Christianity."[18]

Settlement workers and other progressives joined faith with science in their attempts to chart a moral path of progress. They believed, as William

Rainey Harper argued, that Christianity and scientific inquiry both represented the embrace of truth, and they had confidence in the ability of scientific research to produce objective facts that could serve as the basis of ethical public policies. Madeline Wallin, who found the reformist atmosphere of the university exhilarating when she enrolled in graduate school in 1892, explained how the "ground must first be cleared by an intelligent understanding of the facts; by marshalling data; by drawing conclusions only from the most unimpeachable evidence." Wallin was describing the "scientific desire to understand conditions" that motivated Chicago settlement workers. As chair of the philanthropic committee of the university's Christian Union, she worked closely with Hull House and raised funds for the University Settlement prior to founding the Settlement League.[19]

Parrish shared the hopes of the university community that science might act as a guide for the moral reconstruction of social values and policies. Frustrated with southern opposition to gender equality and educational reform, she found feminist possibilities in the progressive potential of science. Experimental psychology offered a view of women as universally human rather than as a subset of humanity defined by reproductive function, as research conducted by women increasingly discredited claims that the divergence of sex characteristics was integral to evolutionary progress. When Parrish enrolled in an experimental psychology course taught by James R. Angell in 1898, one of his female graduate students was beginning dissertation research on theories of inherent sex difference. Helen Bradford Thompson's study, completed in 1900, concluded that there was no scientific basis for the theory of psychological sex differences rooted in biology. She found few patterns of difference in the test results of male and female subjects and attributed the differences that could be measured to disparities in individual experience, such as the differing expectations and treatment of girls in comparison to boys. These conclusions rang true for Parrish. She began to think more critically about the individual and social costs of the differential treatment of girls, especially in regards to the educational aspects of gender socialization.[20]

In a series of essays on female education published in the *Religious Herald* in 1900, Parrish explained why she had come to regard the concept of inherent sex difference as false and harmful. She began her discussion by summarizing popular notions of the value of education, such as "character-building or the attainment of morality" and the transmission of culture. She contrasted this with the treatment of female education as if it "formed a separate and distinct species of the genus education, and as if there were only one mind among women to be trained." Even though the purposes of education were theoretically universal, the education of girls and women was shaped by particular purposes based on assumptions about their future social roles. The only way to resolve the inconsistency between theory and practice, Parrish argued, was to base educational practices on the assumption that there was one "human mind, which, in its fundamental activity is approximately common to all human beings, but which, by reason of heredity and environment, varies widely in individuals of both sexes." Education should be "directed toward the full development of the human being as a human being first" and toward future function second. She concluded that to place artificial limits on intellectual development in the name of social efficiency (preparation for future social roles) was "to defraud the individual of his highest rights, and to prevent the fulfillment of his highest obligations."[21]

Intending the six-part series to serve as a guide for parents in directing their daughters' schooling, Parrish detailed what she regarded as the worst deficiencies in southern female education. One shortcoming was an excessive emphasis on music, art, literature, and languages, and the common practice of allowing girls to specialize in these areas at a young age. Parrish acknowledged that parents who fell into this trap had only the best intentions, as they believed cultural refinement would enable their daughters "to appear well in society," but she warned that using only certain parts of the brain would arrest mental development. Girls needed a balanced and rigorous curriculum to maximize use of neural pathways, ensuring that the "dormant brain cells were roused to activity and organized into vigorously functioning groups." They needed a well-rounded course of study that included history, mathematics, and science, with specialization in foreign languages or fine arts postponed until the last years of college or graduate school, after they had mastered the fundamentals and identified their particular talents and interests.[22]

As a specialist in mathematics and psychology, Parrish had a personal investment in convincing parents that education in math and science would benefit their daughters even though it lacked the social cachet of the arts. She argued that "one of the commonest of our educative fallacies is that a girl cannot learn mathematics." Girls' dislike for the subject was not due to "incapacity," but rather was the result of "bad teaching" and adult claims that "it is a masculine, *not* a feminine study." Parrish noted the practical need for basic skills in daily life, but she described the greatest value of mathematics as its ability to cultivate mental discipline, "sound judgment, [and] truthfulness." The study of science had similar benefits for the development of intellect and character. Laboratory work heightened powers of observation and interpretation, while the study of nature revealed the wonders of the natural world and the "Great Artificer" who created it. Explaining the spiritual enlightenment that could be derived from study of the natural sciences, she observed, "To feel one's self a part of nature, to know it, to love it, is closely akin to knowing and loving God."[23]

In going beyond personal benefits to explore the social value of educating women in science, Parrish revealed the feminist and progressive ideals that were intertwined with her sense of religious purpose. Some of her reasoning was conventional in its focus on the ways in which scientific knowledge could prepare a girl for her future domestic responsibilities, enabling her to "perform well her duties in the household, or in her conjugal and maternal relations." She discussed women's need to understand the science of nutrition, sanitation, and early childhood development so they could produce healthy and well-adjusted children, and their role in the eradication of "social evils" such as alcoholism and opium addiction. However, she abandoned gender conventions in the conclusion of her series of essays by exploding the concept of separate spheres. Noting that women had always been an important part of the "institutional life of the race," Parrish explained the numerous crucial ways in which they were citizens even though lacking the full rights of citizenship. They were the "center of the family," made up a majority of church membership, outnumbered men as teachers, and through their numerous associations performed much of the work of religious charity, philanthropy, and social reform. She was certain that the cooperation of women could resolve social problems, but only if all were "roused from the unconsciousness in which our educational methods have steeped them."[24]

Parrish's final essay presented the reform of female education as the key to the revival of Christianity and the reform of society. An education that imparted both "insight into the play of social forces and an abiding interest in the welfare of humanity" would "destroy the extreme conservatism which renders so many women useless to society," she argued, while also countering "extreme radicalism." Building to a crescendo in her last sentence, Parrish declared that, once women received such training, there would be "more purity and happiness" in the home, "more work in the service of sinning and humanity and less dogmatic theology in the churches," and "more work for the people and less party spirit in politics." Furthermore, enlightened women would demonstrate a "fuller comprehension of the meaning of social relations, instead of the narrow and ignorant caste ambition which now blights the lives of so many husbands and fathers and makes impossible the Christ-life, which is the end of our religion."[25]

Parrish's explicit connection between the reform of education and the reform of society bore the distinct imprint of John Dewey, whose influence she acknowledged at the end of her final essay. She took his graduate seminar in ethics in 1897, the same year he published several key essays on the ethical principles of education. Dewey placed the school at the center of social progress, maintaining that it had a moral responsibility to advance the general welfare by preparing students to assume the responsibilities of democratic citizenship. Educators had an obligation to shift children from a focus on the self to an outer-directed social orientation capable of continually assessing current conditions and needs. As society became more complex, citizens needed trained powers of "observation, analysis, and inference" to determine the appropriate response to changing circumstances. Dewey was adamant in insisting that this goal could be realized only through the cultivation of individual talents and interests, enabling every child to realize and have full command of his or her abilities. The teacher was an important figure in his construction of the role of education, being at once a "social servant" and a "prophet of the true God." Although Dewey explained his educational philosophy in gender-neutral terms, for Parrish it spoke to the ways in which the exclusion of women from universal personhood prevented the development of their abilities and deprived society of the full measure of their contributions.[26]

Pragmatism provided the rationale for Dewey's ethical principles of education, supplying Parrish with the final component of her philosophy of reform. Although Dewey is credited with articulating pragmatic ideals, his insights came from observing the work of progressive women in settlement houses and classrooms. At the heart of their pragmatism was a cooperative process of social experimentation and evaluation that enabled both individual growth and group progress by bringing current practices in line with current needs. Since the human environment was in a constant state of evolutionary change, there had to be a constant process of individual and social readjustment. For institutions and practices to accurately reflect current conditions and meet current needs, they had to be the products of a truly democratic process of evaluation in which all experiences carried equal weight. This process *was* democracy, as Jane Addams argued persuasively in *Democracy and Social Ethics*. Women found in pragmatism justification for the empowerment of female voices, and for southern women it spoke to the illegitimacy of antebellum concepts of gender and education that were not in alignment with postbellum needs. Women who sought independence and public influence had to combat not only the "family claim" of the primacy of individual household needs, but also the "race claim" in which feminine dependency stood as an icon of the superiority of slaveholder culture and the Lost Cause.[27]

As she began to integrate insights from her studies into a comprehensive analysis of southern education, Parrish found reinforcement for her views in the membership of the Association of Collegiate Alumnae. She joined the organization shortly after enrolling at the University of Chicago and founded its first southern chapter in Virginia in 1899. For the first time Parrish found herself in the midst of women who were equally outspoken in their criticisms of inequality and advocacy of universal personhood. In a speech delivered at the annual meeting in 1898, Bryn Mawr College president M. Carey Thomas complained of the persistence of male opposition to educational equality, arguing that even men who taught female students doubted the value of their education. Echoing Parrish's call for a universal psychology, Thomas asked why training in the classics and mathematics would make women worse wives if it did not make men worse husbands. If the bodies of men and women received nourishment from the same material food, would not their intellects benefit from the same college curriculum? She recalled how the first women to attend men's universities were told to open their own institutions and formulate a curriculum suited for female minds. Thomas found it absurd that women should be expected to start from scratch, saying "the shock was as profound as if at some great banquet the women present were to be refused food by their brothers and fathers and told to devise in future a woman's way of dining." Such experiences convinced her that separate institutions for women would inevitably be unequal, especially if run or controlled by men, which required the ACA to monitor their standards and progress.[28]

At the association's meeting in Chicago the following year, Parrish delivered a paper on problems in southern education that included a frank discussion of the impact of region and race on attitudes toward female education. She quoted white opponents of universal education who argued during Reconstruction that it was based on the "absurd and impossible idea of the leveler" and provoked "discontent with the allotment of Providence, and the inevitable gradations of rank." Although such criticisms failed to prevent the establishment of a state school system, the belief that educational equality made social subordinates discontented with their "sphere" continued to hinder the improvement of educational standards. For white women, concepts of a natural order rooted in the antebellum defense of slavery merged with nostalgia for the Lost Cause to produce an approach to female education that no longer met their needs. Parrish explained how during the Civil War the "southern ladies of the old régime" became symbols of the resilience of grace under fire—a metaphor for the Confederacy—leading southern white men to regard them as the "acme of excellence." The antebellum ideal of a female education that focused on basic literacy, housekeeping, etiquette, and the ornamental arts continued to be associated with reverence for the old order, and female seminaries catered to the bias by offering a superficial education supposedly designed to produce ladies.[29]

Speaking from personal experience, Parrish outlined how the inadequacies of female education hampered efforts to modernize public education. Although normal schools had begun to include laboratory work, all too often teacher training was "entirely in the classical or theological direction," completely omitting the "great biological, psychological, pedagogical, ethical and sociological movements of the day." Consequently, the quality of instruction in kindergartens and grammar schools was uneven and the sciences were poorly covered in high schools. Intimately familiar with the plight of less privileged women, Parrish hastened to add that teachers were motivated by a "patient heroism and spirit of self-sacrifice," and their deficiencies were no fault of their own. Speaking of herself in the third person as she often did, she observed that "the older ones were shut out from all opportunity of decent equipment" and "must do what they can in the summer schools to remedy the deficiency." The hundreds of women who flocked to the summer sessions of the University of Chicago proved their eagerness "to take advantage of educational privileges when offered."[30]

Despite her spirited defense of fellow teachers, Parrish was troubled by signs that young southern women were failing to take advantage of the new opportunities available to them. Her generation had longed for greater access to higher education, and she was surprised and disappointed at younger women's apparent lack of interest in attending college. All but four southern state universities were open to women, but their total female enrollment in 1899 was less than the average annual enrollment in Smith College. Parrish realized that some institutions had only reluctantly admitted women and were not welcoming, but she regarded the substandard quality of female secondary schools as a bigger hindrance. Most female teachers had no pedagogical training and were too poorly paid to acquire it, and had to teach numerous topics and act as nurse and chaperone for students as well. Male teachers more often had a college education, but they were likely to doubt girls' intellectual and physical capacity for rigorous study and to see it as unnecessary in any event. As a result, secondary schools were not developing students' interests or stimulating intellectual ambition, much less providing them with the mastery of self and social awareness necessary for societal adjustment and progress. Parrish regretted that girls who graduated from a substandard school labeled a "university" often did not seek college training because they believed they already had it.[31]

Parrish had reason to be optimistic about the future, as southern educators had formed two regional organizations dedicated to addressing the problems plaguing public schools. The Southern Educational Association (SEA), founded in 1890, initially catered to educational administrators and college faculty, but in 1898 its members decided to restructure the organization to include more teacher participation. The committee charged with directing this process, which included Parrish, issued an appeal to "earnest and progressive" teachers across the South to collaborate in creating a system of instruction that unified the work from kindergarten to university. The organizers of the Conference for Education in the South, founded in Capon Springs, West Virginia, in 1898, had an even wider program of reform in mind. When Parrish surveyed state superintendents that year to discover their most pressing needs, the list she compiled from their responses was almost identical to CES goals—the "education of public opinion," centralization of control in state departments of education, better trained teachers, and increased funding for teacher salaries, school buildings, and equipment. CES leaders were equally concerned with improving the quality of secondary instruction, which would pave the way for standardizing and accrediting institutions of higher education by enabling them to raise admission standards and abolish preparatory departments.[32]

Just as she had utilized the Educational Association of Virginia to mobilize support for coeducation, Parrish used the regional groups as platforms for addressing gender inequality in education. In papers presented at the CES in 1899 and the SEA in 1900, she discussed the shortcomings of secondary schools in terms not typically employed by the male leadership. In addition to examining the impact of substandard instruction on female college enrollment, she used her knowledge of psychology to explore the costs to the individual. She expressed concern that teachers lacked the training in psychology, sociology, and pedagogy necessary to effectively guide female students through their teenage years. Adolescence should be a "period of awakening," a time when girls acquired "ideals of vocation and personal consecration" and gained the scientific knowledge needed to understand themselves and the world around them. Instead, all too often they were given haphazard instruction in music and art and were discouraged from freely exploring their interests regardless of where they led. Parrish warned that a girl who passed through this critical stage of emotional and intellectual development "without awakening at all" would be unprepared for the responsibilities of adulthood, and "life will never mean more to her than mere existence," for "she will vegetate rather than live."[33]

While the parents in her audiences may have appreciated her concern for their daughters' right to self-realization, Parrish tread trickier ground in her analysis of the underlying reasons why secondary schools for girls were inferior to those for boys. Directly tackling the role of southern nationalism, she acknowledged white southerners' fondness for the antebellum elite woman and the sectional pride that made them loathe to admit "that anything belonging to that order was defective." She admitted that her own criticisms of the antebellum ideal of womanhood had made her unwelcome in some circles. Parents who admired "ladies noble in character, beautiful in person, [and] gracious in presence" were "apt to consider the college woman abnormal." Parrish expressed her own admiration for the southern lady, but argued antebellum women would be the first to admit that they were ill equipped "for the work which the world needs now, for the vigorous fight with evil in which women MUST take part in the near future." Women could no longer be sheltered from the harsh realities of the world and spared the "stern discipline provided for their brothers," simply to preserve an icon of the past that was irrelevant to current individual and social needs.[34]

Having addressed the regional patriotism underlying southern gender conservatism, Parrish proceeded to analyze the role of men in perpetuating outdated attitudes and practices. She was personally familiar with how they discouraged female academic ambitions by limiting the usefulness of college education for women. As a result of gender discrimination there were few careers available to women that justified the time and expense of earning a degree. They could aspire to become teachers, but even in education the best positions were closed to them. None of the southern coeducational universities employed a "woman professor with a professor's salary," and she was the only one employed at a southern women's college. Even though there were growing numbers of women with doctoral degrees and teaching experience, institutions regularly passed over them in favor of "inexperienced young men with no professional training at all." When universities did hire female instructors, it was because "a good teacher with a small salary is wanted." Parrish confessed that she once thought "women had only to demonstrate their fitness for work and place in order to obtain them" and would have believed impossible what she now knew to be true, that "their very excellence would prove a bar, that men would oppose them because of their superior work."[35]

Continuing her search for the underlying causes of male antagonism to educational equality, Parrish traced its origins to the intimate relations of family and household. In a theme she would return to many times, Parrish argued that men treated woman as a "means to an end rather than an end in herself." They presented marriage as women's natural and highest calling not only to minimize female competition in the workplace, but also because they sought to perpetuate the version of womanhood that pleased them most. Men acted as if "women were created not to realize the highest and best which God has implanted in them, but to assist men in their self-realization, sometimes merely to amuse and please them." This denied women a purpose broader than service to individual men and ignored the universal as well as particular values of higher education—its elevation of character and purpose and its cultivation of an effective, scientific domesticity. It also ignored the fact that some women would never marry, either by choice or by fate, and that some were ill-suited for marriage and motherhood. When Parrish was younger she thought she could persuade men to see the error of this position, but with age came the understanding that the "average man, unselfish as he may be in other respects, is hedonistic in his ethics in this field." She concluded that, while she expected men to continue promoting an ideal of womanhood that gave them pleasure, evolutionary and sacred forces would inevitably produce a new definition of women as "ends in themselves."[36]

Parrish took her message to a national audience in 1901, expanding her analysis in two articles published in *The Independent*. The first was written in response to an essay by Henry T. Finck, a Harvard-educated music critic and self-appointed expert on gender matters. Employing an antiquated sociological approach based on conjecture rather than scientific method, Finck described women's rights activists as a minority composed of "mostly mannish women" who threatened to reverse evolutionary progress and return women's status to that of primitive society. Whereas the womanly woman of the domestic sphere was the product of civilizing forces, coeducation and civil and political equality would produce her opposite, the "hard working, masculine-looking, early-aging savage woman." Parrish, who had encountered similar arguments in her struggle to open the University of Virginia to women, took particular issue with his definition of womanly. It included only superficial external qualities pleasing to men and disregarded internal qualities of character and intellect. She denounced the arrogance of men who assumed the authority to decide what was womanly based on their own personal desires, defining the term to include only those qualities they wanted in a wife. Finck's essay was yet another example of the male tendency to think of women as "things, not persons; as means to an end, not as ends in themselves."[37]

Although Finck's argument was insulting to all women who advocated gender equality, Parrish was especially offended as a member of the Civil War generation. His definition of womanhood was completely at odds with the reality of her life and seemed to deny the value of her many sacrifices for family and community. She made the incongruities explicit in her analysis of his description of the savage woman, refuting Finck's inference that "womanly women do not work hard or age quickly" by pointing to the tremendous toll paid by women who stepped into breadwinner roles while still suffering the heartaches of loss:

> It follows that a woman who uncomplainingly toils all day, and far into the night to support helpless youth or age, the heavy work lining her face and whitening her hair, cannot be womanly, whatever her nobility of character, her culture or refinement. The Southern women who after the close of the Civil War bravely faced their changed conditions and worked hard to support little children left fatherless by the cruel fortune of war seemed to some very good people more womanly as they aged rapidly under the pressure of sorrow and toil than in the heyday of their youth and prosperity; but, of course, those who took that view were accustomed to think of women as rational human beings, not as mere instruments of man's passion or pleasure.

Real womanliness, Parrish countered, consisted of being morally good and true, of becoming what God intended one to become rather than a "mere minister to man's sensual pleasure."[38]

In her second article, Parrish explored the larger social implications of narrowly constructed definitions of "womanly." She argued that perpetuating the conception of women as means to an end was morally wrong and came dangerously close to prostitution, because it made sex the basis of all interaction with men and required women to abandon their duties to the many in favor of giving pleasure to the few. It also stunted the emotional and intellectual development of girls, who adopted a "manwardness" rather than mannishness out of fear that higher education and careers would hinder their ability to marry. Furthermore, allocating only the "gentler virtues" to women left them unprepared for the difficulties of parenting, depriving them of the strength of character and firmness of will necessary to keep adolescent sons and daughters on a moral path. The mother who relied solely on "winsome-ness and soft, refined blandishments" to influence her children was likely to induce in her sons "amused contempt" for women that led to vice rather than righteousness. Since the resolution of social problems required the applica-tion of women's full range of abilities inside and outside the home, Parrish reasoned, women had to assert the right of self-definition; they must decide for themselves the best course of action. Making that decision wisely required teaching girls that "their symmetrical development as individuals is far more important than increase of effeminacy . . . [and] that God has given them no high intellectual potentiality which they should not actualize."[39]

The increasing bluntness of Parrish's tone reflected her frustration with the growing backlash to women's progress. Educated women effectively used scientific research to refute a wide range of evolutionist arguments against equality, only to see them repeatedly resurface in the first few decades of the twentieth century. Some of the most respected male social scientists in the nation continued to assert that feminism was destructive of evolutionary progress because it thwarted the divergence of sex roles. Psychologist and child-study advocate G. Stanley Hall was in the forefront of the attack on educational equality. In contrast to Parrish's concept of a universal human mind, he maintained that gender difference extended to the brain and justi-fied the very emphasis on sex she deplored for its pernicious effects on youth. Hall argued that coeducation was inappropriate during adolescence, because it interfered with the development of distinct sex characteristics during a critical stage of maturation. He insisted that nature and instinct caused ad-olescent boys to reject their mothers and show contempt for male friends who preferred the company of girls; their behavior could not be attributed to "custom and tradition" as feminists claimed, or presumably to the inferi-ority of female education as Parrish argued. Calling for the development of a female curriculum for girls, Hall ridiculed the "cheap idolatry of intellect" that motivated feminists to advocate universal educational standards.[40]

Hall also played a leading role in the attack on women that questioned their competency as teachers. In 1900 young women comprised 58 percent of public high-school students and 63 percent of graduates, leading some male educators and business leaders to suspect that there was something wrong with the schools. Attention focused on female teachers as the problem, because even though they made up only about half of high-school teachers, they comprised 70 percent of all teachers, and their numbers in secondary education had been slowly increasing. Men who felt threatened by the feminization of teaching argued that female teachers were driving away male students. Male (and some female) critics claimed that, while women's innate talent for child nurture made them excellent teachers of young children, they were incapable of effectively teaching adolescent boys. Hall argued that women shrank from the stern methods needed to teach boys discipline and respect for others and blamed female teachers for an increase in male juvenile delinquency. Women's progressive methods of classroom management, which rejected physical intimidation and corporal punishment, were simply too effeminate to inculcate manliness. Other critics went further, endorsing Hall's suggestion that adolescent girls as well as boys would be better served by male teachers, since men supposedly had analytical skills that women lacked. Although these allegations did not result in the exclusion of female teachers from high schools, they perpetuated inequality by justifying the concentration of women in the primary grades and encouraging gender differentiation in curricula.[41]

The groundswell of opposition to educational equality impacted higher education as well, leading the University of Chicago and other institutions to retreat from their commitment to coeducation. The number of women enrolled in colleges and universities increased dramatically after 1870, and by 1900 they comprised more than 35 percent of the student population. Their higher rate of increase in comparison to men was especially noticeable on coeducational campuses, which had more than twice the female enrollment of separate women's colleges. Between 1902 and 1915 numerous coeducational colleges and universities responded with new policies designed to shore up male privilege. Stanford University set an admissions ratio of three males to every female student, Boston University stepped up male recruitment with a "More Men Movement" and established male-only scholarships, and there was a failed attempt at the University of Wisconsin to segregate female liberal arts students. Black higher education provides an interesting contrast. Even though most black institutions were coeducational, women were not a majority of graduates until 1910. Concern that black men were subordinating the needs of women to their own struggle for advancement led black female educators to push for the creation of separate institutions that could nurture female intellectualism and leadership.[42]

At the University of Chicago, some of the same arguments used against coeducation in high schools were marshaled in support of sex segregation of the Junior College (the freshman and sophomore classes) in 1902. President Harper described coeducation as a "pedagogical and social mistake" that hindered the development of womanly women and manly men. Male professors complained that female students were straining the capacity of buildings and public spaces and diminishing the sense of fraternity and scholarly purpose among the men on campus. Marion Talbot perceptively attributed their concerns to the academic success of undergraduate women, who by 1902 outnumbered undergraduate men. Female students comprised only 24 percent of undergraduate enrollment in 1892, but by 1901 this proportion had more than doubled to 52 percent. Even more alarming for the male university trustees, women were effectively competing with men for fellowships and awards. Despite the protests of Talbot, female alumnae, women's organizations, and dozens of their own colleagues, a majority of the faculty voted in support of segregation. While the practical difficulties of maintaining segregated classes made the Junior College experiment short-lived, Talbot perceived women's status to be so imperiled that she attended every board and committee meeting for years afterward to ensure that their interests were represented.[43]

Just as with the attacks on coeducation and female teachers in high schools, attempts to reverse democratic trends in higher education stemmed in part from the discomfort of male professionals who feared the feminization of their fields. John Dewey opposed sex segregation at the University of Chicago, and along with colleague James Tufts came to the defense of women as teachers; however, male professionals who favored equality remained a minority. Talbot soon became disillusioned with university administrators' supposed commitment to employing female professors. After five years the number of female faculty had risen only by two, while men were hired in significantly larger numbers and promoted more quickly than women. Male professors' tendency to channel female graduate students into endeavors defined as feminine—such as work in social settlements, the YWCA, and women's colleges—instead of academic positions in coeducational universities did not bode well for the future. Women found the division of labor less problematic in the 1890s, when the lines of segregation and exclusion appeared to be softening rather than hardening. The integration of science and religion in the Social Gospel movement temporarily muddied notions of essential sex difference and tempered male ambitions with humanitarian ideals. This changed as male scholars became more concerned with establishing their professional credentials. As they strove to prove that their theoretical expertise was superior to women's practical application of knowledge, gendered distinctions such as that between sociologist and social worker became more rigid.[44]

Parrish could see the impact of discrimination in her own field. Women with degrees in psychology were limited to positions in women's colleges and normal schools even if they chose a career over marriage. Parrish was one of twenty-two women listed as psychologists in the 1906 edition of *American Men of Science* and was a pioneer in establishing the new psychology in the South, yet she had no chance of obtaining a position as professor of psychology in a coeducational college or university. Her insightful, sharp critiques of male bias, remarkably similar to those of feminist psychologists in the 1970s, reflected the hurdles women faced in trying to obtain equal footing in the profession. Psychologists such as Edward Thorndike of Columbia University's Teachers College were willing to exploit female graduate-student labor, or to use women to collect data as Hall did through child study, but they rejected women as colleagues. They had no qualms about using their status as experts to promote theories that justified confining educated women to subordinate, segregated positions, and some continued to insist that women should remain in the home. ACA members got the latter message loud and clear when they asked Harvard psychologist Hugo Münsterberg to serve on a conference panel addressing the problems facing women as teachers. After informing the audience that his best advice to female college graduates was to marry and bring "charm and beauty and sunshine into some home," he warned that women's concentration in teaching would "push the men out." It is little wonder that by the early 1900s Parrish had become cynical about the likelihood that male attitudes would change.[45]

The discriminatory response of male professionals to women's progress was exacerbated by national trends that brought northern attitudes on gender and race into closer alignment with the white South. As international competition for access to markets intensified among industrialized nations in the 1890s, Social Darwinist and eugenic theories emerged as convenient justifications for a more aggressive foreign policy. The concept of a hierarchy of peoples in which some were less evolved than others legitimized asserting control over other nations and made racial purity an obsession among white, native-born Americans. Paradoxically, white men who came of age after the

Civil War began to worry that they had become *too* civilized and sought to construct a new manhood that could reassert their dominance over women and more primitive peoples. Theodore Roosevelt led the way in wedding the paternalism of the "white man's burden" to patriarchy, advocating a forceful white manhood imbued with the martial spirit that mirrored the antebellum slaveholder ideal of mastery. Its counterpart was a concept of white womanhood once again stripped to its domestic and reproductive functions, a subset of humanity rather than universally human, and now charged with the preservation of racial purity. Concerned about high birth rates among ethnic and racial minorities, Roosevelt argued that only by prioritizing marriage and motherhood could educated white women prevent national "race suicide."[46]

The intersection of race and sex in nationalist rhetoric had negative implications for all women. The concept of race suicide reinforced the white southern (and increasingly northern) view of black women's moral degeneracy; in a supposedly Anglo-Saxon country they were the wrong kinds of mothers producing the wrong kinds of children, thereby hastening the nation's demise. At the same time, concern for racial purity subjected northern white women to the "race claim" to an unprecedented degree, making the production of children a measure of their racial and national loyalty. The popularization of Social Darwinist theories also deterred white women from looking too closely at the links between gender and race. A mask of scientific expertise obscured the origins of the ideas in a backlash to the demands of women, African Americans, immigrants, and unions, for democratic reforms. White women's rights advocates recognized the threat to their movement and protested the notion that separate spheres was a patriotic necessity, but their defensive posture made them reluctant to risk the damage to their respectability that would likely result from interracial activism.[47] For many, scientific racism encouraged the continued classification of black women by race rather than gender.

While her studies in psychology and sociology sharpened Parrish's understanding of the personal and social costs of gender inequality, her progressive education had a more ambiguous impact on her understanding of race. In the summer of 1899 she took William Isaac Thomas's course on "Race Development of the Mind," which included "comparison of the mental traits of different races, epochs, and social classes." Historians of sociology consider Thomas a racial liberal because he rejected evolutionist theories that legitimized racial discrimination and violence by presenting race differences as innate and irreconcilable. Thomas drew heavily on the work of W. E. B. Du

Bois (especially *The Philadelphia Negro*) and anthropologist Franz Boas in identifying the cultural origins of racial difference and the obstacles to black progress. He insisted on the basic intellectual equality of all human beings and argued that white prejudice could easily be eliminated through greater interracial contact—integration rather than segregation—and the empathy it engendered. However, his conception of the evolutionary development of peoples led him to believe that northern whites had been misguided in trying to provide freedpeople with an education rooted in white culture. He argued that African Americans could not effectively absorb a body of knowledge based on the collective experiences of another race, and endorsed Booker T. Washington's position that industrial education would best fit them for the environment and resources at hand.[48]

Although Thomas's recognition of innate equality and the destructiveness of white prejudice challenged the worst forms of reactionary racism emanating from the South, his concept of race development reinforced southern conservatism on the issue of black education. Both influences are evident in the ACA paper Parrish delivered in the winter after enrolling in his course. In what is the most complete surviving example of her racial views, Parrish was sharply critical of the southern white men who claimed during Reconstruction that education would make freedpeople unfit for manual labor and lead to racial amalgamation. She excoriated white supremacist demagogue James K. Vardaman of Mississippi, who had revived their arguments the previous summer for political gain, dismissing him as a "whiskey-sodden stump politician." However, she was critical of philanthropists who had departed from "sociological principles" in their attempts "to give a primitive people the highest literary and scientific culture without letting the race pass first through an industrial stage." Pointing to Hampton and Tuskegee institutes as educational models deserving of emulation, Parrish envisioned a partnership between "educated white men and women of the South, who know and love the negroes," and "educated colored men and women who are large enough to forget politics and social equality for a while." If these two groups could set aside their prejudices in the interest of "teaching and elevating to self-respect, morality, and financial independence the degraded masses of negroes," she concluded, "the final solution of the problem will be very near."[49]

What Parrish did not foresee was that, in failing to prioritize the struggle for racial equality, whites, however well-intentioned, were leaving a clearer path for white supremacists determined to deal democracy and education a devastating blow. She had learned that women could not achieve equality merely by proving their worth, but scientific theories on race development hindered her ability to apply that lesson to the notion of race uplift. This was a common blind spot among white racial liberals, who generally assumed the necessity of segregation and opposed the worst forms of racial discrimination out of a sense of moral duty (or noblesse oblige) and concern for law and order. They supported the right of African Americans to receive an education and reap the rewards of their efforts through upward mobility, but drew the line at political equality. With a few exceptions, male leaders of the southern movement for educational reform presumed they could end racial conflict by educating whites and worried more about the impact of racism on the economy than on human rights. Parrish's view that African Americans were evolving, and that interracial cooperation was necessary and desirable to facilitate racial advancement, was one of the more progressive positions. It was not until 1920 that white and black women formally joined forces under the auspices of the Commission on Interracial Cooperation, and only in 1930 did white women organize against lynching by forming the Association of Southern Women for the Prevention of Lynching.[50]

It was Parrish's feminism rather than racial liberalism that caused her to lose her position at Randolph-Macon Woman's College. Though she expressed pride in the college's program of study and was fond of female colleagues and students, she had to constantly fight to be treated as the equal of male faculty. She was indignant when the college's board of trustees voted in 1895 to raise male faculty salaries to $1,500 per year while keeping her pay at $1,150. The board responded to her complaint by equalizing salaries the following year, but Parrish continued to protest the exclusion of female faculty from college governance. She refused to suffer silently under a hierarchy of authority in which only men had a vote, and her rejection of southern gender etiquette frustrated RWMC men. Meta Glass, a former student who became her colleague at RWMC, described how in faculty meetings Parrish "moved with surety into a discussion of controversial matters" without introduction or apology. From Parrish's perspective, she was "only a person seeking the heart of the matter," but to male faculty, "she was a lady with whom they often wished violently to disagree and they did not know just how to do it within their code for ladies." Matters reached a breaking point in the fall of 1901, and President Smith asked her to leave at the end of the semester. After everything she had done to create a program of national renown, it was small solace that he allowed her to resign instead of being fired.[51]

Parrish still had significant financial obligations to family and was fortunate to obtain another position at the last minute. She had informally adopted two of her deceased siblings' children, which meant in practical terms that she paid for their education and provided other benefits that might prepare them for successful adulthood. As Parrish put it, she strove to "give them all the advantages necessary to make them the best they can be." At some point in the fall semester, she interviewed for a position as professor of psychology and pedagogy at the Georgia State Normal School in Athens. There is no record of how she learned of the opening, but she made remarks at the annual meeting of the Southern Educational Association in December that indicated she was awaiting confirmation of her hire. While commenting on the teaching of psychology in normal schools, she noted that there was a "prospect" that she might be "promoted from the college to the Normal School," where she would teach psychology. She must have received notification shortly afterward, as she assumed her new duties in February 1902.[52]

As Parrish packed her bags and prepared to leave for Georgia, white delegates at Virginia's 1901–2 state constitutional convention eliminated a Reconstruction clause asserting the equal rights of all citizens and approved suffrage laws that disfranchised most black men and many white voters. As in southern states with similar suffrage restrictions, a new literacy requirement further politicized black education. After debating an assortment of discriminatory proposals, delegates approved revisions that mandated segregated schools, reduced the minimum length of the school year, and made it easier for local officials to divert state funds to white schools. Since convention leaders knew that most voters would not approve their retreat from democracy, they decided to proclaim the constitution rather than submit it to a referendum.[53] The full implications of an ascendant reactionary racism for universal education, and for the connections between racial and sexual politics, would become obvious to Parrish shortly after her arrival in Athens.

CHAPTER FOUR

The Limitations of Reform

L eaving Virginia in the midst of a constitutional convention that tied educational reform to black disfranchisement proved to be an ill omen for
Celeste Parrish. As attempts to eliminate black men from the electorate
reached a frenzied peak around the turn of the century, she moved to the only
Deep South state that had not yet enacted the literacy and understanding
clauses that enabled constitutional disfranchisement. Parrish had reason to
be optimistic about her future; even though she had to leave RMWC, her
professional achievements had attracted regional and national attention from
reformers concerned about the state of southern education. Her efforts to
improve teacher training had gained the respect of leaders of the Southern
Education Board and won her a promising new position at the Georgia State
Normal School in Athens. On the other hand, her field of activism broadened
just as universal education became a target of white supremacists intent on
crushing African American aspirations for equality. Drawing upon the most
vicious aspects of scientific racism, they linked black literacy with moral
degeneracy and the rape of white women, using appeals to white manhood
that undermined the southern movement for educational reform.[1] As the
race claim became more coercive, the conservatism of male reformers and
women's lack of formal political power left Parrish reliant upon female networks of support.

Although Parrish did not stay in Virginia long enough to witness the end
results of the constitutional convention, she could have predicted the outcome based on the pattern of events in other states. In 1890, Mississippi became the first state to adopt a constitutional requirement that voters be able
to read and write a section of the state constitution. South Carolina (1895),

Louisiana (1898), North Carolina (1900), and Alabama (1901) adopted similar constitutional provisions, followed by Virginia in 1902. Delegates at the constitutional conventions created legal loopholes designed to prevent the disfranchisement of illiterate whites, such as the understanding clause (allowing voters to explain a section of the constitution read aloud) and the grandfather clause (for direct descendants of men eligible to vote in 1867), but these were temporary measures set to expire anywhere from three months to eight years after enactment. White as well as black education was politicized by literacy requirements, since access to schools could determine access to suffrage. Illiterate southerners soon found that disfranchisement stripped them of the political leverage necessary to obtain a fair share of educational funds, making the problem a self-perpetuating one. For black southerners, this meant that Progressive Era reforms aimed at improving educational standards disproportionately benefited white schools.[2]

When Parrish accepted the job in Georgia, it was not obvious that the link between suffrage and black literacy would become the political flashpoint there that it had been elsewhere. In 1899 and again in 1901, Democratic state representative Thomas W. Hardwick failed to get legislative approval for a bill that would have asked Georgia voters to approve a literacy test and understanding clause. Some Democrats might have wanted to retain black voters as potential leverage in factional battles within the party, but for the most part they simply thought the amendments were unnecessary. There was no threat to white control, as voters had been subject to a cumulative poll tax since 1877 and most counties held whites-only primaries well before it became state policy in 1900. The state also contained influential white men who were supportive of black education. These included University of Georgia chancellor Walter B. Hill and Hoke Smith, an attorney and trustee of the Peabody Education Fund who served on the Atlanta School Board for a decade beginning in 1897.[3] Both men were members of the Southern Education Board committee organized to direct Georgia's campaign for educational reforms.

The state's white clubwomen also provided leadership in educational reform. They formed the Georgia Federation of Women's Clubs (GFWC) in 1896, and a year later assisted the state school commissioner in compiling a report on the status of public education in Georgia. The federation published a brochure documenting the many inadequacies of the state system, and members used it to support their campaigns for public kindergartens, industrial education, school libraries, and compulsory attendance laws. They soon added local taxation and federal funding for schools to their agenda. When the state legislature was slow to respond to their demands, women's clubs bypassed foot-dragging politicians by taking direct action in the community. They found local sponsors for model schools, funded the training of model-school teachers, conducted book drives for libraries, improved school furnishings and grounds, and established their own educational institutions (such as Tallulah Falls School). Chancellor Hill's wife, Sallie Barker Hill, directed women's work for the SEB state campaign committee.[4]

Georgians' participation in the southern movement signaled a receptiveness to innovation and reform that was attractive to Parrish. Increasing the numbers of professionally trained teachers was a necessary part of the campaign to narrow the gap between southern and national educational standards, and the primary purpose of the coeducational Georgia State Normal School was to provide better trained teachers for rural schools. Georgia State Normal School faculty were active in the Southern Educational Association, and the school president, Eugene Cunningham Branson, was a founding member. Branson informed Parrish when he hired her that he wanted her to direct a complete overhaul of the teacher-training program. As she explained it, he wanted the pedagogical work "expanded, kept in harmony with the best educational thought, and, at the same time, adapted to the needs of the country schools." He immediately charged her with conducting a survey of rural schools as a first step toward determining what changes should be made.[5]

The goals of the normal school reflected its origins in a larger regional movement that initially was driven by the expansion of public school systems during and after Reconstruction. In response to a shortage of trained teachers, most southern states opened their first normal schools in the 1880s and 1890s. Students usually were from low-income households, older than the average college student, and had considerable work experience. As illustrated by Parrish's experiences in Virginia, normal schools provided an education for women and racial and ethnic minorities excluded from more prestigious state institutions. The Georgia legislature created GSNS as a coeducational institution in 1891, having already authorized the establishment of Georgia Normal and Industrial College in Milledgeville (GNIC, now the coeducational Georgia College and State University) for white women two years earlier. Women also could get teacher training in the state's two coeducational land-grant institutions, the white North Georgia Agricultural College in Dahlonega (now the University of North Georgia) and Georgia State Industrial College for Colored Youth outside of Savannah (now Savannah State University).[6]

The opportunity to assist in the professional development of young men and women who had experienced hardships similar to her own appealed to Parrish's ethic of service. There were 452 students enrolled in 1903, most of whom were teachers, principals, and superintendents with minimal formal education. In comparison to the relatively privileged RMWC students whose parents could afford tuition at a private college, normal-school students were from humble households and could not have acquired professional training without the state's offer of free tuition in exchange for a pledge to work in public schools. A national magazine described students as mountain boys and country girls who performed menial labor and went without meals to pay for their travel to Athens and the cost of boarding at the normal school (about eighty-five dollars for the full term). Parrish's goal was to inspire these students with the "the possibilities and potentialities of the New Education." She envisioned graduates spreading across the state, going "forth gladly to serve in the lowliest places" and introducing rural children to "the joy of a life of full, free, and efficient service."[7]

Eugene Branson shared Parrish's commitment to rural uplift, although his path of professional advancement had been somewhat smoother than hers. He also started his career as a public-school teacher while acquiring an education piecemeal. He attended Trinity College (now Duke University) for two years between 1878 and 1880 and enrolled in Peabody Normal College in Nashville for at least one semester in 1883. Also like Parrish, Branson regularly attended the annual meetings of the CES and SEA and was active in other regional and national education associations that advocated progressive reforms. The most striking difference in their professional lives was Branson's ability to move easily into administrative positions due to the gendering of opportunity that Parrish often criticized. He served as high-school principal and city school superintendent in North Carolina before moving to Georgia, where he became superintendent of Athens schools while still in his mid-twenties. He left that position to become professor of pedagogy, first at Georgia Normal and Industrial College for women and then at the GSNS. School trustees promoted him to the office of president only a year before Parrish arrived.[8]

Parrish's hire was part of Branson's ambitious plan to put the State Normal School on firmer professional and financial footing. The state legislature created the institution in 1891 but did not make provisions for annual appropriations until 1894. The campus initially consisted of a single building, which severely limited the number of students who could be boarded, and only one dormitory had been added when Branson assumed the presidency.

The curriculum in 1901–2 focused on common-school and high-school subjects, but the hire of Parrish and three other faculty members enabled the addition of the first college-level courses the following year. At first, Branson remained in charge of pedagogy, giving Parrish responsibility for supervising the model school, an elementary-school class housed on campus to enable students to observe and practice teaching. She also created courses in logic, ethics, and psychology—including "introspective and experimental work"— and advised Branson on the hire of a new principal and teacher for the model school. The expansion of the faculty allowed instructors to specialize in their course offerings rather than covering numerous fields, and a new School of Domestic Arts and Sciences offered study in physiology, home economics, home administration, and domestic chemistry. Due to legislative inaction, the improvements were largely dependent upon philanthropic donations.[9]

Parrish's initial focus on the model school reflected her concern that the practical side of the teacher-training program did not meet professional standards. American normal schools used a confusing mixture of labels for the public schools associated with their programs—alternately calling them model, practice, demonstration, and laboratory schools—but ideally, they contained both model and practice components. Normal-school students first observed expert teachers modeling effective methods, and later, usually in their senior year, demonstrated their mastery of those methods by teaching. "Critic teachers" then evaluated their performance, a role Parrish had filled at the Virginia State Female Normal School. Most programs preferred to house model schools on campus rather than having students practice their skills in local schools, to ensure that expert teachers provided the modeling and supervision. Very few established laboratory schools in the sense that John Dewey used the label, to indicate experimentation in organizational structure and methods.[10]

Even though she rarely received public recognition or credit after her death, Parrish was vital to the fundraising efforts that made dramatic improvements to the model school possible. Shortly after her arrival in Athens, she arranged a meeting with George Foster Peabody, a native Georgian and SEB member who was known for his philanthropy. Parrish subsequently persuaded him to furnish an experimental psychology laboratory and to pledge more than $13,500 to construct a new practice school. When completed in 1903, Muscogee Elementary School was an impressive three-story brick building with a library, gymnasium, bowling alley, playrooms, kitchen, workshop, and museum. Unlike the small model school it replaced, it was staffed with teachers who had been carefully chosen and trained by Parrish in progressive methods. She stressed that only teachers who had a "broad and thorough" education and demonstrated the "sympathy with mankind that comes of earnest sociological study and evidences itself in the effort to improve social conditions nearest at hand" would be hired for the practice school. Moreover, not all normal-school students would be allowed to practice teaching in Muscogee Elementary; only those with proven abilities and whose lesson plans were "accepted as worthy" would be able to assist faculty.[11]

The practice school allowed Parrish to fuse social science and Social Gospel influences, employing the progressive methods of Dewey while imbuing future teachers with an enthusiasm for social betterment. She was careful to distinguish between the purposes of the practice school and those of the model schools that Georgia clubwomen were establishing to serve as guides for school improvement in surrounding communities. Muscogee Elementary School could in no way be considered a model for rural communities, because it had resources that they were unlikely to ever have; instead, its purpose was to produce teachers who would "make the school a social center" and "develop the community life in the best possible way." Its guiding philosophy was the new education's progressive approach that integrated intellectual, social, and spiritual knowledge, and it was organized on the premise that "elementary education should grow out of and be centered around the life and experience of the child." Practice schoolteachers did not teach separate, discrete subjects, but involved students in projects that integrated science, mathematics, history, and manual and industrial arts. Rather than relying on traditional authoritarian methods of discipline, they appealed to students' interests and encouraged "the self-control which is the result of developing character."[12] The first few years of running the school were very demanding for Parrish, as she had to simultaneously train teachers, supervise normal-school students, and reassure parents and colleagues who were skeptical of her unorthodox methods.

As her duties expanded to include full responsibility for psychology and pedagogy in addition to directorship of the practice school, Parrish had to deal with the lingering effects of a public controversy that erupted during her first semester in Athens. It was related to a discussion she had with the freshman class in April 1902, when she was asked by a student to share her views on white responsibilities for black education. According to one of the students present, Parrish explained that she had instructed black teachers in summer institutes and would do so again. When a female student interrupted to say that she would never consent to teach blacks, Parrish sharply replied that if that were the case she should "be made to stop teaching." The student responsible for the outburst, Love M. McDaniel, was a public schoolteacher who was infuriated by the reprimand and lodged a formal complaint accusing Parrish of advocating social equality of the races. The faculty launched a full investigation to determine exactly what had been said, and after examining the evidence concluded that McDaniel's charge was false and Parrish had done nothing wrong. Branson announced the outcome of the investigation to the students in a chapel talk, but the matter did not end there. More than a year and a half later, in December 1903, the normal school board of trustees conducted another investigation of the event in hopes of extinguishing a whirlwind of publicity surrounding it.[13]

The incident became part of a public controversy when opponents of educational reform used it to cast doubt on the racial loyalties of Parrish and the normal school. The *Macon Telegraph* printed a sensational account just prior to the trustees' meeting, erroneously claiming that Parrish told her class "the highest honor ever paid her was when she was tendered the principalship of a colored school," and that she was "urging the policy of sending out teachers from the normal school to engage in the work of educating the negroes of the state." Readers would have readily understood the underlying meaning of the latter statement. Roughly 80 percent of the state's public schoolteachers were women, and normal-school students had to pledge to teach in the public schools for two years after graduation. The article's wording deliberately conjured up the image of delivering white female bodies to black male students, teachers, and principals. The newspaper further stated that Parrish's words had the hearty approval of "Mr. Baldwin and his associates," meaning the overlapping memberships of the SEB and GEB, because of their support for the education of both races. Apprehending the threat the article posed for both the normal school and educational reform, Parrish issued a quick denial of its claims.[14]

Although no one revealed the article's sources, the origins of its sentiments lay in recent events that linked racial equality and black political empowerment with interregional cooperation and universal education. Southern Democrats commonly used the specter of social equality—a phrase denoting integration, miscegenation, and racial amalgamation—to discredit Republicans and third-party challengers. Even after they had effectively disfranchised black men, Democrats continued to argue that any political division among white voters would result in "Negro domination" and social equality. The success of the cumulative poll tax and white primary in decimating the black vote in Georgia did not prevent Democrats from once again accusing Populists of threatening to empower blacks by splitting the white vote in the 1904 elections. This influenced People's Party presidential candidate Tom Watson, a Georgian, to change his position on black disfranchisement. In the 1890s he championed interracial cooperation among farmers and urged white men to resist Democrats' cynical manipulation of race prejudice; however, by 1904 he had become convinced that white men would never unite behind the banner of populism and defeat the Bourbon Democratic machine unless race was removed as a political factor. In September, Watson promised to deliver Populist votes to any Democratic reform candidate who would commit to the constitutional disfranchisement of blacks. The horrendous Atlanta race riot of 1906 was only one result of the intense racist rhetoric that accompanied the successful gubernatorial campaign of Hoke Smith, who accepted Watson's offer, and his opponent Clark Howell.[15]

As Watson transformed his position on race, he formulated an appeal to southern white manhood that was sharply critical of the model of interregional cooperation underlying the southern movement for educational reform. In the early 1900s his numerous speeches and publications combined bitter sectionalism with agrarian ideology, portraying the South as a region under siege from condescending northern capitalists determined to succeed where Reconstruction had failed. This time the threat came not from military occupation, but from the insidious and corrupt influence of businessmen who were luring unwary southerners to their destruction with the promise of economic development. Appealing to the antebellum elite ideal of manhood, Watson argued that northern capitalists measured social progress by crass material standards—by increases in the numbers of schools, churches, and businesses—without regard to qualities of character such as honor and virtue. Moreover, northerners had no respect for the South's culture and wrote histories that disparaged its role in the nation's past. Appealing to the wounded pride of embattled white farmers, Watson described the antebellum planter as the "lordliest man that ever walked this continent" and urged his audiences to combat the northern image of southerners as the nation's "black-sheep" in need of "much charity and pardon." What white southerners needed most, he concluded, was for northerners to stay out of their affairs, especially those related to the "Negro Question."[16]

Even though Watson did not specifically target the southern movement, he created problems for its reformers by maligning northern influence and encouraging the reactionary tendencies of whites opposed to black education. Much like the People's Party, Georgia's white Populists had never been particularly responsive to black needs. The Alliance legislature of 1890–91 created the Georgia State Industrial College for Colored Youth, but only because the second Morrill Act put states at risk of losing federal funding if they did not admit black students to white land-grant colleges or create separate ones for them. Alliance men also tried to limit black school funds to the amount of taxes paid by African American property owners, a proposal revived by white supremacists in 1900 and 1904. Atlanta journalist and political operative John Temple Graves broadcast the extremist defense of discrimination in his numerous speaking engagements. In addresses at the New York Chautauqua and University of Chicago commencement in 1903, Graves vigorously asserted that African Americans were members of an inferior race that could not be redeemed through education. Claiming that criminality increased as blacks became more educated, Graves warned that with knowledge came ambition and resentment at the limits imposed by white prejudice. Racial conflict was "irrepressible and inevitable," since whites would never relinquish their dominance as the superior race.[17]

Extremist arguments against black education appealed to the biases of southern white educators who already were skeptical of its value. At the 1900 meeting of the SEA, University of Virginia professor Paul B. Barringer endorsed Mississippian James Vardaman's position that southern states should place white needs first. He cautioned that literacy increased black "criminality and physical depravity," and providing African Americans with industrial education would only lead to race war by increasing economic competition with whites (an argument also made by Graves). That same year Professor John R. Straton of Mercer University in Macon, Georgia, published an article in the *North American Review* that questioned the efficacy of black education. He cited evidence purporting to show that black immorality and crime—and especially rape—increased with black literacy. Although Straton declined to identify literacy as the causal factor, he argued that education could not hasten the evolutionary progress of an inferior race. He warned that trying to advance African Americans too far, too quickly, would result in their physical and mental degeneration; they had to pass through an industrial phase before they could benefit from the education of an advanced race.[18]

Theories of black degeneracy and appeals to sectional pride soon became interwoven in a campaign to discredit the SEB and GEB. Writer Edward Ingle and *Manufacturers' Record* editor Richard Hathaway Edmonds led the way, launching a propaganda war against what they labeled "Ogdenism." They depicted the northern leadership of the two boards and the Rockefeller dollars that funded them as part of a conspiracy to reprise Reconstruction through financial means, using education to promote racial equality while bribing whites into acquiescence with the promise of philanthropic donations. Ingle and Edmonds were contemptuous of southern board members who made critical remarks about their region in acknowledging the need for reforms, and they regarded the rush of southern "hat-holding" applicants for GEB funding as humiliating and emasculating. It may be true, as board members suspected and historians have argued, that Edmonds acted in the interests of manufacturers who were concerned about the impact of educational reform on child labor.[19] Edmonds also may have worried that publicizing southern backwardness would discourage outside investment in the region; however, the argument that the southern movement was an insult to the independence and honor of southern white men had a broad appeal that extended well beyond the manufacturing class.

The persistence of sectionalism in national politics served to further the impression that educational reform was part of a northern conspiracy to reconstruct the South by bringing its white men to heel. Between 1900 and 1905, Republican congressmen made repeated efforts to punish southern states with black disfranchisement laws by reducing their representation in Congress, and the Republican Party made reduction a plank in its national platform in the 1904 presidential campaign. Although the only substantive result of the proposals was new restrictions on gerrymandering, periodic revival of the reapportionment issue kept southern politicians up in arms and led some to call for repeal of the Fifteenth Amendment. Southern critics tied Robert Ogden to the controversy through his membership in the Union League Club of New York City, which in December 1903 called for federal enforcement of the Fourteenth and Fifteenth amendments and reduction of southern congressional representation. Despite accusations of his complicity, Ogden previously had helped persuade club members to table similar resolutions for fear that a federal legal challenge would further consolidate southern white support behind the Democratic Party and exacerbate racial tensions. The resulting atmosphere of intolerance would lead to repression of free speech, especially academic freedom, thereby dooming reform efforts and leaving the "best people of the South" unable to protect blacks.[20]

Ogden's conservatism did nothing to dissuade Edward Ingle. In a series of articles (some of which were reprinted as pamphlets) he summarized many of the beliefs underlying attacks on Ogden and the southern movement. Pointing to the fact that GEB and SEB board members frequently used the phrases "universal education" and "the democratization of education" in describing their goals, Ingle complained that they intended to provide the same education to all children regardless of race. This was "dangerous" for southern race relations, as it raised expectations of equality in the minds of African Americans. Ingle found the timing of the reform movement suspicious, noting that it was launched after a handful of states had established literacy requirements for the vote. This suggested to him that "the inspiration of Ogdenism was the determination to give the negro full weight at the polls in the South." He also highlighted the potential of the boards to undercut white control of resources through a direct infusion of philanthropic and federal funds. Ingle observed that Ogden's son-in-law, Hampton Institute treasurer Alexander Purves, had a plan for black land cooperatives that included agricultural education similar to the farm demonstration work funded by the GEB. Furthermore, CES leaders and board members openly advocated a revival of something akin to the Blair Bill, which would have provided federal funding for southern public schools.[21]

The fact that Ogden appeared to lack the white southerner's repugnance for social contact with blacks gave some credence to Ingle's claims. Critics were able to hold up his personal life, and especially his close friendship with Booker T. Washington, as an example of hidden motives. When Washington visited New York City, Ogden's every word and action were scrutinized by men who suspected that a secret agenda of social equality underlay the educational reform movement. That he hugged or walked with his arm around Washington, called him a "personal friend," dined with him, and kept him as a guest in the Ogden home, all became signs of a "negro-loving obsession" in the minds of men who themselves appeared obsessed. Thomas Dixon Jr., author of *The Leopard's Spots* and *The Clansman*, reveled in the attention he got in the press from calling Ogden a "negro worshiper." He accused Ogden, who was managing partner of Wannamaker's Department Store in New York City, of allowing black men to seat themselves at the tables of white women and girls in the store restaurant. In statements published in southern newspapers, Dixon put quotation marks around the word "southern" in all references to the SEB and called the board a cover for "the most insidious, dangerous movement against Southern sentiment since the war."[22]

The timing of the attack on Parrish and the normal school was no coincidence, as board influence had been steadily growing in Georgia. Branson made a trip to New York City in the fall of 1901 to lobby for hosting the next Conference for Education in the South in Athens, and he took advantage of the opportunity to meet with philanthropists to solicit donations for the normal school. His mission was successful on both counts. When the conference met in Athens in April 1902, William Baldwin and Wallace Buttrick informed participants assembled at the normal school that the GEB was pledging $7,500 in scholarship funds for female students and would match any additional money raised by Georgia clubwomen up to another $7,500. The Georgia division of the United Daughters of the Confederacy (UDC) was in the process of raising funds for a women's dormitory, Winnie Davis Hall, and Buttrick also committed the GEB to half the remaining balance if UDC members could match it by January. In March 1903 a group of men that included Branson, University of Georgia chancellor Walter B. Hill, and state school superintendent W. B. Merritt, met in the office of Governor Joseph M. Terrell to form an educational campaign committee to spearhead the drive for reform. The SEB promised to fund the committee's first year of work.[23]

Ogden had good reason to fear that academic freedom was endangered, as southern educators who defended black civil rights had been the targets of white-supremacist attacks. Professor Andrew Sledd of Emory College (now Emory University) in Oxford, Georgia, published an article in the *Atlantic Monthly* in 1902 in which he dared to admit two inconvenient truths. Directly refuting extremist justifications for racial violence, he argued that lynching was motivated purely by base prejudice and that the vast majority of its victims were not rapists. Even though he believed African Americans were members of an inferior race, Sledd maintained that white Americans had an obligation to respect their inalienable rights and to give them a fair chance to realize their potential. His essay was included in the July edition of the journal, and by the second week in August public pressure had convinced college trustees he must resign. The following year an article by Professor John Spencer Bassett of Trinity College held Democrats to account for their opportunistic appeals to race and labeled racial discrimination un-American. He agreed with Sledd that merit and ability should be the determinants of one's station in life, regardless of race. Fortunately for Bassett, Trinity president John C. Kilgo chose to take a stand for intellectual freedom, and along with alumnus Walter Hines Page of the GEB successfully opposed trustees who wanted the historian to resign.[24]

Unlike the outcry against Sledd and Bassett, the charges against Parrish were highly gendered and sexual in nature. The intent to repress academic freedom is clear, since her remarks were part of a classroom discussion not intended for public consumption, but the strategy of the attack differed. White supremacists made explicit connections between education and the threat of rape and miscegenation in an effort to deny African Americans an avenue of upward mobility that might increase their political influence and restrict access to cheap labor. Attempting to justify the use of violence to enforce white dominance, extremists claimed that lynching was the primal response of white men to assaults on the safety and purity of white womanhood. Their argument was so persuasive that prominent Americans continued to accept that lynching was provoked by rape long after Ida B. Wells-Barnett's numerous publications had proven otherwise.[25] However, their legitimacy depended on white women accepting the myth of the black-beast rapist. In reprimanding her student for expressing disgust at the thought of teaching blacks, Parrish rejected the race claim. The accusation that she supported social equality of the races was a ritual through which she could be forced to acknowledge the need for protection from black men, thereby declaring her identification with white men on race grounds and her dependency upon their superior physical and political power.

In defying the extremist dynamic of white gender relations, Parris represented a threat despite her lack of formal political power. Unlike most women engaged in social reform, she had constructed a life free of relations of dependency and was truly "out of control." The problem was not just her feminism or her attitude toward black education, but the fact that she challenged conventional gender roles from outside the bounds of marriage and promoted interracial cooperation from an independent position of public authority. As an educator who trained thousands of public schoolteachers, she played a key role in the socialization of young white women and through them could impact the attitudes of future generations. Her belief in white responsibility for black welfare, however conservative or patronizing it may appear in retrospect, undermined white-supremacist propaganda by encouraging female students to reject the notion that contact with African American boys and men was physically dangerous and morally disreputable. Her integration of social gospel and progressive ideals made it appear un-Christian and socially irresponsible to deny anyone the ability to realize his or her God-given potential. Since white men who launched public attacks on respectable white women risked dishonoring themselves, those targeting Parrish used anonymous suggestions of impropriety to publicly discredit and shame her.

In contrast, even the most outspoken and abrasive of feminists was safe if she accepted the race claim, as the case of Rebecca Latimer Felton shows. Felton, the wife of former Congressman William H. Felton, used the temperance and woman suffrage movements as platforms for verbally flogging white men who she believed were neglecting their familial obligations. Bitter at the devastation of the Civil War, Felton wanted men to compensate for the hardship they had wrought by providing institutional protections and equal opportunities for poor white women who had no male providers. Although she denounced the rape of black women in the convict-lease system as an example of male abuse of power in the 1880s, in the next decade she began focusing on the mythological black rapist as a more powerful symbol of white men's failures. Felton openly advocated lynching in 1897 and later instigated the public attack on Andrew Sledd. She regarded vigilante violence as a grim but necessary reminder to white men that it was their own failure to protect and provide that left their wives at the mercy of black rapists.[26] While her support for woman suffrage challenged male political control, in asserting white female dependency and sexual purity in opposition to black male aggression Felton upheld the interlocking construction of white heterosexuality and white supremacy.

Parrish directly refuted such notions of sexual endangerment in the September 1901 issue of the *Southern Workman*, the journal of Hampton Institute. She intended her essay to appeal to the practical sensibilities of southern whites who interacted daily with African Americans whom they employed. Parrish began by explaining that she twice hired a black man to serve as driver when she had to travel alone to a remote rural district to visit a critically ill friend. She described how the men performed their duties in a professional and kindly way despite poor weather and her obvious distress. Parrish then alluded to white women's exaggerated fears of rape by noting that she, her friends, and the livery where she rented the wagon "felt it a mere matter of course to rely upon the Negro. Not one of us thought of danger. That thought came to me only when, much later, someone asked me if I thought such a journey was safe." She went on to give another example of black fidelity, that of a scrupulously honest housekeeper who acted as nurse and financial agent for Parrish during a prolonged illness. Parrish's personal vignettes attempted to ground southern whites in the realities of racial interdependence by highlighting the mutual trust that normally characterized their interactions with African Americans.[27]

Forced to defend her racial views and lacking the protective mantle of matrimony, Celeste Parrish turned to other educators for support. She apologetically told University of Georgia chancellor Walter B. Hill that she had thought there was nothing in Love McDaniel's complaint "to hurt my influence in the South or to cause a Sledd-like sensation." She was fortunate that Hill, a normal-school trustee, had a personal stake in resolving the controversy. He was elected to the SEB in January 1904, served as chair of the Georgia educational campaign committee, and acted as the board's valued advisor on racial issues. His impeccable southern credentials and grounding in the Social Gospel made him the ideal face of reform in Georgia. He was a leader in the campaign for state prohibition and author of the local option bill, and his speeches and writings on black education expressed a conservative Christian humanism that embraced the brotherhood of races. He perfectly threaded the middle road prized by northern philanthropists, condemning demagoguery, lynching, and repression of free speech, while endorsing a combination of industrial and classical education for blacks and the Tuskegee approach to race uplift. Hill wanted to settle the normal-school conflict as quickly and quietly as possible to prevent the local campaign from being crippled at the starting gate.[28]

Despite publicly denying that she received a statement of support from "Baldwin and associates," Parrish had the sympathy of SEB members who understood the nature of her predicament. When she informed Wallace Buttrick (of both the GEB and the SEB) during one of his visits to Athens that she was being attacked in the press for supporting black education, he replied that board members would stand by her. She also spoke with George Foster Peabody about the incident, who relayed the information to Robert Ogden. In Ogden's correspondence with Parrish about donations to the normal school and other matters, he expressed sympathy for the "unjust attacks" she had to endure. He realized that it was difficult for reformers to convince white southerners of the need for universal education when extremists were arguing it would increase crime and sexual violence among blacks. He also appreciated Parrish's quiet efforts to keep him informed on developments in black education in the Athens area. Even though Ogden regarded academic freedom as essential to reformers' ability to refute racist falsehoods, the propaganda war waged by Ingle and the *Manufacturers Record* convinced him that leadership on the issue must come from within the South. Reluctant to intervene and provoke fresh accusations of northern interference, Ogden confided to Parrish that he saw hopeful signs in the positive outcome of Bassett's case.[29]

Ogden knew of conditions in Georgia partly through the work of board member and CES field agent George S. Dickerman, who received numerous reports of hostility toward whites engaged in black education. One white educator in North Georgia told Dickerman, "For a southern man to take up the work as it should be done would be to close to him all other work in educational lines. He would need to be certain of continued employment, if, as is the case with me, the support of his family depended on his daily earnings." He added that he had lost friends as well as career opportunities in his seven years of work in black schools. Atlanta University chaplain Edward T. Ware also complained to Dickerman of white hostility. Ware wrote that white southerners accused Atlanta University of promoting social equality by seating black students and white teachers at the same tables in the school dining room and by encouraging blacks to realize their potential. He was grateful that there were "many yet in the southern work who will not burn incense to this god of prejudice," but he was pained by reformers supposedly committed to universal education who did not accept Atlanta University's "principle of fairness and justice."[30]

The need to minimize the appearance of SEB influence put Parrish in an awkward position, forcing her to rely on her Baptist faith and the loyalty of colleagues and students to provide her defense. At the December hearing members of the normal school's entire senior class testified that Parrish had not made the statements attributed to her by the *Telegraph*. The remarks she did make were in response to a question from a male student, A. D. Hammock, who was the school superintendent for Rockdale County. Hammock was a staunch supporter of the normal school, and his political savvy was evident in his careful interpretation of Parrish's comments. He argued that she had only meant to convey that southern whites should be in charge of black education to ensure the preservation of racial harmony. She had reprimanded McDaniel for lacking the true educator's generosity of spirit, since white teachers should be willing to extend to blacks "a helping hand in the school room if conditions really demanded it." In a backhanded reference to the vulgarity of racist extremists, Hammond added that he had never heard Parrish "make a statement that would have offended the well informed, refined southern gentleman." Student testimony, along with the prior faculty investigation that found Parrish "guilty of nothing worse than expressing a generous Christian interest in a backward race," gave the board of trustees more than sufficient grounds for exoneration.[31]

While the *Telegraph* article grossly distorted the facts in other areas, it was accurate in claiming that the classroom incident had soured relations between Parrish and the normal-school president. Branson demonstrated poor judgment in deciding to conduct an investigation into McDaniel's accusations without informing Parrish beforehand. When he announced that McDaniel would meet with the faculty, Parrish assumed it was to issue a reprimand for the insulting language of the student's letter of complaint. She was hurt and offended to discover that her own professional integrity was being questioned and that it was she who was "on trial." She no longer trusted Branson to represent her interests, and a climate of mistrust grew between the two. When Branson heard rumors that Parrish told students he was behind the articles in the *Telegraph* and had treated her badly, he was outraged and again showed poor judgment. He took his complaint to the board of trustees and was embarrassed at the December hearing when the rumors proved to be false. By that time, his differences with Parrish had become a matter of public knowledge in Athens and a topic of gossip among educators statewide. In January, Branson insisted on another investigation by the board, this one into "his acts and doings as President."[32]

Walter Hill was understandably alarmed, fearing that simple misunderstandings were developing into a full-fledged scandal that would harm the state's educational campaign and leave no one unscathed. Knowing that Parrish had been forced out of her previous position, Hill worried that her career would suffer irreparable damage if she had to leave the normal school because of her differences with Branson. He was concerned enough to ask George Foster Peabody to try to secure a position for her elsewhere. Hill also was anxious about the impact a second hearing might have on Branson, since some of the trustees found his rash reaction to baseless rumors offensive. Branson's reluctance to give a woman the benefit of the doubt and his willingness to publicly air his grievances with her seemed ungentlemanly to say the least. This outcome was ironic. Branson was distressed that students might think he had mistreated a woman and had hoped the first hearing would clear his name. He must have seen the looks of disapproval on trustees' faces when he made his accusations at the December meeting, because in a January letter to trustee W. B. Merritt he asked for a full review of his record as president and "as a man" as soon as possible.[33]

The second board investigation was just as nasty and divisive as Hill feared it would be. Branson, who testified first at the April hearing, accused Parrish of being insubordinate and uncooperative. One example he gave to support this claim was her supposed refusal to allow him to oversee expenditures for the new practice school. He testified that, when he asked her to place all orders on his desk for prior approval, she responded by saying "she would not degrade herself like a negro by so doing." Branson further alleged that Parrish was "inconsiderate of the health of the students by requiring too much work of them." A physician who treated one of Parrish's female students for "nervous strain" testified that Parrish reprimanded him for agreeing with the student that an excessive workload was the cause of the malady. Perhaps the most damaging evidence was a letter Branson solicited from William Smith of Randolph-Macon Woman's College stating that Parrish had been forced to resign because she could not work in harmony with the faculty and president. Branson also provided a letter from "nearly all of the members of the faculty of that college stating that Dr. Smith's position in the matter was correct." He reinforced those assertions by accusing Parrish of upsetting normal-school colleagues by making critical remarks about their teaching methods.[34]

It is revealing that the male president and faculty of RMWC closed ranks with the male president and faculty of the normal school in an attempt to paint Celeste Parrish as disruptive and insubordinate. All of the women faculty took Parrish's side, and all but one of the GSNS men sided with Branson at the 1904 hearing. The underlying cause of the gendered divisions was male educators' resistance to treating female colleagues as equals. As Parrish observed more than once, male administrators guaranteed the subordination of female faculty by hiring them for only the lowest-paid, lowest-ranked positions. Women's exclusion from the state universities of Virginia and Georgia further served this end by denying them access to the education and professional connections that facilitated the upward mobility of men. Parrish was an exception, as her study at Cornell and the University of Chicago exceeded the credentials of the average normal-school educator of either sex, including Branson. She thought she had made it clear to Branson that her acceptance of the GSNS position was contingent upon it being defined as expert consultant rather than classroom teacher, only to find her judgment questioned and her advice often resented. She admitted in her testimony to the board that she occasionally had been "emphatic" and "untactful" due to her "intense desire to build up the work of the school," but she denied being insubordinate and disagreeable.[35]

As in her dealings with RMWC faculty, Parrish's problems stemmed partly from her refusal to adhere to a gendered code of behavior that was premised on an assumption of female dependency. In her view, postbellum conditions and new scientific insights required a revised gender etiquette that recognized women's equality of intellect and right to independence. Parrish had to become self-sufficient at a young age and acquired a strong will and tenacious spirit of necessity; she had no time for false modesty and deferential posturing, and no patience for male professionals who expected it. This confused and even offended men unaccustomed to dealing with women who lacked all feminine artifice, influencing some to interpret her behavior as manly. One account of her participation in the Georgia educational reform campaign noted that "she had very much the mind and the manner of a man on the public platform" and "was frank and even abrupt and blunt in making her points." Parrish also had no use for fashionable hair or clothing or conventional notions of a fashionable body, all of which focused women's energies on sexual attractiveness rather than intellect and character. According to RMWC colleague Meta Glass, she was proud of her thirty-six-inch waist.[36]

Ironically, given her rejection of stereotypical femininity, male colleagues found it difficult to see Parrish as anything other than an embodiment of her sex. When Branson looked at her he saw a middle-aged woman not much older than his wife. He had a family who considered him "Lord and Master" of the household and a wife whom he called Lottie, but who always referred to him as Mr. Branson. Accustomed to the deference of subordinates, he did not seriously consider that Parrish had herself earned the right to deferential treatment. Instead, he told Hill he attributed her "peculiarities to physical conditions incident to her period of life," presumably meaning the hormonal changes of perimenopause. Hill was relieved rather than dismayed at this reduction of Parrish the accomplished professional to Parrish the irrational woman, thinking it would allow Branson "to deal with even an annoying situation with the saving grace of humor."[37] It did not.

Parrish's conflict with Branson provided a case in point for her argument that men who were progressive on other issues could not be counted upon to support gender equality. Branson was well known and respected by the leaders of the southern movement, had the backing of progressive male educators and politicians in Georgia, and was a pioneer in the field of rural sociology. Historians have allowed these attributes to largely obscure his fundamental conservatism on gender and race issues. One of his colleagues at the University of North Carolina, where Branson chaired the Department of Rural Social Economics after leaving Georgia in 1914, described him as an "unreconstructed southerner." Branson frequently made autocratic decisions directly impacting Parrish's work, and when she questioned or objected to his directives he labeled her insubordinate. Even though Parrish was almost ten years his senior, he had been supervising female teachers since his early twenties and considered her lack of subservience a personal affront and a burden he should not have to bear. His patronizing attitude is evident in a letter to Hill in which he expressed the hope that she would eventually "settle down in her work happily and be as useful to the school as she is capable of being."[38]

Since Branson did not share Parrish's racially liberal views, the controversy surrounding her remarks on black education worsened his irritation with her. Perhaps it was the pangs of his own conscience that caused him to jump to conclusions when he heard that she had blamed the *Macon Telegraph* articles on him. In an essay published in *World's Work* in March 1902, he lauded the "wisdom" of Samuel Armstrong, founder of Hampton Institute, for recognizing that "any scheme of education for the Negro must preserve for him the best results of slavery." Arguing that industrial education was necessary to enable African Americans to live "in safety" among white southerners, Branson declared that white farmers fled the countryside "to escape the danger to their families of nameless crimes of violence by the worst class of Negroes." While he presented education for manual labor as a corrective for black criminality (apparently including black men's alleged propensity to rape), when it came to economic issues Branson usually equated black success with white failure. He often claimed that African American farmers were gaining ground while white farmers threw in the towel, arguing that rural reform was necessary to prevent a further blackening of property ownership and the agricultural economy.[39]

Parrish found she could not count on Walter Hill's support either, showing how women's lack of formal political power could disadvantage them professionally even with men who favored women's rights. Hill was married to a prominent advocate for women's civil and political equality, Sallie Barker Hill, and he publicly defended the campaigns for coeducation and woman suffrage. However, Hill privately believed that Branson had made a critical mistake in publicly addressing Parrish's grievances. He thought Branson should have remained silent and simply exercised his prerogative not to renew her appointment. Then, if Parrish demanded an investigation of her dismissal, she would have to appeal from a subordinate position and Branson would retain the upper hand. The "misfortune" of Branson's demand for a complete review of his relationship with Parrish, Hill reflected, was that "it put him and her upon precisely the same footing." He was concerned for Parrish, but thought it was more important to retain Branson, who as a man had political connections that could be worked to the advantage of the normal school. Parrish sensed that Hill was not in her corner. Fearing that she had been misrepresented, she insisted that she had "tried so hard to do right and to placate Mr. Branson" and begged Hill to "*please* try to regain and keep the 'suspended judgment'" until he had heard all the evidence.[40]

The board of trustees never issued a final determination for the hearing in 1904 because the governor of Georgia intervened before its members concluded the investigation. Prior to the board meeting scheduled for early June, Governor Terrell contacted trustee Lawton Evans to say that airing the normal school's dirty laundry just as the General Assembly was scheduled to convene might lead to a reduction in state appropriations. Evans and Hill met with Branson to ask him to reconsider his statement that irreconcilable differences prohibited him from continuing to work with Parrish. As a result, lawyers representing Branson and Parrish hammered out a set of resolutions to govern their professional relationship, which included the creation of a Prudential Committee to enforce the terms of the agreement. Hill was optimistic that the conflict would finally come to an end, but the governor's intervention only postponed its resolution.[41] Branson had said and done things that could not be rescinded. The letters he obtained to impugn her record at RMWC were not something she could easily forgive, and her presence at the normal school was a constant reminder of embarrassments he would rather forget.

Parrish coped with the contentious environment by creating female networks of support that provided the stability her professional life lacked. Like many other "new women" who chose careers over marriage, she constructed alternative forms of household and family that were compatible with female independence. Sometime between 1902 and 1905 she adopted a daughter, Charlotte "Lottie" Jarrell, from a DeKalb County orphanage. Jarrell thrived in her new home, engaging Athens children in civic-improvement projects and later becoming active in student government and the Young Women's Christian Association at South Georgia State Normal School (now Valdosta State University). Parrish also came up with a sensible plan for resolving the problem of housing for single GSNS teachers. She rented a home near campus that in 1910 included six teachers as boarders—Carlotta Alexander, Mary Creswell, Elsie Gibb, Kate Hicks, Mary Mitchell, and Laura Smith.[42] It was doubtless a welcome substitute for the isolation and anonymity of a commercial boardinghouse, especially for the three teachers who were in their thirties. For Parrish the arrangement replicated the intimacy of Randolph-Macon Woman's College, where living and dining on campus enabled her to mentor younger women.

Sharing a household created close friendships between Parrish and the female faculty of the normal school that well outlasted their employment in Athens. John Collier, a sociologist best known as architect of the "Indian New Deal" in the Franklin D. Roosevelt administration, provided a rare glimpse into the personal lives of the teachers in his memoirs. Collier was born and grew up in Atlanta and began hiking the Southern Appalachian Mountains when he was in his late teens. In the summer of 1904 he acted as a guide for Parrish and "her young women co-workers of the practice school" on a two-week hike through the Georgia and North Carolina mountains. Accompanied by Collier's brother and his best friend, the group walked during the day and camped at night, enduring many rainstorms along the way. Parrish did not let her age—almost fifty-two—or heart condition keep her from climbing to the top of Blood Mountain, where the hikers spent the night. According to Collier, she played a critical role in his intellectual development by introducing him to the works of John Dewey and G. Stanley Hall. He described her as a "marvelous thinker and teacher" with a "warm and selfless heart."[43]

Collier's account is only one example of how Parrish's regional reputation gave her a broad circle of acquaintances that facilitated integration into social life in North Georgia. When Rebecca Douglass Lowe of the Atlanta Woman's Club (AWC) assumed the presidency of the General Federation of Women's Clubs in 1898, she appointed Parrish to serve on the educational committee. Parrish and two other committee members conducted an exhaustive survey of the educational work of the nation's federated clubs and provided Lowe with a summary report that documented the impressive scope of women's activities in support of public schools. Lowe presented the findings at the SEA meeting in New Orleans in December, most likely at Parrish's suggestion, as she also was presenting a paper at the conference. In addition, Parrish had a prior acquaintance with Sallie B. Hill, whose daughters Mary and Parna enrolled in Randolph-Macon Woman's College in 1900. Hill accompanied the girls to Lynchburg in the fall to help them get settled, and the three visited with Parrish over a meal in the dining hall. Parna seemed especially impressed with Parrish's knowledge of psychology and often mentioned her in letters to family members. Both she and her mother were members of the Athens Woman's Club, which Parrish joined shortly after moving to Georgia.[44]

Just as in Virginia, Parrish wasted no time in engaging in a wide range of activities that transcended the division between public and private that characterized the careers of most male professionals. Having decided to apply her talents to teacher training rather than pursuing laboratory research and the "rewards of high scholarship," Parrish was attracted to child study as a democratic form of inquiry that bridged the gap between the formal knowledge of scientists and teachers and the practical knowledge of mothers. In response to male critics who denigrated the value of observational research conducted by untrained mothers, Parrish countered that their reservations only proved that the education of future mothers should include "a systematic study of the sciences of life and mind, together with their practical application." While the concept of scientific motherhood could have undemocratic consequences when it shifted authority to professional experts, Parrish's goal was to achieve the reverse, to include women in the creation of formal knowledge and elevate the status of mothering. As she had done in Lynchburg, during her first semester at GSNS she offered a series of public lectures on child study for teachers and mothers in Athens.[45]

Parrish's dedication to improving child development through intelligent parenting led her to found the Georgia chapter of the Congress of Mothers in the summer of 1905. Many leaders of the organization, renamed the Parent-Teacher Association, wanted to raise the status of motherhood to keep women in the home; however, the group also attracted reformers such as Parrish who shared a concern for child welfare but embraced a broader public role for women. Parrish envisioned elementary education as ideally a partnership between mothers and teachers and regarded the formation of PTA chapters as a method of achieving this goal. Teachers would educate mothers on the benefits of child study and the new education, while parents would gain allies in shaping their children's educations to meet individual needs. In preparation for the first annual meeting of the state Congress in 1906, top officials from Georgia's federated clubs joined Parrish in issuing a call to all women's groups to send delegates. When the women convened in Atlanta in April, advocates of public kindergartens and child labor reform had prominent places on the program, and Parrish gave an address in which she provided an overview of the educational philosophy guiding her work at GSNS and the practice school.[46]

Georgia clubwomen who shared her progressive vision of child development gave Parrish the respect and recognition that she often failed to receive at the normal school. Immediately following the first meeting of the Mothers' Congress, three women published reports on their visit to the practice school with the intention of convincing others to make the trek to Athens. Passie Fenton Ottley carefully explained the basic elements of the new education—its focus on developing potential, appealing to interest, and providing a holistic unification of knowledge—that avoided the monotony of rote memorization and made children want to learn. Mary Mitchell Brown explained how teachers patiently encouraged children to develop powers of attention and self-control rather than using force to maintain discipline. Calling Parrish "one of the most noted exponents of the new educational methods in this country," Brown described classrooms of alert, cooperative, and engaged children. Annie E. Johnson, chair of the education committee of the Georgia Federation of Women's Clubs, reminded readers that when clubwomen first decided to establish model schools they had to send young women to New York and Massachusetts to obtain the teacher training that Parrish now provided at the normal school.[47]

The authors of the article on the practice school were illustrative of the state's leading female educational reformers. Both Ottley and Brown had served as officers of the Atlanta Woman's Club, which studiously researched current issues and was the most vocal of all federated clubs in its advocacy of educational reform. Passie Ottley was from Mississippi and had attended a Virginia seminary before enrolling in Mississippi Woman's College (now Mississippi University for Women). She maintained a regular column in the *Southern Educational Journal* in the 1890s, and later studied sociology at the University of Chicago and managed the Georgia Federation's Tallulah Falls School. Mary Brown was from Ohio and a graduate of Lake Erie Female Seminary (now Lake Erie College). She played a key role in raising scholarship funds for female GSNS students and spoke publicly on the need for cooperation between women's clubs and educators. Annie Johnson was born in New York and attended a private school in Paris, France, before marrying a Georgia lawyer. As president of the Georgia Federation between 1897 and 1901, she promoted the establishment of model schools and edited the GFWC official organ, *The Southern Woman*. She later became associate editor of a newspaper in which she held majority ownership.[48]

Parrish also found like-minded women in the Athens Woman's Club. The teachers and University of Georgia faculty wives who comprised a majority of its members had made education a priority since the club's founding in 1896. Parrish joined a planning committee for the establishment of a free kindergarten only a few months after becoming a member. When fellow member Mary Ann Lipscomb began efforts to found a school for mountain whites a year later, Parrish helped draw up the formal proposal for Tallulah Falls School in Rabun County and participated in the funding drive. The mountains of northeast Georgia must have reminded her of home, because she also agreed to organize a fundraiser for the struggling Rabun County public high school and was one of three Athens residents whose donations equipped its domestic science room. In addition, as a member of the Laura Rutherford chapter of the United Daughters of the Confederacy she served on a committee tasked with raising money for a girls' dormitory at the high school. Despite her many obligations, she was rarely too busy to give lectures and addresses when women's groups came calling, frequently appearing on the programs of the GFWC meetings and the Gulf States Convention of the YWCA.[49]

Parrish found that Georgia clubwomen were engaged in a battle for educational equality that was almost identical to the one she had led in Virginia. Even though white women had access to three state institutions—the normal school, the women's college, and North Georgia Agricultural College—none of them came close to matching the quality of the male-only University of Georgia and Georgia Institute of Technology. Beginning in 1896, federation officials twice petitioned University of Georgia trustees to admit women for graduate study and continued to lobby the legislature for an enabling bill after their requests were denied. Rosa Woodberry of the Athens Woman's Club was one of two female teachers who repeatedly appealed to trustees to grant graduate credit for their individual work with university professors. Prominent clubwomen also endorsed Rebecca Latimer Felton's 1898 letter to the *Atlanta Constitution* calling for the admission of women to the textile school at Georgia Tech. In an editorial published in May 1902, Parrish argued that, since southern states lacked the means to establish "really good women's colleges," the logical solution was to admit women to male colleges and universities and "strengthen them by all the funds which would otherwise go to the establishment of more women's colleges." She found that Georgia's university men were no more convinced that those in Virginia that coeducation was feasible and desirable.[50]

Concerned that southern institutions were not making adequate progress in improving the quality of female education, in 1903 Parrish took direct action to hasten the pace of change. While teaching at the University of Tennessee's Summer School of the South in July, she and a group of female participants decided the time had come to create a regional organization of college-educated women. Parrish, Lillian Wyckoff Johnson, and Emilie McVea presided at the founding meeting of the Southern Association of College Women in Knoxville. The Association of Collegiate Alumnae provided them with an organizational template, but its restrictive definition of collegiate study excluded almost all southern institutions, leaving most southern women ineligible for membership. SACW founders cast their net more broadly, opening membership to graduates of the twelve southern colleges affiliated with the Association of Colleges and Preparatory Schools of the Southern States. They aimed to circumvent male opposition to educational equality by creating a separate network of women dedicated to promoting, improving, and standardizing the work of southern women's colleges.[51]

The SACW tackled the "distinctly southern" problems that Parrish had been discussing for the previous five years. As its members explained in their second annual meeting in 1904, they sought to create a "distinct line of demarcation between the secondary school and college," to nurture in young women "a desire for college training," and to provide financial assistance to "ambitious girls who are debarred from colleges by lack of means." Members vowed to be supportive of institutions striving to improve standards and to be unsparing in their criticisms of those that were not, and to work for the "improvement of the elementary schools of the south, especially those of the rural districts." SACW members hoped to create a smoother path to college for the young women who came after them, and their policies reflected the democratic ideals underlying Parrish's ethic of service. Unlike most women's organizations that offered financial aid to college-bound young women, the SACW provided grants rather than loans. Atlanta women founded a Georgia chapter in March 1905 and welcomed the ACA to a joint meeting in their city in November. On the third day of the conference, attendants traveled to Athens, and Parrish gave them a tour of the normal school.[52]

The founding of the SACW was one indication that Celeste Parrish had learned some hard lessons regarding the gendered limits of reform in her professional life. The racialized attack on her respectability and the failure of Eugene Branson and Walter Hill to acknowledge her importance to the normal school proved that in the eyes of most southern men—reactionary and progressive—she could not escape the particularized category of sex. She was not overly cynical in thinking that no feminine achievement would be great enough to earn the right of equality, and that the only real hope lay in separate organization. However, while female networks enabled women to draw upon a variety of interlocking organizations in gathering data, mobilizing public opinion, and pressuring political leaders and institutions, they could not completely compensate for the interlocking and mutually reinforcing structures of male dominance in the home, workplace, and legislature. Women's political power ran on a different track than men's, one that gave them little protection from discrimination. Unfortunately, Parrish had not learned her last hard lesson on that count.

CHAPTER FIVE

The Refuge of Service

A t first it appeared as if Celeste Parrish's networks of support would make the tension at the Georgia State Normal School tolerable, but by 1910 it was clear that conditions would not significantly change, and her departure was inevitable. Rancor continued to tinge her interactions with Eugene Branson, who had learned his own lessons from the hearings of 1903 and 1904 and would not make the same mistakes twice. He was not alone in finding her assertion of professional equality untenable. First the normal-school faculty and then its board of trustees divided into separate and hostile camps, with almost all men backing Branson's claim that she was a disruptive influence. Parrish's participation in the southern movement proved to be her salvation, as its leaders controlled the philanthropic funds that provided her with yet another last-minute alternative to unemployment. Her new position as state rural school supervisor for North Georgia fulfilled her ideal of community service while eliminating much of the friction produced by daily interaction with men who could not accept her as a peer. Even though the new duties were taxing for a woman nearing retirement age, her work with rural parents, students, and teachers was a return to her roots and a capstone befitting the career of a consecrated woman.

It did not take long for another conflict to arise between Branson and Parrish, but its quick resolution suggested that compromise was still possible. In 1905 he tried to promote one of the practice-school teachers, Mildred Shepperson, to the principalship of Muscogee Elementary. It was an obvious ploy to curry favor with George Foster Peabody, her uncle and a generous donor to both the normal school and the University of Georgia. Branson acted as if the position was part of the spoils of office to be distributed at his discretion, telling Shepperson that he wanted her to have the job without discussing the matter with Parrish beforehand. Branson put Parrish in an awkward position, as she genuinely liked Peabody and his niece, but believed Shepperson lacked the experience and training necessary to be principal. Branson's plans were thwarted by the intervention of Robert J. Guinn, chair of the GSNS Board of Trustees, who argued the promotion should be Parrish's decision. Shepperson subsequently took Parrish's advice regarding the need for further training and left for the University of Chicago.[1]

For the next five years, Branson and Parrish avoided any further public airing of their differences and seemed to make the best of a difficult situation. Branson backed her annual reappointment, and when he attempted to resign for health reasons in 1906 she introduced a faculty resolution expressing support for his continued leadership. In November 1907 she turned down an offer to replace Jere M. Pound, who had resigned his position as professor of pedagogy at Georgia Normal and Industrial College to become state school commissioner. According to an Athens newspaper, she carefully considered the opening at GNIC before deciding "the call of duty was to remain in her present position." The prospect of severing her association with Branson must have been tempting, but she was reluctant to abandon Muscogee Elementary School. Two of her former students, Muscogee principal Laura Smith and teacher Mary Creswell, had followed her advice and were attending University of Chicago summer sessions. Parrish finally had faculty who understood and appreciated her attempts to integrate the practical world of everyday life with the educational experiences of the school. The establishment of the GSNS Mothers' and Teachers' Cooperative Club extended this understanding to the school community by fostering friendships between teachers and parents and giving Parrish a forum for the promotion of progressive pedagogy.[2]

Parrish continued to immerse herself in the educational work of organized women and generously contributed her expertise to their school-reform campaigns. Clubwomen responded with enthusiasm when the SEB educational campaign committees asked them to build grassroots support for reform by founding school-improvement clubs. In 1904 Sallie Hill became the first president of the Georgia School Improvement Club (GSIC), one of six state organizations affiliated with the Women's Interstate Association for the Betterment of Public Schools. Parrish, who had worked for three decades to adapt modern methods and practices to the conditions prevailing in rural schools, was well equipped to provide guidance to clubwomen and rural parents. Her ethic of service and friendship with Sallie Hill made her amendable to the community-outreach work that male reformers expected of women. She spoke at meetings of rural teachers on "community work," addressed the annual meetings of the GSIC, and participated in conferences for farmers' wives staged by Hill at the State College of Agriculture in Athens. At the 1909 conference Parrish addressed rural women on "The Need of Mothers' Co-operative Circles in Our Suburban and Rural Districts."[3]

It was not until 1910 that the relationship between Parrish and Branson finally reached an impasse. Branson's conflicts with Parrish apparently convinced him that the joint appointment of chair of pedagogy and director of Muscogee Elementary held too much authority for a woman; it muddied the chain of command between president and faculty, as a female director was likely to side with the female teachers. In a deliberate act of provocation, he submitted the resignation of Muscogee Elementary principal Laura M. Smith to the board of trustees without Smith's knowledge or consent. Even though Smith landed on her feet, obtaining an assistantship at the University of Chicago that allowed her to complete her bachelor's degree, Parrish was angered by Branson's callous treatment of her former student. He cleverly laid the groundwork for new charges of insubordination by steadfastly refusing to discuss any of Parrish's complaints with her. This left her no recourse but to appeal his actions to trustees, even though directly contacting them violated a policy she had agreed to in 1904 that required teachers to approach the board only through Branson. The board had been restructured and enlarged since the earlier conflicts and now contained a representative from each of the state's congressional districts, plus two from Athens and two from the state at large, few of whom had any personal acquaintance with Parrish. In addition, Robert Guinn, who previously defended her authority over the practice school, was no longer on the board.[4]

Branson then let the other shoe drop, announcing that he was implementing a new track in the teacher-training program that would be under the supervision of a subordinate faculty member. The new track would allow graduates of four-year, accredited high schools who had at least seven months' teaching experience to graduate from the normal school in only one year. Although Parrish was head of the Department of Pedagogy and director of Muscogee Elementary School, under the new plan she would have no control over curriculum and instruction for the shorter course of study or supervision of its student teachers in the practice school. Even more disturbing, the teacher Branson had chosen to head the course, Alice Prichard, disliked young children and had been a disruptive influence in the practice school before Parrish assigned her to other duties. When Prichard worked as Parrish's assistant she was constantly at odds with the Muscogee teachers and eventually announced her intention to resign, stating that she "hated the work" and "disapproved of the policy and management of the school." Branson had previously admitted to Parrish that Prichard was "morbidly sensitive" and "born without a skin," yet his proposal essentially made her co-head of pedagogy with authority over the very teachers she detested. It was the kind of autocratic move that Parrish had found so objectionable in her early years at GSNS, as Branson did not bother to consult with her while formulating the plan.[5]

Since the normal-school president was determined that Prichard would return to the Department of Pedagogy (she had left to assist in mathematics), Parrish came up with alternative duties for which the young woman was better fitted. Prichard had proven her ability to teach adults when she successfully conducted "review C" work, a half-year course offered to teachers preparing for state examinations. Her limited training had not been a problem, because the state school superintendent dictated the books and course of study. Parrish proposed that Prichard be permanently assigned to the review course, freeing more qualified teachers to focus on advanced pedagogical instruction and the day-to-day operations of Muscogee Elementary. Parrish also suggested giving Prichard sole control of exam review, believing her emotional peculiarities would be less troublesome for other faculty if she worked independently of them. The time and effort Parrish expended in coming up with a compromise solution was wasted, as Branson steadfastly refused to discuss the matter with her in person. Much to her frustration, after telling her to put her thoughts in writing, he ignored the proposal outlined in her letter and vaguely suggested that he would address the issue at a later date.[6]

Parrish was understandably alarmed, as Prichard's erratic behavior had the potential to reverse years of hard-won progress at the practice school. When Muscogee Elementary first opened, Parrish had to carefully cultivate the trust of skeptical parents by convincing them that the incorporation of student teaching would not diminish the quality of their children's education. She worried that her entire program of educational reform would be destroyed if Prichard upset the delicate balance between normal and elementary instruction. Parrish could lose the support of parents if inadequately trained normal-school students were allowed to teach in the practice school, and Prichard would disrupt the entire operation of Muscogee Elementary if she provoked petty quarrels with its teachers. Faculty already were upset about the possibility of having to work with a woman whom they described as a "disturbing element" in their letter of protest to Branson.[7]

Parrish's anxiety increased as Branson continued to undermine her position at the normal school. He implemented the new short course in the fall of 1910, placing it under the direction of Prichard without responding to Parrish's pleas for clarification of the new administrative chain of command. Learning from his missteps in the 1903–4 controversy, Branson followed Walter Hill's earlier advice to maintain the upper hand and kept his silence until the time came for her reappointment. Parrish correctly interpreted his casual dismissal of her concerns as evidence that he was plotting to orchestrate her removal, and in the early months of 1911 she left no stone unturned in search of other employment. She repeatedly wrote Hollis Frissell, principal of Hampton Institute, to arrange a meeting with him. Since he saved only his replies, it is uncertain whether she sought a job at Hampton or wanted his endorsement of her plan to found a girls' school. She needed the backing of prominent men to obtain philanthropic funding for the school and sent her proposal to University of Georgia chancellor David C. Barrow in hopes of enlisting his help, but he showed little interest. Unlike the previous chancellor, Walter Hill, who cared for Parrish because of her friendship with his wife and daughters, Barrow's allegiances lay only with Branson. He returned Parrish's plan to her with the noncommittal remark that it presented a "most attractive school."[8]

David Barrow proved more helpful when it came to Parrish's search for a position associated with the southern movement's rural reform campaign. The Peabody Education Fund and the General Education Board jointly funded two positions in southern states—the female organizers of school-improvement associations, also called SIA field agents, and male rural school supervisors. The former worked in association with organized women and teachers to found clubs and build community support for schools, while the latter were officially part of state departments of education and focused on improving teaching and school administration and promoting legislative reforms such as local taxation. Parrish was highly qualified for both of these positions and marshaled letters of recommendation from an impressive array of leading educators and reformers that included Chancellor Barrow, state school commissioner M. L. (Marion Luther) Brittain, and Governor Hoke Smith (a trustee of the Peabody Fund). When she attended the meeting of the Conference for Education in the South in April, she took the opportunity to speak with SEB members about the possibility of future employment. She made a point of approaching Wickliffe Rose, who also served as general agent for the Peabody Fund, and Robert Ogden.[9]

A note of desperation crept into Parrish's correspondence with board members as the spring semester drew to a close without any definitive offer of a job. As she explained to one board member, Wickliffe Rose was annoyed at the letter-writing campaign she launched, since he already had told her that she would have a position if he could arrange the funding. The pending dissolution of the Peabody Trust was going to deprive the Peabody Education Fund of about half of its financial resources, and Rose was reluctant to make promises until he could find alternate sources of income. Parrish became alarmed when another board member suggested that fund trustees would have to eliminate support for the rural work, and she wrote to Rose in May to ask for reassurance. She bluntly stated that she was "on the eve of being ejected from the State Normal School of Georgia" and had solicited letters of recommendation to assure him that she still had the respect and confidence of leading citizens, faculty, and students. She also wanted to justify her hire, to avoid the appearance that Rose was using his position to dispense favors to a friend. She informed him that she was willing to "be entirely silent and passive under indignities" at the normal school if she could be certain of another job, but otherwise she needed to develop an alternate strategy.[10]

Parrish's desperation stemmed from the fact that a lifetime of supporting family members had left her without the financial means to cope with joblessness. She described herself as a "woman in helpless distress" in her appeal to Rose. She informed him that she had "a family to support" and had been expending all her salary on the education of her adopted children. Her most pressing concern in 1911 was her daughter, Lottie Jarrell, who was sixteen years old and planning for college. The school Jarrell entered in 1914, the South Georgia State Normal College for women, was tuition-free, but Parrish still had to purchase books and a uniform wardrobe and pay fees and monthly boarding charges. Furthermore, she was nearing her fifty-ninth birthday and had made no preparations for retirement. As she explained to Rose, "When I lose my work here it is necessary that I have other work. I could not fall back on savings, because I have none. I would sweep the streets rather than ask for work which I could not do well. But, I *know* and you tell me that *you* know that I can do a much needed work in the South."[11]

In adopting Jarrell and treating young relatives as her own children, Parrish had assumed the same familial responsibilities as her male colleagues, but without the privileges that eased the burden for men. She did not get the preferential treatment given male heads of households that acknowledged their familial obligations with promotion and higher pay. Branson treated women who had to be self-supporting as objects of charity, bestowing upon them subordinate positions in the normal school as an extension of his patriarchal duties. Parrish's rejection of this gendered construction of professional relations elicited hostility that further disadvantaged her financially. She told Rose that she had feared there would be "subtle attempts" to keep her from finding work in Georgia and had "absolute proof of one successful attempt" and "strong reason to believe that others have been made." Whether the handiwork of Branson or someone else, the efforts to blacklist Parrish left her reliant upon the broad network of friends and acquaintances she had constructed through decades of educational leadership. Even though she was asking for well-earned consideration (which she felt the need to stress in her letter to Rose), it was embarrassing and humiliating to have to beg for a job, or in her words, to "seem anxious to an undignified extent."[12]

Parrish did not let the awkwardness of the situation prevent her from asserting the right to be treated as a professional. She informed A. P. Bourland of the SEB that, while she very much wanted "work in the field along the general line of the uplift of the school and home life of the state," she was not particularly interested in "the precise work" Sallie Hill did prior to her resignation for health reasons in January 1911. Even though the women who responded to male appeals to form school-improvement associations were experienced community activists with a sophisticated understanding of the political climate in which they worked, men did not view them as full partners in the southern movement. This is evident in Charles W. Dabney's lengthy history of the movement, which includes detailed biographical sketches of male participants while completely omitting women. Perhaps because they regarded women's work as voluntarism rather than professional service, most leaders of the Conference for Education in the South treated the female campaigns as a sideline at the annual meetings. In 1906, women gave their oral reports in the male school superintendents' meeting, but afterwards CES officials segregated them in a single women's meeting with other female speakers that was not always included in printed proceedings. In expressing a preference for work appropriate for someone with her knowledge and experience, Parrish was refusing to acquiesce to a gendered division of reform that replicated women's subordination in the professions.[13]

The marginalization of female reformers in the CES irritated Georgia clubwomen who had long played an integral role in the educational reform campaigns in their state. Shortly after attending the 1910 meeting in Little Rock, Passie Fenton Ottley of the Atlanta Woman's Club complained that women's participation in the annual programs was limited to school-improvement association reports and a brief address by a representative of women's clubs from the state in which the conference met. She argued that conference leaders' focus on school-improvement associations obscured the full extent of women's activities in at least two ways. First, she noted that the associations were part of larger female reform networks. In some states the education committee of the state federation conducted the school-improvement work as part of its duties, while in others the federation worked closely with the SIA and state board of education. Second, Ottley observed that the educational work of federated women was not limited to forming school-improvement clubs, but rather encompassed a wide range of activities that included fund-raising and lobbying for legislative reforms. She concluded that, "since the conference is along all lines of educational endeavor a sort of clearing house for such effort in the south, it seems a pity that its 'proceedings' should fail to embody so large a slice of woman's work in this section."[14]

Georgia clubwomen's attention soon turned to Parrish, as the public conclusion of her final confrontation with Branson and the GSNS trustees left her in dire need of allies. When she approached the GSNS Board of Trustees with her concerns, instead of responding they bowed to Branson's wishes and approved her dismissal on May 26. Prior to the meeting, she tried to discover the charges against her and asked the acting president of the board for an investigation and hearing similar to those held in 1903–4. Knowing that an investigation would likely have the same embarrassing result for Branson as before, the president told her that there were no specific charges to investigate—Branson merely claimed irreconcilable differences. The strategy of autocratic disengagement that Walter B. Hill outlined seven years earlier worked perfectly. Denied the ability to launch a defense, she became jobless at the age of fifty-eight. The board did not bother to inform her of its decision, forcing her to read about it in the newspapers. As they had done with Laura Smith, Branson and the trustees announced that Parrish had resigned, but they could not maintain the pretense when the head of the normal-school English Department and all but one of the Muscogee Elementary School teachers resigned in protest. Branson and the newly named board president, Athens lawyer Thomas J. Shackelford, then went on the offensive, disseminating lies and half-truths that slandered Parrish. Ironically, Shackelford employed the same phrase that the practice-school faculty had used to describe

Prichard, claiming Parrish had long been a "disturbing element" at the normal school.[15]

Georgia clubwomen were outraged at the shabby treatment of Parrish and immediately sprang to her defense. They issued statement after statement to the press expressing their appreciation and respect for Parrish's selfless commitment to public service and passionate advocacy of educational reforms. The GSNS Teachers and Mothers Co-operative Club approved a resolution detailing how she had solicited the funds to construct the practice school and somehow managed to shape it into an "embodiment of advanced pedagogical principles" on limited resources. The Atlanta Federation of Women's Clubs, representing seven organizations with a total membership in the thousands, lamented that the greatest loss was to the state's schoolchildren. Other women's clubs echoed the city federation's claim that teachers trained by Parrish were effective educators who spread her zeal for community uplift across the state. Sallie Heard, who had cofounded Georgia Sorosis in 1892 in honor of the New York Sorosis women's club, spoke of her experiences as manager for the Traveling Library of the South. She testified to the efforts of Parrish's former students to build school libraries and their frequent requests for books on pedagogy and school improvement. The Athens Woman's Club similarly lauded Parrish's "brilliant achievements and untiring and successful efforts in the service of the women and children of the state." Clubwomen also called for an investigation into Parrish's firing and pressured the Department of Education to create a position for her. They had some leverage in the latter demand since they had done invaluable work for the state school commissioner for more than a decade.[16]

Atlanta clubwomen had special reason to empathize with Parrish's plight, as many of their members were educators engaged in their own struggle for professional equality. Two days after the GSNS Board of Trustees fired Parrish, Principal Nettie Sergeant of the Atlanta Girls' High School appeared before the city school board to protest the fact that male teachers at the Boys' High School were paid almost 73 percent more than female teachers who taught the same courses at her institution. Observing that women's cost of living was the same as men's, she called the disparity an "inhumanity to women" that might drive them to "militant suffragism." When board member George Hope offered the usual justification that men had families to support, Sergeant quickly responded that many women did as well. Despite her able defense and the mayor's assurances that board members agreed with her, the board of education repeatedly deflected responsibility for inequality, alleging that the matter must be decided by the city council. When female teachers finally received raises in the fall, first-year teachers at the girls' school still made only about 57 cents for every dollar paid first-year teachers at the boys' school. City officials continued to ignore their requests for more resources.[17]

Viewing Parrish's plight as part of this larger struggle, clubwomen took offense at the gendered nature of normal-school administrators' attacks on her. Claiming that trustees were only thinking of the good of the normal school, Shackelford bluntly told reporters, "We believe that a man should head the pedagogical department." Speaking at a University of Georgia alumni banquet several days later, he arrogantly dismissed clubwomen's demands, saying that the "board of trustees is infallible" and "petitions in petticoats will not be regarded." The Atlanta Federation of Women's Clubs fired off a strongly worded resolution to normal-school trustees arguing that ability, not sex, was the only fair measure of fitness for a position and Parrish had proven that "a woman can be the peer of any man in the theory and practice of pedagogical psychology." Despite their protests, Branson and the trustees hired a man, C. H. Bruce, to replace Parrish, and when he left after only a year they hired another man to take his place. Even petitions in pants were not tolerated if they opposed the gendered hierarchy; the only male professor to side with Parrish, Fred Orr, resigned in September when the trustees ignored his threat to leave if they did not dismiss Branson.[18]

Parrish and her supporters were gratified when former board chair Robert Guinn laid bare the petty jealousies and gendered motives of her male critics. At first he was reluctant to speak with reporters, but when he heard of the efforts to impugn Parrish's character and abilities he exploded with indignation. In a statement that must have given Parrish great pleasure, Guinn said that she was a disturbing element only "in so far as splendid ability and superior services shall disturb those who are envious of such qualities, and whose jealousy of the influence that such qualities win, moves them to the most exasperating system of nagging." Ever since the earlier investigations, Branson had resented normal-school students' loyalty to Parrish, as well as the loyalty of the graduates whom she hired to teach in the practice school and boarded in her home. This resentment lay behind Shackelford's accusation that she monopolized students' time, Branson's decision to create a separate program under the independent control of Prichard, and the firing of the talented and able Laura Smith. As Guinn thoughtfully remarked, if Parrish had been a man with political connections or a woman who was willing to compromise her integrity and meekly do as she was told, she would still have a job. Branson regarded her as a competitor and a threat because she did not conform to the gendered construction of authority that required deference to men, and her lack of formal political power left her vulnerable to retribution when she resisted his attempts to humble her.[19]

Although Celeste Parrish's friends in high places made no apparent attempt to intervene in her dispute with Branson, they eased the sting of her dismissal by creating a new position for her. At the end of June, Governor Hoke Smith announced that he was using a $5,000 award from the Peabody Fund to finance a series of rural educational rallies. He appointed Parrish to join current school commissioner M. L. Brittain, former commissioner Jere Pound, and rural school supervisor R. H. Powell (already paid through the Peabody Fund) in directing the work. As part of her duties Parrish made numerous public-speaking appearances and regularly published articles in *School and Home* and the local press. The rallies were timed to put pressure on the Georgia legislature to approve a bill that would facilitate the consolidation of rural schools and the creation of uniform licensing standards for teachers, among other reforms. When the educational bill passed in August, it provided a more permanent basis for Parrish's work by creating three state-funded rural school supervisor positions with annual salaries of $2,000. Her supporters ensured that the wording of the bill did not exclude women from the position, and in September Hoke Smith named her one of the three new supervisors. As the state superintendent explained in his annual report, her "years of service in Virginia and Georgia" had proven she was a "first rank" trainer of teachers, making her an excellent choice for the position.[20]

The creation of the rural school supervisor positions was the result of persistent efforts by the General Education Board to encourage educational reform by providing start-up funds. GEB donations persuaded southern states to implement numerous educational programs, including farm and home demonstration work, children's agricultural clubs, and supervision of rural schools. By 1914 it had contributed almost $16 million to education in the South. Its work was enhanced by the contributions of other philanthropies, most notably the Peabody, Slater, and Jeanes funds. The GEB and Peabody Fund shared the costs of maintaining rural school supervisors in eleven southern states in addition to Georgia, and their aid helped convince state leaders to officially sanction the work. Shortly after the Georgia legislature created the three new positions, State Department of Education officials approached Wallace Buttrick of the GEB about the possibility of obtaining funding for a fourth supervisor who would work with black schools. The GEB agreed to assume responsibility for the salary and expenses of the "special supervisor" for black schools, George Godard, and the Slater Fund helped finance the black teachers' institutes that he organized.[21]

Even though Godard had the most impossible task—improving rural black schools throughout the state—the scope of work for the other supervisors was daunting. Each had responsibility for one-third of the state's counties, roughly divided into southern, middle, and northern sections. Their primary duty was to visit individual schools and provide normal training for teachers in five-day summer institutes, acting as a corrective to the uneven quality of institutes organized and run locally. State officials also expected them to lay the groundwork for educational improvement along broader lines. In every community they were to enlist the support of women's clubs and meet with county school officials and business and professional groups to create unity of purpose. This was the southern movement's template for educational re-form, one based on the belief that giving parents and local leaders a sense of investment in public schools was the key to permanent progress. Just as with the school-improvement clubs and educational rallies, the larger goal was to build grassroots support for reforms such as local taxation, school consolida-tion, and compulsory attendance. CES leaders had agreed upon these goals for rural school supervisors at a special meeting held in conjunction with the annual conference held earlier that year.[22]

Parrish's new position could not have been better fitted to her abilities. She had regularly taught institutes since graduating from the Virginia State Normal School more than twenty-five years earlier. Her experiences as a rural educator and a leader in the movement to professionalize teaching gave her a thorough understanding of the problems and needs of rural schools. She brought formidable skills to community work that had been honed in decades of organizational activism, and her establishment of the Georgia Congress of Mothers and success at forming mothers' clubs proved that she was adept at gaining the cooperation of teachers and parents. Equally importantly, she had an excellent relationship with the state's clubwomen and a close familiarity with their educational work. Everything Parrish had learned, every skill she had cultivated since her early years of teaching in Virginia, could be applied to the conditions prevailing in rural Georgia. Her belief that individual needs were social needs and that individual development was central to the success of households and communities could finally find full expression in commu-nity work.

With characteristic selflessness, Parrish asked for the most challenging of the three regions assigned to rural supervisors. Her field of work encompassed forty-eight counties, the bulk of which were located in the far northern and northwestern parts of the state where the Blue Ridge Mountains abutted the foothills of the Southern Appalachians. She regarded the teachers in mountain schools as most in need of help, arguing that their isolation was responsible for "the passivity, the hopelessness and the absolute indifference which sometimes creeps gradually upon a teacher who might have been a blessing to the school." She found that the academic skills of the average teacher were "much below the standing of a graduate of a high school." Parrish was determined to reach every school even though travel conditions were physically trying for a woman of sixty. She had to navigate her horse and buggy across rugged terrain and primitive roads that were difficult in the best of circumstances and perilous in the worst. To reach all the counties, Parrish had to hold institutes during most months of the year, but snow and ice made roads impassable in the winter, and heavy rains presented problems in warm weather. Mary Creswell, a former student and boarder who resigned from Muscogee Elementary when Parrish was fired, described an incident in which her mentor and a group of teachers narrowly escaped disaster while crossing a flooded stream. The water was deeper than they realized, causing the horses to flounder as the dangerous current began to sweep the wagon downstream. Parrish calmed the frightened women by singing a hymn as the horses regained their footing and pulled the wagon to shore.[23]

The difficulty of reaching every school in every county required Parrish to maximize the impact of her presence through extensive community outreach. When making individual school visits she encouraged broad participation by providing public lectures and giving local residents a place on the program. She arranged for ministers to meet with teachers, invited physicians to address them on public health issues, enlisted the help of local women's clubs and missionary societies, attended farmers' meetings, and held evening events for parents to maximize attendance. To ensure that her efforts would have lasting influence, she counseled teachers on the relationship between education and community uplift, urging them to seek further training and "to consecrate themselves more fully to their work." She pushed parents and teachers to form Home and School clubs to promote further school improvements and lessen the isolation of rural life. When necessary, Parrish also led children in cleaning up school grounds and organized them into corn and canning clubs and Junior Civic Leagues. She conducted all of these activities in addition to instructing teachers in better methods, helping to found county educational associations, and assisting in campaigns for legislative reforms.[24]

Parrish's position as rural school supervisor had much in common with the Jeanes supervisors who performed similar work in rural black communities. Philadelphia Quaker Anna T. Jeanes donated $1 million to establish the Negro Rural School Fund, more commonly known as the Jeanes Fund, in 1907. The GEB administered the funds to counties to pay the salaries of teachers who supervised instruction in industrial education in rural black schools. In 1912, sixteen Georgia counties had a Jeanes teacher, who made on average only $322 for seven months of work. The teachers, almost all of whom were black women, engaged in a broad range of community work. They made home visits, organized parents, formed school-improvement clubs, and initiated fundraising campaigns for better buildings and equipment. White officials such as George Godard, who assumed general supervision of the state's Jeanes teachers in 1913, viewed industrial education as preparation for manual labor, but the teachers regarded it as a tool of race uplift. They shared many of Parrish's beliefs about the ability of manual skills and domestic science to improve the quality of homelife and raise rural standards of living. Also like Parrish, they tried to lay the foundations for long-term progress by courting the support of clubwomen and local officials.[25]

Even though Celeste Parrish was better compensated for her work than were the Jeanes teachers, her pay did not come close to covering the costs of providing services to forty-eight counties. Supervisors' annual salary of $2000 with $666 for expenses was grossly insufficient, and the state legislature provided no additional funding for institutes. Parrish struggled to find innovative ways to maximize the use of time and resources, such as by rotating the locations of institutes within counties so she could make evening visits in different communities each year. In 1914 she pressured public and private educational institutions to provide assistance by sending them copies of a CES resolution calling for their cooperation with state officials in providing teacher training. Almost all pledged their support, and eleven institutions paid the salary and travel expenses of at least one faculty member who served as institute instructor. The following year Parrish implemented a plan to hold two-week institutes at Emory College, the Berry School (a private industrial school for mountain children in Rome), North Georgia Agricultural College, and three district agricultural high schools. By inviting the participation of teachers from nearby counties at each location, she was able to combine between eight and ten county institutes in each session while doubling their length and drawing upon the faculty and resources of the host institutions.[26]

The combined institutes were both effective and popular with teachers, but Parrish had to use her own salary to keep the work going. The centralized two-week institutes had greater operational costs in comparison to five-day local sessions, but she could not charge tuition because public schoolteachers could not afford to pay it. At first most instructors agreed to donate their time, believing that the state would finance the work once it was established. When the funding failed to materialize, it was obvious that Georgia legislators expected to continue to obtain their professional services for free. Parrish understood the importance of institute income for poorly paid educators and was embarrassed to repeatedly ask them to make the sacrifice. In 1917 she assumed personal responsibility for paying the travel and boarding costs of volunteers. The next year, her last as rural supervisor, she flatly refused to ask for volunteers "because the exigencies of the war and the needs of the Government have already made such large demands upon the time and energy of the teachers." She was able to hold four combined institutes, but only because the presidents of Georgia Normal and Industrial College and the State College of Agriculture promised to pay their faculty to participate.[27]

Parrish's network of female reformers was critical to her ability to carry out her duties despite the parsimony of men in government. The women she singled out for recognition in her annual reports to the state legislature illustrate the value of her organizational connections. In her 1913 report she thanked Mary E. Barnwell, Nellie Thorne Osgood, and Blanche Potter Spiker for their voluntary assistance with numerous institutes. Barnwell was a member of the Georgia chapter of the Southern Association of College Women and served as director and teacher for Atlanta's Sheltering Arms free kindergarten. Osgood was an artist, art teacher, and member of the Atlanta Woman's Club, and Spiker served on the executive board of the Georgia Federation of Women's Clubs and operated a private dance school in Atlanta. In 1914 another AWC member, Mary Walton Hunter Wiggs, used her position on the finance committee of the Georgia Congress of Mothers to secure funding for home economist Elizabeth Holt to assist Parrish in teaching institutes and organizing parent-teacher associations. Female educators located in Parrish's assigned counties also generously donated their services, as did Mary Creswell, who was now director of home economics at the College of Agriculture and head of girls' canning club work for the extension service.[28]

Parrish's efforts to involve clubwomen in rural reform were motivated by more than financial necessity, as she believed that rural-urban cooperation was crucial to resolving the poverty and isolation that plagued the countryside. To overcome "the detachment which many city women feel with regard to the country teacher and the country school," she brought rural and urban women together so that they could "come to know and respect each other." She asked women's clubs to send representatives to teachers' institutes and encouraged them to take part in discussions. She also arranged special meetings for rural women and had experienced clubwomen on hand to help them form their own clubs. Having clubwomen sponsor social events for teachers and mothers was yet another way that Parrish tried to "prepare the way for sympathetic cooperation" in tackling the problems of school communities.[29]

The organization of rural women served the further purpose of increasing the political power of women's clubs by extending the rural reach of the female reform network. Clubwomen quickly recognized the value of Parrish's proposal to organize Home and School clubs into county federations affiliated with the Georgia Federation of Women's Clubs. As GFWC leader and AWC member (and farm manager) Nellie Peters Black explained it, affiliation would make farm women "part of the great body of 25,000 women who are doing such big things in Georgia." She envisioned a rural network of "country clubs" that empowered rural women to make demands of local officials, coordinating their efforts to procure funding for school improvement, home extension services, and county boards of health. When it came to school reform, Parrish could verify that clubwomen's assistance was invaluable in countering the indifference of local and county officials, as they provided speakers for the 1911 educational rallies and consistently responded to her calls for help with institutes. Women's groups provided food and entertainment, helped organize parents' and children's clubs, promoted county educational fairs, and adopted rural schools to ensure that improvements continued after Parrish left.[30]

She repaid their loyalty by using her status as an accomplished professional to bring attention to the value of their activism, providing the public recognition denied them by the CES. She highlighted their contributions in her annual reports to the state legislature and published an article in the *Atlanta Constitution* in 1912 that gave a historical overview of their educational work. Parrish wrote the article as "a tribute to women who have rendered worthy service in a great cause," and an "acknowledgement of much needed and most competent help" in her own work. She described clubwomen's successful efforts to organize communities in support of schools, provide scholarships for teachers, and establish model schools and public kindergartens. Parrish con-

tinued to lend her professional expertise to the Georgia Federation by chair-
ing its rural schools committee and monitoring the progress of its Tallulah
Falls School. Her evaluation of the federation school was included in a survey
of Rabun County schools published by the State Department of Education
in 1914. She was critical of its facilities and what passed as industrial work,
but continued to visit the school and publicized its steady improvement. Its
director, Lucy Lester Willet, used Parrish's letter of commendation to raise
funds for the perennially cash-strapped institution.[31]

In addition to enhancing her value to organized women, the greater authority and autonomy Parrish enjoyed as a rural supervisor finally provided
her career with the stability that was lacking at the normal school. She became close friends with Mell Duggan and his wife, Sarah, and enjoyed cordial
relations with the male rural school supervisors. She praised them for their
accomplishments and sprang to their defense when the *Atlanta Constitution*
erroneously credited a University of Georgia professor with their work for
local taxation. Moreover, as an appointee of Hoke Smith she was now publicly associated with the progressive faction of Georgia's Democratic Party
and could count on its backing. Smith and state school superintendent M. L.
Brittain knew what it was like to be the target of unfair political attacks, as
Tom Watson had launched a bitter war of words on both men after they refused to do his bidding. In 1915 Parrish was one of thousands of signatories
on a petition asking the governor to commute the sentence of Leo Frank, an
Atlanta factory manager whom Watson campaigned to get unfairly convicted
of murder and who was subsequently lynched. She sent a personal letter of
condolence to Frank's widow after his death, saying she was one of the "many
Christian women who have never wavered in their belief in your husband's
innocence."[32]

Parrish also found security in the rewarding personal life she was able
to construct after relocation to Atlanta, where her office in the Department of Education was headquartered. The city's progressive community
included many men and women from outside the South and provided a hospitable home for the southern women who led the state's educational and
child-welfare reform campaigns. Parrish joined the Atlanta Woman's Club and
strengthened her ties of friendship with prominent activists such as Nellie Peters Black and Passie Fenton Ottley, who appreciated her professional talents
and commitment to gender equality. Domestic and professional relationships
overlapped as they had in Athens, reflecting the ways in which inadequate
pay and common interests created a sense of camaraderie among educators.

She soon took up residence in the home of Merrill and Minnie Belle Hutchinson, who taught music and drama in a private girls' school operated by AWC member Rosa Woodberry. The Hutchinsons had moved from Boston after visiting friends in Atlanta in 1908, and they were able to establish their own residence by taking in other teachers as boarders. Minnie Belle, who also was a member of the AWC, assisted Parrish with teachers' institutes.[33]

With the insecurities of the Georgia State Normal School well behind her, Parrish was able to make better use of her talents and abilities. She contributed articles to instructional manuals for teachers and conducted a survey of Atlanta's public schools, which, while not rural, fell within her territory as supervisor. Since Brittain gave her only two weeks' leave from her regular duties to complete the survey, she did not have time to visit all of the city's schools and had to choose a representative sample. Parrish chose to visit only white schools, probably because African American women had conducted a thorough investigation of black schools the previous year that well documented the devastating effects of inadequate funding. After two weeks of inspection and observation, Parrish submitted a report that provided critiques of buildings and grounds, equipment and materials, courses of study, and teaching methods. Her main recommendations in the latter two areas mirrored her goals for rural schools: replacing rote memorization with an emphasis on creative and critical thinking; adapting methods to the temperament and interests of children; and making content relevant by grounding it in the environment of the surrounding community. While these were common progressive strategies for making schools more efficient, her further suggestions for how to improve the quality of teaching and narrow the gap between school and home were less typical.[34]

The survey was a common way for progressive school officials to justify the reforms they wished to implement, but Parrish's report differed from most in that it did not promote a corporate model of reorganization that centralized authority in the hands of educational administrators. She agreed with the need for administrators to set and enforce teaching standards, but argued for allowing teachers greater flexibility and control in the performance of their duties. She insisted that most teachers were very conscientious and doing "the best they could under the conditions." One of the biggest obstacles to improvement, in Parrish's view, was the city superintendent's rigid control of the curriculum. He dictated the exact material included in tests and held teachers accountable for student performance, which made teachers and students "so anxious over the examinations which they knew would be taken from the text book" that they spent most of their time "memorizing the words which they knew they would be examined upon." Parrish also criticized the weekly normal sessions that were meant to provide continuing education for teachers, because they focused on familiarity with basic subject matter rather than on the best teaching methods for each subject. She identified inadequate funding as another major obstacle and urged the city council to increase appropriations. Her report singled out the Girls' High School as one of the buildings most in need of replacement, describing in detail how it was unhealthy, unsafe, and "absolutely unfit for use."[35]

Parrish's recommendations found favor among Atlanta's progressive Democrats, not all of whom shared her underlying motives. Hoke Smith, who was president of the Atlanta Board of Education between 1897 and 1903, and Robert Guinn, who became its president in 1914, were genuinely interested in educational reform, but they were not above using educational issues for political ends. Guinn solicited Parrish's study partly to embarrass city superintendent William M. Slaton, who was the governor's brother and part of a rival faction in the Democratic Party.[36] Parrish did not let Guinn's plans to oust Slaton influence her report; she was sharply critical of the superintendent in some areas, but also provided a comprehensive list of his praiseworthy accomplishments. She knew that most problems long predated Slaton's tenure and were the result of inadequate funding and the city council's control of finances. Her recommendations included reforms that were advocated by organized women and parent-teacher groups as well as progressive Democrats, such as a local tax controlled by the school board, better pay for teachers, and expansion of industrial education. Her description of the abysmal conditions at the Girls' High School, which had not improved since a physician blamed them for his daughter's death two years earlier, highlighted another central concern of women.[37]

In addition to voicing the concerns of teachers and clubwomen, Parrish used her report to promote a model of cooperative democratic community that stood in sharp contrast to men's self-serving political machinations. She believed the city was not doing enough for the children of mill workers and suggested building a new school for the Exposition Mills neighborhood with "playgrounds, gymnasium, baths, assembly rooms, shops, library, kitchen and dining room." The grounds would include a "teachers' cottage and a group of able and consecrated teachers who would be willing to live among the people, and give themselves in their service." Asserting that making schools the center of community life was "no more than justice to the people," she urged the school board to establish a few social centers to initiate the work. She made the same recommendation after revisiting the mill school four years later, condemning the "still miserable conditions" and "civic and corporate short-sightedness" behind the lack of progress. Even if "humanitarian interest were forgotten and Christianity non-existent," she scathingly remarked, "the good business man should be ashamed to allow so much waste of profitable material."[38]

Even though she had definite ideas on how to improve public schools, unlike school reformers such as Guinn who sought to impose their will on the public, Parrish respected the right (and need) of citizens to make decisions for themselves. Her report outlined a process for revising the public school curriculum that began with the formation of a committee composed of representatives from industry and commerce, the professions, the skilled trades, public utilities, Associated Charities, the courts, men's and women's clubs, churches, and homes. The representatives would "tabulate the needs that have come under their observation," and members of a course-of-study committee with educational expertise would use their recommendations to make the necessary curricular adjustments. Parrish's belief in community-based, collaborative reform was equally evident in her critique of philanthropic efforts. She was convinced that changes had to originate in cooperative public initiatives to be effective, and was sharply critical of groups such as the Southern Mountain Education Association that founded rural schools in which the surrounding communities had no investment or influence. She acknowledged that dispensing charity was gratifying for donors, but argued that the "best work of the philanthropist would be to arouse the people to an impelling sense of needs and then to allow them to work out their own salvation."[39]

Parrish knew from her rural community work that men and women must be aroused to a sense of their needs, since school improvements that came only from teachers would lapse when the teachers went elsewhere. She traveled many miles to reach isolated areas in an effort to convince parents that education was critical to the success of future generations. One of her assistants described a typical evening meeting in a "remote rural mountain community": "In the dim light of flickering oil lamps she told them that, while they now owned their land and were in possession of rights and privileges as citizens of Georgia, that if they did not educate their children and give them better advantages than they, the parents, had had, people from other states would come in and possess their lands and develop the resources which should be the heritage of Georgia children." Parrish was echoing the concerns of southerners who worried that outside business interests such as lumber syndicates and mining companies were exploiting the region's natural resources with no concern for environmental damage or the future prospects of local residents. She wanted to impress upon North Georgians that the outside world was changing and that their attitudes toward education had to change accordingly if they wished to remain on the land. She urged them to strive to meet the state guidelines for a Standard County School and to embrace reforms that violated a tradition of local autonomy.[40] Local taxation and consolidation of schools might cede some authority to others, but the policies also gave parents more control over their children's futures.

Parrish's vision for how schools could better meet public needs was strongly influenced by the industrial education movement. Progressive reformers believed that instruction in manual skills could address a variety of problems facing American communities. In urban areas, it was a way to adjust the curriculum to meet the needs of an increasingly diverse school population, keeping working-class youth out of factories with the lure of preparation for the workplace. In the countryside, it could stem rural-to-urban migration by giving students the scientific knowledge and skills necessary to increase farm income and bring the quality of homelife closer to urban living standards. A national debate raged over exactly how to implement industrial training, especially courses that were vocational in orientation. John Dewey feared the undemocratic tendencies of many proposals. He thought industrial education might minimize class differences by giving children appreciation for manual labor, but feared it would have the opposite effect if implemented in separate schools for working-class children. Humanist educators, especially black scholars such as W. E. B. Du Bois, shared his concern about the undemocratic tendencies of curricular differentiation. They knew that its implementation often institutionalized the biases and agendas of interest groups, which betrayed the democratic promise of education as a source of self-realization and a common national culture.[41]

For Parrish, the ability of industrial education to meet both individual and social needs exemplified the democratic promise of progressive education. In the primary grades it served the important purpose of integrating school and home by using household activities to teach basic principles of science and mathematics. In the higher grades, instruction in manual training and domestic science provided boys and girls with skills that could benefit them as wage earners and members of households while also reducing poverty and mortality rates. Parrish advocated making space for industrial education in the curriculum by eliminating less useful elements, such as courses in Greek and Latin and higher mathematics. She argued that study involving advanced scientific expertise or the skilled trades appropriately belonged in separate technological and vocational schools; however, there was much practical knowledge remaining that was central to preparation for the "fundamental duties of citizenship, namely, those of family maintenance and community upbuilding." It was an obligation of schools as public institutions to provide knowledge "necessary to any high degree of community welfare." These statements drew explicit connections between individual welfare and the greater public good, rejecting the notion that personal development was purely a private concern.[42]

Although she believed that industrial education was beneficial for all youth, most of Parrish's public statements focused on its value for rural communities. Echoing earlier statements by agrarian groups, she depicted the inclusion of basic mechanical and agricultural science in country schools as a necessary departure from the elitist educational systems of the past that served only the needs of the privileged few. When it came to domestic science, Parrish's support for putting homemaking on a scientific basis was driven partly by her concern that rural families were suffering unnecessarily. She knew the hardships households endured due to illness and premature death, and was convinced that instruction in nutrition, sanitation, and the production and preservation of food would safeguard family health. To persuade rural audiences to accept the substitution of industrial education for part of the classical school curriculum, Parrish would ask students to raise their hands if they planned to attend college. In most cases there were only two or three college-bound students out of a group of a few hundred, which reinforced her argument that a college-preparatory approach failed to meet public needs. She did not oppose the right of individuals to freely explore their interests but thought courses of study should take into consideration the lives that most students would lead after graduation.[43]

As with African American educators and industrial education, female educators were divided on the issue of domestic science. Ellen Swallow Richards, cofounder of the ACA and architect of modern home economics, wanted to create a field for women in the sciences by professionalizing domesticity. Programs such as the Household Administration course of study at the University of Chicago, headed by Marion Talbot and Sophonisba Breckinridge, created careers for women who otherwise were excluded from academic positions. Schooling women in nutrition, sanitation, and early childhood development also created a pathway to municipal housekeeping by giving them expertise in public health issues. On the other hand, the creation of separate domains of knowledge was problematic for groups struggling to achieve equality. Difference almost always equated with inequality, which led elite women's colleges to resist including domestic science in their curricula. Talbot received little faculty support when she offered a course in domestic science at Wellesley, and the subject was eliminated from the curriculum after she left for the University of Chicago.[44]

Parrish fully explained her reasons for supporting domestic science education in an article published in *Educational Review*. She was responding to a previous essay by M. Carey Thomas, president of Bryn Mawr College and a leading member of the Association of Collegiate Alumnae. Thomas argued that gender differentiation of the curriculum was unnecessary and undesirable, since intellectual abilities were not sex-linked, and providing men and women with the same education ensured successful marriages. Parrish agreed that there was no justification for limiting women's freedom of choice and no need for separate courses in high school and most college work. Where she differed was in her pragmatic assessment of actual conditions. She accurately predicted that changes in attitudes and behavior would occur very slowly, resulting in the development of gendered courses of study as "sex prejudice" and "time-honored customs" led professional women to specialize in services for women and children. She also questioned Thomas's brusque dismissal of domestic science based on the assumption that equality required sameness. There was a practical need for a division of labor in households with young children, Parrish argued, and since women would likely continue to have primary responsibility for childrearing it was not foolish—as Thomas had claimed—to recommend that they study nutrition, sanitation, and child psychology. As passionately as she supported gender equality, Parrish could not ignore the importance of intelligent mothering for children and the society in which they lived.[45]

Many of Atlanta's parents and students appeared to share Thomas's skepticism about the value of domestic science. While domestic science courses were popular in rural areas where women were less likely to work outside the home or farm, students who lived in urban areas with white-collar employment opportunities for women found business and commercial education more attractive. It was no coincidence that when Parrish inspected the Girls' High School she found the domestic science equipment in storage. In contrast, demand had quickly exceeded space for a business course of study offered in 1888, and a commercial course introduced in 1907 was so popular that it became a separate institution—the English-Commercial High School—after only three years. Even these programs retained a strong academic component, and parents resisted including industrial education in the curriculum even though most students were not college bound.[46] Cultural polish, like business skills, had obvious value for those with aspirations for upward mobility, while domestic science was associated with domestic service and women's unpaid labor in the home. Rather than basing the curriculum on an objective assessment of current social needs, parents and students—much like M. Carey Thomas—wanted it based on their hopes for the future. The tension between the two positions was difficult for Parrish to bridge in the area of home economics, as it seemed to pit the healthy development and adjustment of children against women's struggle for equality.

Although domestic science never achieved the degree of public acceptance Parrish hoped it would, she continued to insist that household needs deserved a greater share of public funding. In 1910 she had worked hard to build support for a bill to add home economics to the institute work of the State College of Agriculture, but women were not included in extension services until the General Education Board and the Smith-Lever Act of 1914 provided funding. After becoming rural school supervisor, she used her annual reports to lobby for expansion of the work. In 1914 she begged the legislature to create a director of home economics in the Department of Education, so that Elizabeth Holt's work in rural schools could be continued on a more permanent basis. The following year Parrish raised the issue again, stressing how "unhappiness, inefficiency, illness, poverty, and death might be sensibly lessened in Georgia by a strong, good woman" who could assess the needs of rural households and direct her work accordingly. Parrish expressed appreciation for the assistance provided by the State College of Agriculture, but decried its "desultory and unsystematic" nature. Home economists Mary Creswell, Lois Dowdle, and Bessie Stanley Wood were happy to help with institute work and community visits, but could do so only when not engaged in their home-demonstration and canning-club duties. In 1916 Parrish repeated her request for the creation of a statewide position for a home economics professional, and suggested the legislature make the teaching of home economics a requirement for all public schools.[47]

As Parrish filled her days with activities promoting the welfare of other households and communities, she finally took steps to secure her own permanent home. In August 1914 she began preparation for retirement by buying four acres of land adjacent to the home of Mell and Sarah Duggan in Rabun County. She built a "rustic cottage" on a hill overlooking the town of Clayton, planted apple trees and Scotch broom transplanted from Pittsylvania County, Virginia, and told her friends that she intended to write as soon as she could make the time. Her primary financial obligation to family was fulfilled in 1916, when daughter Lottie graduated from college. Lottie soon married James Stump of Valdosta and settled into adult life with her new husband and his parents, who owned a farm where the young couple initially lived. When Parrish turned sixty-five, she made arrangements to purchase additional acreage from J. N. Justus, the neighbor who had sold her the first piece of land. In 1917 he extended a loan with terms that would allow her to purchase another seven acres in four installment payments over the next two years. Because of the difficulties of travel in cold weather, Parrish mainly used the cottage as a summer home and continued to live in Atlanta with the Hutchinsons during the rest of the year.[48]

Even as she looked forward to a much-deserved rest, Celeste Parrish's demanding work schedule began to have a detrimental effect on her health. An administrator of Young Harris College recorded the hectic pace of activities he witnessed at an institute in 1914. On the first day, Parrish gave talks in the morning, afternoon, and evening, and on the second day she worked with teachers on methods, made two more presentations, organized a mothers' club, and gave a canning demonstration. The administrator was impressed with the energy of a "lady of her age," which then was about sixty-two. Prior to 1916 she was still working every month of the year, with the bulk of the institutes falling in the months of May–July and November–December. Although the exact nature of her illness is not documented in the surviving public records, she had a long-standing heart problem, and by 1917 she was seeking medical care and had to curtail her school visits and community work. When her heart finally gave out a few months before her sixty-sixth birthday in September 1918, she had worked every month that year with the exception of April. As Mary Creswell explained it, "she kept at work holding teachers institutes and traveling through the mountains until she became too ill to recover."[49]

Celeste Parrish labored to fulfill her ideal of public service until the moment she took her last breath. In her annual reports she described the consecrated teacher as someone who regarded professional development as a form of public service and embraced educators' responsibility to improve "the life of the community in which their school is located."[50] For those who took their responsibilities seriously, public service came at a cost. The creation of combined institutes eased Parrish's burden of travel for teacher training, but they could not include all of her counties, and she would not neglect community work. A teacher in Winder, a Barrow County mill town where Parrish made monthly school visits for four years—even though it was not in her assigned territory—described her mentor's demanding professional philosophy: "Miss Parrish, one of our state supervisors, says that when a teacher has taught from Monday morning until Friday afternoon, she has given to the community just one half what she is due it. She says that what the visiting teacher may do, and the influence she may exert, when she is not engaged in the school room, is of inestimable worth, and constitutes one half of her work. During these extra hours with children and patrons she can forge links in the 'golden chain' that time will never sever."[51]

It is not surprising that the state school superintendent found it difficult to replace Celeste Parrish. Part of the problem was the low pay, which the legislature had not increased since creating the rural supervisor positions. After being turned down by the first four men to whom he offered the job, M. L. Brittain urged the General Assembly to increase the salary by 50 percent and the expense allowance by almost 35 percent. Male educators who had the same regional stature as Parrish also had more options, and they were not likely to assume such arduous duties unless adequately compensated. Parrish would have been irreplaceable even with the enticement of higher pay, however, because she carried a heavy burden of professional and public service that extended well beyond her official job duties. As rural supervisor she combined the school-improvement activities conducted by women with the educational reforms of the southern movement headed by men, both of which integrated the professional goals of teacher associations with progressive prescriptions for economic development and social stability. She also pursued a line of work with clubwomen and home extension agents that was not undertaken by her male colleagues, providing lectures and demonstrations in domestic science to lighten rural women's burden of work and to promote female professional careers.[52]

To understand the meaning of Parrish's death, one has to consider the terms on which she lived her life. Her mutualist ideals were strongly rooted in the Social Gospel—in the belief that working for the betterment of society was a Christian duty—but the roots of her passion for educational reform and rural uplift lay in her personal experiences with deprivation after the Civil War. She refused to give in to despair when she lost her parents and inheritance, and instead stubbornly adhered to a course of self-improvement so she could realize her potential and keep her family from falling further into poverty. The injustice of the obstacles she faced as a woman gave her a special sympathy for the plight of young women and a fierce and uncompromising position on their right to equality that carried her through the most difficult days of her career. Parrish's summers at the University of Chicago informed and reinforced her belief in the democratic promise of education as well as her commitment to service. Education had done so much to heighten her self-awareness and social understanding that she wanted to spread its blessings to as many southerners as possible. Sarah Duggan and Lottie Jarrell Stump, who were with her when she died, reported that Parrish's last words were, "I am not afraid to die, but there is much work I would like to do."[53] While it seems terribly unjust that she did not have a chance to enjoy retirement in North Georgia, according to the values that guided her life course, to die in the performance of public service was fulfillment of the highest ideals of family, community, and citizenship.

Conclusion

As Georgia's educators and clubwomen commemorated the life of Celeste Parrish in the months following her death, they simultaneously waged a campaign to completely restructure the administration of Atlanta's public schools. Their efforts to make the school board a popularly elected body divorced from politics represented the culmination of decades of female political activism. Parrish's contributions were substantial, as she helped lay the groundwork for the movement by encouraging the organization of teachers, parents, and communities in support of school improvement. In initiating the establishment of the Parent-Teacher Association in Georgia and promoting a model of community-based democratic reform, she provided Atlanta women with a method and a rationale for grassroots mobilization that enabled them to successfully challenge sexism and incompetence in the management of city schools. While Georgians found many appropriate ways to posthumously honor Parrish, women's extraordinary role in the victorious school-board campaign of 1918 was perhaps the best memorial to her legacy of service.

Parrish died just as the battles for coeducation and woman suffrage were gaining ground, and it was only natural and fitting that her closest friends thought of women's rights as they honored her in death. After Superintendent M. L. Brittain declared her "Georgia's ablest woman" in his funeral address, Mell Duggan amended the statement to "free it from the limitations of sex," labeling her "Georgia's ablest educator" instead. At the next annual meeting of the Georgia Educational Association, in May, Duggan introduced a resolution to endorse the woman suffrage amendment and announced a fundraiser to establish an endowed chair in Parrish's name at the University of Georgia, where she had taught summer normal sessions for years. A group of school-teachers tried to perpetuate a tradition of female leadership in the state's Department of Education by launching a campaign to have her position offered to Laura Smith, her former student and supervisor of Atlanta's elementary schools. Although Smith had a solid reputation and many admirers in the city and state bureaucracies, Parrish remained the only woman to serve as rural school supervisor in Georgia.[1]

Parrish was able to witness significant progress in one of her most passionately held and deeply personal causes, the struggle for coeducation, in the two years prior to her death. The barriers to women's admission to the University of Georgia began to deteriorate in 1916, when the state legislature heeded the requests of university administrators and opened the regular sessions of the Graduate College to female students. In February 1918, Parrish's determined lobbying and the exigencies of war helped convince the College of Agriculture Board of Trustees to implement a course of study in home economics for female juniors and seniors. Even though limiting enrollment to specific programs and classes of students were strategies for minimizing the numbers of female students on campus, state officials had finally provided women with access to professional degree programs. Parrish must have been especially pleased when College of Agriculture president Andrew Soule hired Mary Creswell to head the School of Home Economics. Creswell, who visited Parrish only a few months before her death, described how her mentor eagerly pored over the new program of study and provided detailed critiques of the scope and content of each course.[2]

At a public memorial service held in Atlanta, the attention of clubwomen, teachers, and Parrish's former pupils turned to these events as they discussed the best way to honor her life. Her friends supported the Stewart County Teachers' Association campaign to raise money for a monument for her grave, but they also sought a way to commemorate her living legacy in the state's schools. Nellie Peters Black suggested that the Georgia Federation of Women's Clubs establish a scholarship in Parrish's name. Duggan, who also spoke at the service, proposed that it be awarded to women attending the University of Georgia. The university's board of trustees had recently endorsed the admission of women to the College of Agriculture and announced that female students would be admitted to the School of Education beginning with the 1919–20 school year. Attendees at the memorial service agreed that establishing the first women's university scholarship in Parrish's name was an appropriate tribute for someone who had fought for decades to widen women's access to higher education. With the Atlanta Woman's Club in the lead, Georgians contributed enough money to provide two scholarships for the first female students to enter the university in the fall of 1919.[3]

The opening of the University of Georgia to women was a remarkable achievement, as many of the South's top public universities continued to resist coeducation for decades. The University of Florida admitted women in 1947, followed by Clemson University and the Georgia Institute of Technology in the 1950s. Parrish would have been disappointed but unsurprised to learn that the University of Virginia was one of the last holdouts. University alumni fighting in France during World War I took the time to write to legislators who were considering a coeducation bill, protesting that "the traditions of their alma mater should not be desecrated" by the admission of women. A Virginia woman found their letter ironic, considering "that an equal opportunity for women in a State institution is a logical part of the democracy for which they are struggling." After a long campaign by clubwoman Mary Munford, state officials begrudgingly established a coordinate college for women, Mary Washington College, in 1944. The University of Virginia did not become fully coeducational until 1971, when a lawsuit forced the issue. The University of North Carolina finally capitulated the following year and established the same admissions requirements for men and women.[4]

The Southern Association of College Women made impressive gains in another of Celeste Parrish's main causes, the improvement and standardization of female colleges in the South. Between 1911 and 1916, the Committee on Standards of Colleges compiled numerous reports that publicized the inadequacies of institutions calling themselves colleges and universities. Committee chair Elizabeth Avery Colton's 1916 pamphlet, *Various Types of Southern Colleges for Women,* so angered administrators from institutions categorized as "nominal and imitation colleges" that they threatened to bring libel suits against the SACW. They did not follow through, no doubt deciding that litigation would only bring more negative publicity and that improvement was the most constructive response. There were only two women's colleges that offered four years of college study in 1903, but by 1918 the number had increased to seven. Many others dropped the label of "college" or closed their doors. The determined crusade of the SACW committee influenced male and coeducational institutions to improve their standards as well. Colton's studies documented the steady progress of all southern institutions belonging to the Southern Association of Colleges and Secondary Schools. The number that offered four years of college-level study increased from three in 1904 to twenty-seven in 1917. SACW members were not able to get state legislatures to establish effective standards for awarding college charters, but their campaign raised public awareness of the resources that a legitimate institution should have.[5]

The impact of Parrish's activism is more difficult to quantify in the realm of everyday life, but the significance of her mentoring and leadership should not be overlooked. As a member of the first generation of college-educated southern women to enter teaching after the Civil War, she had to forge new paths for female educators. Whether by promoting laboratory work for undergraduates or urging junior colleagues to continue their education, in numerous ways Parrish continually battled to break down the barriers to female academic achievement. She also insisted that female public-school teachers and college faculty be treated as professionals, with the right to democratic governance and authority over their work in the classroom. Throughout her career, Parrish stood as an exemplary model of dignified independent womanhood for the thousands of young students and teachers whom she mentored. Her incisive analysis of the injustice of denying women universal personhood expressed prescient insights regarding the origins and impact of inequality that feminists rediscovered for themselves decades later.[6]

In the several years surrounding Parrish's death, Atlanta clubwomen demonstrated the power of a central aspect of her philosophy of reform—her faith in a cooperative, grassroots approach to change. They had founded the Atlanta School Improvement Association (ASIA) in February 1915 in response to a school-board decision to implement double sessions in a handful of white schools. About a month later, the ASIA Executive Committee appointed a woman in each ward to form a committee to inspect schools and report back in two weeks. The ward-inspection committees included working-class women, and the executive committee appointed a white woman to conduct school inspections and confer with black women before compiling a report on African American schools. ASIA leaders quickly moved to get labor unions and businessmen on their side, launching a publicity campaign regarding the poor state of Atlanta schools that was an embarrassment to city officials. With the help of African American community leaders, including the women associated with the Neighborhood Union, the ASIA was able to get the city council to retract plans for double sessions prior to the opening of the school year.[7]

Even though ASIA members achieved their main goal of abolishing double sessions, conflict continued to plague women's relations with the board of education and city council. Much of the tension stemmed from factional in-fighting among city officials. Mayor James G. Woodward was constantly at odds with Alderman Jesse Armistead, who as chair of the council finance committee also sat on the school board. Since Armistead was an advocate for teachers and allied with organized women, the mayor and his faction frequently thwarted proposals that women supported. After the council voted to equalize the pay of male and female teachers, the mayor claimed that the intention was not to raise women's salaries to match those of men—which would require additional funding—but rather to take the amount already spent on salaries and distribute it more equitably. He further argued that it would be "excessive" to pay teachers at the Girls' High School the same as those at the Boys' High School. Councilmen approved the mayor's proposal to cut funding for Girls' High faculty salary increases and to completely eliminate funds for the city's normal training school, which effectively fired the school's female principal and instructor. Armistead's faction was tricked into voting for the measures with the false promise that the funds would be restored at a later date.[8]

At times it appeared that misogyny, as much as politics, was at the heart of factional differences in the city council and school board. This was particularly clear at a board meeting in which members discussed the appointment of a woman to head the English-Commercial High School, a girls' school that had recently become coeducational through the incorporation of the commercial department of the Boys' High School. A majority of board members voted to reappoint Annie P. Wise, who served as principal before the merger and had twenty-three years of service in Atlanta schools. Some, however, thought it inappropriate to have Wise in a position of authority over the man who had headed the Boys' High Commercial Department. Board member Harvey Hatcher was irritated at the thought that female influence was behind the move, and complained that Wise's appointment made him question "whether the board is directing the teachers or whether the teachers are running the board of education." He imperiously declared that "a man ought to be in charge of the new school, for it is a man's job, for which no woman is qualified." Mayor Woodward also wondered if the board was "controlled too much by the teachers." Before adjourning, council members adopted a new teacher salary schedule that slightly increased the salaries of women while leaving significant gender disparities in pay.[9]

The ASIA defeated another attempt to implement double sessions in the fall of 1917, but it was not until the city council conducted an investigation of school administration the next spring that women were able to fully express their grievances. The inquiry was sparked by the complaints of Boys' High School teacher W. F. Dykes, who accused Superintendent J. C. Wardlaw and high-school supervisor Charles Culver of hiring a male teacher who was pacifist, atheist, and pro-German. Dykes's true gripe was that he had recommended another man for the position, but he used the sensational charge of wartime disloyalty to force city officials to give him a hearing. His additional charge of "Prussianism" in the school system was well founded, however, and women eagerly seized the opportunity to air complaints that had been building for years.[10] Although not all women shared Dykes's distain for Wardlaw and school-board president R. J. Guinn, they resented the autocratic manner in which male administrators had implemented new policies, as well as city officials' callous treatment of female teachers, principals, and supervisors.

Women's bitter criticisms of policies introduced by R. J. Guinn have misled some historians into thinking that they opposed progressive reform, when it was the method of implementation that was the root cause of discontent. It was Guinn who had hired Celeste Parrish to conduct a survey of Atlanta schools in 1914, and many of the reforms he subsequently imposed on teachers were her recommendations. For example, she suggested that the school board consider merit when raising teacher pay rather than basing salaries purely on seniority. Parrish's intention was to reward teachers who demonstrated a commitment to professional development and public service, but in the hands of city officials the policy became an arbitrary cost-cutting measure. Guinn created a merit system in which supervisors observed and evaluated teachers on several occasions, and then placed them in salary groups based on their average scores. Women complained that supervisors often were too busy or too poorly trained to conduct effective evaluations, and they objected to the policy of keeping the evaluations secret. Principal Fannie Spahr found the secrecy grossly unfair in cases where teachers were demoted, since it was difficult for them to improve if they did not know what needed improvement. Teachers with decades of experience testified that their pay had been cut under the merit plan, a result they suspected was intentional, as it had reduced expenditures on teachers' salaries by $15,000.[11]

Women who criticized Guinn's autocratic style of administration often praised his advocacy of progressive reforms. ASIA president Effie Foreman began her testimony by describing how he had aggressively promoted double sessions at a Tenth Street PTA meeting, telling school patrons he was determined to stay on the board of education until he could get them implemented. While Foreman objected to his apparent willingness to run roughshod over the rights of parents, she conceded that Guinn had introduced "many valuable changes in the Atlanta school system." Elementary school supervisor Laura Smith also gave Guinn credit for introducing many positive reforms, but she argued that "no reforms, however good, should be instituted without the approval and the complete understanding of those who are to be chiefly responsible for them—namely, the teachers." The testimony of both Foreman and Smith suggests that it was Guinn's reluctance to submit policies to a process of public review and approval, as Parrish had strongly recommended in her survey, that provoked the most resentment.[12]

While women obviously valued the opportunity to openly express their displeasure with male governance, they used the hearings to promote a specific set of reforms. They sought structural changes that would make school administrators more accountable to parents and teachers. Many who testified remarked that the school board needed to be separated from the city council and made an autonomous body with its own source of funding. Laura Smith complained that the present school board was too large, too affected by ward politics, and too dominated by the city council, which elected its members and controlled its finances. One solution was to create a smaller board composed of members who were popularly elected by both men and women. Smith also criticized the board's undemocratic style of administration. Echoing a common refrain in women's testimony, she maintained that it was not always the reforms but the method of their adoption that caused problems. Smith argued that the board needed to thoroughly research policies under consideration to see what other cities were doing, and then discuss their findings with teachers before implementing any changes.[13]

Members of the city council were not interested in democratic methods of administration, and in refusing to accept the school probe committee's recommendations they forced reformers to appeal to legislators for revision of the city charter. The council voted to strike the section of the committee's report that recommended creating a five-member school board elected at large, as well as the section advocating board control of city revenue dedicated to schools. Some aldermen complained bitterly about the behavior of women, whom Hatcher called "an audience of hissers and handclappers." Lucy Marion Peel, a prominent clubwoman, issued a public statement decrying the dishonorable behavior of public officials, warning, "This may not be woman's work, but we will make it ours." Within a few weeks reformers had gained the support of the entire Fulton County delegation in the state legislature. The bill that passed in early August provided for the creation of an elected five-member board with complete administrative control of schools, including the educational portion of city revenue. Even though Atlanta voters had approved proposals in the July primary to make the city-superintendent position elective and allow women to serve on the school board, these reforms were left out of the bill. In the latter case, it was because the state constitution required school-board candidates to be eligible voters.[14]

When it began to appear that city officials were determined to continue business as usual despite the charter revisions, women took steps to ensure that the new system of administration would truly represent public interests. Acting like petulant children, Hatcher and other council members withheld the funds needed for teacher raises and the installation of heating and furnishings in three school buildings under construction. Current board members began to announce their candidacy for the December election, which suggested the new board would strongly resemble the old one. As school supporters began expressing a desire to choose their own candidates, members of three organizations—the PTA, ASIA, and Wake-Up-Daddy Movement (another school reform group)—held a mass meeting on September 24 to create a single movement under the banner of the Atlanta School Improvement Association. Attendees chose Edgar A. Neely to serve as president and authorized him to create a committee of ten members, half of whom were to be women, to construct a list of preferred candidates and report back in two weeks.[15]

The creation of a grassroots political movement proved to be more difficult than reformers expected, which made their success all the more remarkable. They had to repeatedly postpone a second mass meeting, first because Atlantans were busy with the city's third Liberty Loan drive, and then because city health officials banned all public meetings due to the influenza epidemic. To cope with the ban, ASIA leaders established a democratic process for the selection of a school-reform ticket that could be conducted through outdoor meetings at each of the city's schools. They instructed school patrons to hold meetings to choose delegates to represent them at district meetings, after which delegates at the district meetings would nominate candidates for the school board and choose delegates to represent them at a mass meeting. Since the city's ten wards had been divided into five districts for the purposes of school-board representation, the ASIA plan required considerable cooperation across school communities. Participants had to agree to accept the majority's choice of candidates at each step in the process and to vote the entire school reform ticket at the polls. It was an ingenious plan to bypass ward politics and ensure that school patrons in each district obtained the candidate of their choice even though the elections were at-large.[16]

The plan worked remarkably well despite efforts to derail it. The city lifted the ban on public gatherings in late October, just in time for the district meetings to conclude. Two of the current board members, George Eubanks and James E. Hickey, tried unsuccessfully to corrupt the process at the local level to secure a place on the reform ticket. Hickey even created a sham school-improvement club with anti-reform alderman I. F. Styron as its president, but his machinations did not succeed in making him the candidate of choice for District One. After the ASIA announced its slate of candidates on November 21, women hit the streets, distributing campaign literature and circulars that described the poor conditions prevailing in Atlanta schools. They canvassed the city, holding ward and community meetings to maintain interest in the election, and the positive public response made them increasingly optimistic about the possibility of a clean sweep for the reform ticket. One ASIA leader bragged the week before the election that the organization's campaign machinery was "well oiled and running with clock-like precision." She was certain that citizens who understood what was at stake would vote against dilapidated schools and in favor of a living wage for teachers; they would "make democracy a fact and not a theory to be discussed by politicians."[17]

The election results fulfilled reformers' expectations, as voters turned out in large numbers to support the reform candidates. The three who ran uncontested received thousands of votes, and anti-reform candidates Hickey and Eubanks lost by substantial margins. The *Atlanta Constitution* declared the election a "victory for the mothers and fathers and teachers and ordinary citizens" whose voices usually were not heard. Referring to the ASIA, an unnamed city official claimed, "You can't beat a movement like that." Whereas PTA chapters previously had been focused on issues that impacted their own schools and neighborhoods, the ASIA linked them together for the first time in a citywide movement. The wards with the most active Parent-Teacher Associations had a larger voter turnout and a larger majority win for the reform candidates running for contested seats.[18] When Celeste Parrish founded the Georgia Congress of Mothers in 1905, she would have been surprised to know that in little more than a decade it would wield enough power to remake Atlanta school governance.

Parrish was too ill to actively participate in the citizens' revolt and did not live to see its outcome, but she surely followed the events throughout the summer and viewed them as a healthy manifestation of democratic ideals. Guinn and other board members had implemented many of the recommendations included in her school-survey report, but they ignored her suggestion that they include all members of the community in the decision-making process. Caught up in internecine struggles for political power, members of the school board and city council simply handed down decisions and suppressed dissent until teachers and parents could take it no longer. As Parrish often warned, reformers ignored public opinion and excluded popular participation at their own peril. She would have been proud of the sophisticated campaign launched by organizations she had a hand in founding, and whose members she had a hand in training in community work. Ever true to her democratic ideals, she knew that, while democracy carried its own set of problems, it was the only sure path to lasting progress; there was no way around the difficult, time-consuming process of grassroots organization and cooperation. In the most discouraging moments of demagoguery and divisiveness—of which Celeste Parrish experienced many—it was and is an insight worth remembering.

NOTES

1. Biographical sketches of Parrish list her birth year as September 12, 1853, a mistake that apparently first occurred after the Civil War when she was orphaned and under the guardianship of an uncle. Her recorded age in the U.S. Census records for 1860 and 1870 suggest that the online database compiled by Edmund West, *Family Data Collection—Births* (Provo, Utah: Ancestry.com, 2001), is correct in listing her birth date as November 16, 1852.

2. Pittsylvania County Land Books, 1861–1865, County Courthouse, Chatham; F. Lawrence McFall Jr., *Danville in the Civil War* (Lynchburg, Va.: H. E. Howard, 2001), 2–4; Lynda J. Morgan, *Emancipation in Virginia's Tobacco Belt, 1850–1870* (Athens: University of Georgia Press, 1992), 23; Frederick F. Siegel, *The Roots of Southern Distinctiveness: Tobacco and Society in Danville, Virginia, 1780–1865* (Chapel Hill: University of North Carolina Press, 1987), 68–74, 100–102, 105–17.

3. Alison Goodyear Freehling, *Drift Toward Dissolution: The Virginia Slavery Debate of 1831–1832* (Baton Rouge: Louisiana State University Press, 1982), 243–46; Morgan, *Emancipation in Virginia's Tobacco Belt*, 20–21; Siegel, *Roots of Southern Distinctiveness*, 81–82; Nannie May Tilley, *The Bright-Tobacco Industry, 1860–1929* (1948; rpt. New York: Arno Press, 1972); Federal Census Slave Schedules for 1850 and 1860, Pittsylvania County, Northern District.

4. Census statistics for Pittsylvania County drawn from ICPSR Archive, Study 3, Historical, Demographic, Economic, and Social Data, the United States, 1790–1970, University of Virginia Geospatial and Statistical Data Center, fisher.lib.Virginia.edu/; Siegel, *Roots of Southern Distinctiveness*, 80–83, 99–100.

5. Sarah L. Hyde, *Schooling in the Antebellum South: The Rise of Public and Private Education in Louisiana, Mississippi, and Alabama* (Baton Rouge: Louisiana State University Press, 2016); Edgar W. Knight, *Public Education in the South* (Boston: Ginn and Co., 1922); Thomas Jefferson, "A Bill for the More General Diffusion of Knowledge," in *Crusade Against Ignorance: Thomas Jefferson on Education* (New York: Teachers College, Columbia University, 1961), 83–92; Robert J. Vejnar II, "A Battle to Preserve Republican Government: Antebellum Virginia's Struggle Over Public Education," MA thesis, James Madison University, 1992, 8–10; Jennings L. Wagoner Jr., *Jefferson and Education* (Monticello, Va.: Thomas Jefferson Foundation, 2004), with preface by William G. Bowen, 33–43.

6. Gillie A. Larew, "Celestia Parrish," *Virginia Journal of Education* 35 (May 1942): 342; Celeste Parrish, "Problems and Progress of Universal Education in the South," *Publications of the Association of Collegiate Alumnae*, ser. 3 (February 1900): 50–51, first and second quotes from 51; third quote from Celeste Parrish, "My Experience in Self-Culture," in *The Early Life Story of Miss Celeste Parrish, Noted Georgia Educator* (Atlanta: Georgia State Department of Education, 1925), 1.

7. Jane Turner Censer, *The Reconstruction of Southern White Womanhood, 1865–1895* (Baton Rouge: Louisiana State University Press, 2003), 51–83; Catherine A. Jones, *Intimate Reconstructions: Children in Postemancipation Virginia* (Charlottesville: University of Virginia Press, 2015); Jeffrey W. McClurken, *Taking Care of the Living: Reconstructing Confederate Veteran Families in Virginia* (Charlottesville: University of Virginia Press, 2009); Amy Feely Morsman, *The Big House After Slavery: Virginia Plantation Families and Their Postbellum Domestic Experiment* (Charlottesville: University of Virginia Press, 2010).

8. Quote from A. D. Mayo, *Southern Women in the Recent Educational Movement in the South,* ed. Dan T. Carter and Amy Friedlander (1892; rpt. Baton Rouge: Louisiana State University Press, 1978), 57; Celeste Parrish, "Some Defects in the Education of Women in the South," *Proceedings of the Second Capon Springs Conference for Christian Education in the South, 1899* (Raleigh: Edwards and Broughton, 1899), 68–69.

9. Cornelius Jacob Heatwole, *A History of Education in Virginia* (New York: Macmillan, 1916), 100–123, 137–210, 235–39, 280–304; Richard Lowe, *Republicans and Reconstruction in Virginia, 1856–1870* (Charlottesville: University of Virginia Press, 1991), 160–81; *Virginia School Report, 1871: First Annual Report of the Superintendent of Public Instruction of Virginia, for the Year Ending August 31, 1871* (Richmond, Va.: Superintendent of Public Printing, 1871), 14–15, 132–42.

10. *Virginia School Report: Second Annual Report of the Superintendent of Public Instruction, for the Year Ending August 21, 1872* (Richmond, Va.: Superintendent of Public Printing, 1872), 2–3; Elsa Barkley Brown, "To Catch the Vision of Freedom: Reconstructing Southern Black Women's Political History, 1865–1880," in *African American Women and the Vote, 1837–1965* (Amherst: University of Massachusetts Press, 1997), ed. Ann D. Gordon et al., 66–99; Glenda Gilmore, *Gender and Jim Crow: Women and the Politics of White Supremacy in North Carolina, 1896–1920* (Chapel Hill: University of North Carolina Press, 1996), 31–38; Evelyn Brooks Higginbotham, *Righteous Discontent: The Women's Movement in the Black Baptist Church, 1880–1920* (Cambridge, Mass.: Harvard University Press, 1993), 19–31. On the Richmond Colored Normal School, see Hilary Green, *Educational Reconstruction: African American Schools in the Urban South, 1865–1890* (New York: Fordham University Press, 2016), 67–84.

11. Jane Dailey, *Before Jim Crow: The Politics of Race in Postemancipation Virginia* (Chapel Hill: University of North Carolina Press, 2000), 27–31; James T. Moore, "Black Militancy in Readjuster Virginia, 1879–1883," *Journal of Southern History* 41 (May 1975): 167–86; *Virginia School Report, 1882: Twelfth Annual Report of the Superintendent of Public Instruction for the Year Ending July 31, 1882* (Richmond, Va.: Superintendent of Public Printing, 1882), 59, 64–65; *Virginia School Report, 1884: Fourteenth Annual Report of the Superintendent of Public Instruction, for the Year Ending July 31, 1884* (Richmond, Va.: Superintendent of Public Printing, 1884), 140–42.

12. Quotes from Parrish, "My Experience in Self-Culture," 3. Information on Parrish's family comes from U.S. Census records, Pittsylvania County records, and the genealogical research of Ronnie Walker, a descendent of her mother's side of the family (hereafter referred to as the Walker Papers).

13. Susan B. Carter, "Incentives and Rewards to Teaching," *American Teachers: Histories of a Profession at Work* (New York: Macmillan, 1989), ed. Donald Warren, 49–62; Amy Thompson

McCandless, *The Past in the Present: Women's Higher Education in the Twentieth-Century South* (Tuscaloosa: University of Alabama Press, 1999), 83–84; Michael Dennis, *Lessons in Progress: State Universities and Progressivism in the New South, 1880–1920* (Urbana: University of Illinois Press, 2001), 201–3; quote from "Miss Laura Smith Declares Finance Committee at Fault," *Atlanta Constitution,* June 21, 1918.

14. Roberta D. Cornelius, *The History of Randolph-Macon Woman's College from the Founding in 1891 through the Year of 1949–1950* (Chapel Hill: University of North Carolina Press, 1951), 20, 31; Gail Apperson Kilman, "Southern Collegiate Women: Higher Education at Wesleyan Female College and Randolph-Macon Woman's College, 1893–1907," PhD diss., University of Delaware, 1984, 85–97; letter, G. D. Haupin to Helen Peak, March 1, 1939, Randolph College Archives. The salaries of faculty at state institutions were included in the annual *Virginia School Report.*

15. Edwin G. Boring, "Edward Bradford Titchener, 1867–1927," *American Journal of Psychology* 100 (Autumn-Winter 1987): 376–94; Christopher D. Green, "Scientific Objectivity and E. B. Titchener's Experimental Psychology," *Isis* 101 (December 2010): 697–721. Titchener contributed notes to the first piece of research that Celeste Parrish published in the *American Journal of Psychology,* "The Cutaneous Estimation of Open and Filled Space," *American Journal of Psychology* 6 (January 1895): 514–23.

16. Frank S. Murray and Frederick B. Rowe, "Psychology Laboratories in the United States Prior to 1900," *Teaching of Psychology* 6 (February 1979): 19–21, and "A Note on the Titchener Influence on the First Psychology Laboratory in the South," *Journal of the History of the Behavioral Sciences* 15 (July 1979): 282–84; Helen Peak, "The Parrish Laboratories of Psychology at Randolph-Macon Woman's College," *Journal of Experimental Psychology* 24 (May 1939): 551–53; Cornelius, *History of RMWC,* 46–47.

17. John Dewey, *The School and Society* and *The Child and the Curriculum* (1900, 1902; rpt. Chicago: University of Chicago Press, 1990), 31–37, 132–33; John Dewey, "The School as Social Center," *The Elementary School Teacher* 3 (October 1902): 73–86; John Dewey, "Democracy in Education," *The Elementary School Teacher* 4 (December 1903): 193–204; Jay Martin, *The Education of John Dewey* (New York: Columbia University Press, 2002), 199–203; Robert B. Westbrook, "Schools for Industrial Democrats: The Social Origins of John Dewey's Philosophy of Education," *American Journal of Education* 100 (August 1992): 401–19; Mary Jo Deegan, *Jane Addams and the Men of the Chicago School, 1892–1918* (New Brunswick, N.J.: Transaction Publishers, 2005), 251–53. See also Robert B. Westbrook, *John Dewey and American Democracy* (Ithaca, N.Y.: Cornell University Press, 1991).

18. John Dewey, "My Pedagogic Creed," in Dewey and Albion W. Small, *My Pedagogic Creed by Prof. John Dewey,* also *The Demands of Sociology upon Pedagogy by Prof. Albion W. Small* (New York: E. L. Kellogg & Co., 1897), 3–18, first quote from 16; Celeste Parrish, "Discussion," *Southern Educational Association, Journal of Proceedings and Addresses of the Eleventh Annual Meeting held at Columbia, S.C., December 26–29, 1901* (n.p.: The Association, 1902), 199–203, second quote from 201; *Forty-First Annual Report of the Department of Education to the General Assembly of the State of Georgia for the School Year Ending December 31, 1912* (Atlanta: State Printer, 1913) (hereafter *Forty-First AR*), 42–43.

19. Deegan, *Jane Addams and the Men of the Chicago School,* 9–13, 36, 45–48; Charlene Haddock Seigfried, *Pragmatism and Feminism: Reweaving the Social Fabric* (Chicago: University of Chicago Press, 1996), 44–66; Ellen Fitzpatrick, *Endless Crusade: Women Social Scientists and Progressive Reform* (New York: Oxford University Press, 1990), 28–36; Lynn D. Gordon, *Gender*

and Higher Education in the Progressive Era (New Haven, Conn.: Yale University Press, 1990), 88–102; Marion Talbot and Lois Rosenberry, *The History of the American Association of University Women, 1881–1931* (Boston: Houghton Mifflin, 1931), 3–14; *Publications of the Association of Collegiate Alumnae,* ser. 3, no. 3 (February 1900), quotes from 67. See also Mary Jo Deegan, *Annie Marion MacLean and the Chicago Schools of Sociology, 1894–1934* (New Brunswick, N.J.: Transaction Publishers, 2014).

20. Parrish, "Problems and Progress of Universal Education," 58–61, first quote from 50; "Report of the State Female Normal School at Farmville, Virginia," 13–14, in Appendix, *Virginia School Report, 1885: Fifteenth Annual Report of the Superintendent of Public Instruction for the Year Ending July 31, 1885* (Richmond, Va.: Superintendent of Public Printing, 1885).

21. Parrish, "Some Defects in the Education of Women in the South"; Celeste Parrish, "The Education of Women in the South," *Southern Educational Association Journal of Proceedings and Addresses of the Tenth Annual Meeting Held at Richmond, Va., December 27–29, 1900* (Richmond, Va.: The Association, 1901), 45–62; Celeste Parrish, "The Womanly Woman," *The Independent* 53 (April 1901): 775–78; Celeste Parrish, "Woman's Problems," *The Independent* 53 (October 1901): 2582–85.

22. "The Purpose and Policy of the SACW," *Fourth Annual Report of the Southern Association of College Women, 1906,* 5–6, Box 1, Folder 1, American Association of University Women, Georgia Division Records, Georgia Department of Archives and History; "Southern Association of College Women," *The Chautauquan* 59 (June 1910): 96–98; Dorothy D. DeMoss, "'A Fearless Stand': The Southern Association of College Women, 1903–1921," *Southern Studies* 26 (Winter 1987): 249–260; Talbot and Rosenberry, *History of the American Association of University Women,* 46–56; Elizabeth Colton, "The Past and Future Work of the Southern Association of College Women," *High School Quarterly* 6 (July 1918): 224–30.

23. James D. Anderson, *The Education of Blacks in the South, 1860–1935* (Chapel Hill: University of North Carolina Press, 1988), 83–87; Dennis, *Lessons in Progress,* 8–12; James L. Leloudis, *Schooling the New South: Pedagogy, Self, and Society in North Carolina, 1880–1920* (Chapel Hill: University of North Carolina Press, 1996), 145–50. For a detailed account of the southern movement written by one of its participants, see Charles William Dabney, *University Education in the South* (Chapel Hill: University of North Carolina Press, 1936), vol. 2.

24. Leloudis, *Schooling the New South,* 155–64; William A. Link, *A Hard Country and a Lonely Place: Schooling, Society, and Reform in Rural Virginia, 1870–1920* (Chapel Hill: University of North Carolina, 1986), 113–15; Rebecca S. Montgomery, *The Politics of Education in the New South: Women and Reform in Georgia, 1890–1930* (Baton Rouge: Louisiana State University Press, 2006), 71–88; Anastatia Sims, *The Power of Femininity in the New South: Women's Organizations and Politics in North Carolina, 1880–1930* (Columbia: University of South Carolina Press, 1997), 89–102; *Report of the Commissioner of Education* (Washington, D.C.: Government Printing Office, 1908), vol. 1: 315–16.

25. "Meaning and Purpose of the Muscogee Elementary School," *Georgia State Normal School Bulletin, 1909–1910,* 62–66, Box 8, State Normal School Records, 1894–1933, Hargrett Manuscript Collection and University Archives, University of Georgia Libraries, Athens (hereafter NSR); "Georgia's Training School for Teachers," clipping from *Pandora, 1903,* Box 3, Folder 4, NSR; Celeste Parrish, "An Educational Development in Georgia," *The Elementary School Teacher* 6 (November 1905): 131–45; Louise Anderson Allen, "Silenced Sisters: Dewey's Disciples in a Conservative New South, 1900–1940," *Journal of the Gilded Age and Progressive Era* 5 (April 2006): 119–37.

26. First quote from "Miss Celeste Parrish: Her Address on 'The Educational Outlook in Vir-

ginia,'" clipping, *Richmond Dispatch*, March 23, 1902, Section 8, Folder 1, Lila Meade Valentine Papers, Virginia Historical Society, Richmond (hereafter VHS); "Branson Tells Board His Side," *Atlanta Constitution*, April 15, 1904; second quote from "Teachers Resent Action of Board," *Macon Telegraph*, May 30, 1911.

27. Thomas R. Dew, *Review of the Debate in the Virginia Legislature, 1831–'32*, rpt. in *The Pro-Slavery Argument, as Maintained by the Most Distinguished Writers of the Southern States* (Philadelphia: Lippincott, Grambo, & Co., 1853), 287–490; George Frederick Holmes, "Ancient Slavery," *De Bow's Review* 19 (November 1855): 559–78, and vol. 19 (December 1855): 617–37, quote from 567; George Fitzhugh, *Sociology for the South, or the Failure of Free Society* (Richmond: Virginia State Agricultural Society, 1853), 23–25, 213–20; Marjorie Spruill Wheeler, *New Women of the New South: The Leaders of the Woman Suffrage Movement in the Southern States* (New York: Oxford University Press, 1993), 16–17. See also Drew Gilpin Faust, *A Sacred Circle: The Dilemma of the Intellectual in the Old South, 1840–1860* (Philadelphia: University of Philadelphia Press, 1977).

28. Christie Anne Farnham, *The Education of the Southern Belle: Higher Education and Student Socialization in the Antebellum South* (New York: New York University Press, 1994), 30–32, 174–80; Elizabeth Seymour Eschbach, *The Higher Education of Women in England and America, 1865–1920* (New York: Garland, 1993), 141–43; Elizabeth Fox-Genovese, *Within the Plantation Household: Black and White Women of the Old South* (Chapel Hill: University of North Carolina Press, 1988), 46–47, 256–59; Joan Marie Johnson, *Southern Women at the Seven Sister Colleges: Feminist Values and Social Activism, 1875–1915* (Athens: University of Georgia Press, 2008), 15–21; Thomas Woody, *A History of Women's Education in the United States* (New York: Science Press, 1929), vol. 2: 253–54, 269–70.

29. Parrish, "The Womanly Woman," 776; Parrish, "Some Defects in the Education of Women in the South," 62; *Minutes of the General Faculty* 13: 408–20, Albert and Shirley Small Special Collections Library, University of Virginia; quote from "Branson Tells Board His Side."

30. "Club Women Ask Investigation," *Atlanta Constitution*, June 4, 1911; *Fortieth Annual Report of the Department of Education to the General Assembly of the State of Georgia for the School Year Ending December 31, 1911* (Atlanta: State Printer, 1912), 26–27; *Georgia State Board of Education Minutes and Correspondence, 1870–1923*, 263–64, Georgia Department of Archives and History; Dabney, *Universal Education in the South* 2: 219–23.

31. Gillie Larew, "Celestia Parrish," in *Adventures in Teaching: Pioneer Women Educators and Influential Teachers* (Richmond: Virginia Iota State Organization, Delta Kappa Gamma Society, 1963), 234–41, quotes from 241; Parrish, "My Experience in Self-Culture."

32. Ronald E. Butchart, *Schooling the Freedpeople: Teaching, Learning, and the Struggle for Black Freedom, 1861–1876* (Chapel Hill: University of North Carolina Press, 2010), 55–57, 67–69; Adam Fairclough, *A Class of Their Own: Black Teachers in the Segregated South* (Cambridge, Mass.: Belknap Press, 2007), 62–68; Green, *Educational Reconstruction*, 15–34; Jones, *Intimate Reconstructions*, 161–69.

33. Joyce Antler, *The Educated Woman and Professionalization: The Struggle for a New Feminine Identity, 1890–1920* (New York: Garland, 1987); Penina Migdal Glazer and Miriam Slater, *Unequal Colleagues: The Entrance of Women into the Professions, 1890–1940* (New Brunswick, N.J.: Rutgers University Press, 1987); Gloria Moldow, *Women Doctors in Gilded-Age Washington: Race, Gender, and Professionalization* (Urbana: University of Illinois Press, 1987); Rosalind Rosenberg, *Beyond Separate Spheres: Intellectual Roots of Modern Feminism* (New Haven, Conn.: Yale University Press, 1982); Margaret W. Rossiter, *Women Scientists in America: Struggles and Strategies to 1940*

(Baltimore: Johns Hopkins University Press, 1982); Barbara Miller Solomon, *In the Company of Educated Women: A History of Women and Higher Education in America* (New Haven, Conn.: Yale University Press, 1985).

34. Miriam R. Levin, *Defining Women's Scientific Enterprise: Mount Holyoke Faculty and the Rise of American Science* (Hanover, N.H.: University Press of New England, 2005); Patricia Ann Palmieri, *In Adamless Eden: The Community of Women Faculty at Wellesley* (New Haven, Conn.: Yale University Press, 1995); Patricia Albjerg Graham, "Expansion and Exclusion: A History of Women in American Higher Education," *Signs* 3 (Summer 1978): 759–73.

35. Deegan, *Jane Addams and the Men of the Chicago School*; Gordon, *Gender and Higher Education in the Progressive Era.*

36. Gilmore, *Gender and Jim Crow*, 63–72; Steven Kantrowitz, *Ben Tillman and the Reconstruction of White Supremacy* (Chapel Hill: University of North Carolina Press, 2000), 214–20, 260–61; Joel Williamson, *The Crucible of Race: Black-White Relations in the American South Since Emancipation* (New York: Oxford University Press, 1984), 111–19.

37. Mary E. Creswell, "Personal Recollections of Celeste Parrish," typed manuscript, Celeste Parrish Memorials, Hargrett Manuscript Collection and University Archives; "Miss Celeste Parrish, Noted Georgia Educator, Is Dead," *Atlanta Constitution*, September 9, 1918; "Memory of Miss Celeste Parrish is Honored at Dinner Meeting of Kappa Gamma Delta Fraternity Here," *Athens Daily Banner*, February 19, 1940; *Tribute to a Pioneer Teacher: Celeste Parrish* (Danville, Va.: Delta Kappa Gamma Society, Iota State Organization, 1941); Meta Glass, "Reminiscences of Miss Parrish," *Virginia Journal of Education* 35 (May 1942): 343; Larew, "Celestia Parrish," *Virginia Journal of Education* 35 (May 1942): 342–46; Elise Gibbs, "Celeste Parrish," *Some Georgia Historical Sketches* (Atlanta: Hubbard Printing, 1943), 69–71; Archie Swanson Beverley, "A Tribute to a Great Leader," *Religious Herald*, February 24, 1949, 14, 23. In contrast to women's accounts of Parrish's contributions to education, a male faculty member of the Georgia State Normal School, E. S. Sell, mentions Parrish only in passing and gives the school president, Eugene Cunningham Branson, credit for her accomplishments (Sell, *History of the State Normal School, Athens, Georgia* [n.p., 1923]).

38. The only historians who give Parrish more than a passing mention are Allen, "Silenced Sisters," and Amy Friedlander, "A More Perfect Christian Womanhood: Higher Learning for a New South," *Education and the Rise of the New South*, ed. Ronald K. Goodenow and Arthur O. White (Boston: G. K. Hall, 1981), 72–91.

CHAPTER ONE

1. In *Confederate Daughters: Coming of Age During the Civil War* (Carbondale: Southern Illinois University Press, 2008), Victoria E. Ott argues that southern white women who came of age during the 1850s tended to romanticize the Old South and accept antebellum notions of feminine domesticity. In *The Reconstruction of White Southern Womanhood*, Censer similarly finds that the generations of women born before 1820 and between 1820 and 1849 were less likely than Parrish's generation to challenge gender constraints.

2. Edward Ayers, *In the Presence of Mine Enemies: The Civil War in the Heart of America, 1859–1863* (New York: W. W. Norton, 2003), 85–88, 102–7, 120–23; Freehling, *Drift Toward Dissolution*, 239–62; James I. Robertson Jr., "The Virginia State Convention of 1861," *Virginia at War: 1861*, ed. William C. Davis and James I Robertson Jr. (Lexington: University Press of Kentucky, 2003), 1–25.

3. One of the most complete lists of Confederate soldiers from Pittsylvania County has been compiled by McFall in *Danville in the Civil War,* appendix I. Genealogical information on the Parrish and Walker families referenced here comes primarily from 1860 county census returns and the work of Ronnie L. Walker, a descendent of Parrish's mother's family who shared with the author his meticulous research in county and state archives, hereafter referred to as the Walker Papers.

4. Letter, Rebecca Tredway to Rawley White Martin, December 8, 1862, Rawley White Martin Papers, Folder 2, Southern Historical Collection, Manuscripts Division, Wilson Library, University of North Carolina–Chapel Hill (hereafter SHC); William H. Sims to Phebe H. Bailey, August 4, 1864, Bailey Family Papers, Section 8, Folder 3, VHS; William Blair, *Virginia's Private War: Feeding Body and Soul in the Confederacy, 1861–1865* (New York: Oxford University Press, 1998), 33–37, 39–40, 46–47; McClurken, *Taking Care of the Living,* 29–33; McFall, *Danville in the Civil War,* 15, 18–30; Robert Enoch Withers, *Autobiography of an Octogenarian* (Roanoke, Va.: Stone Printing, 1907), 209.

5. Letter, Rebecca Tredway to Rawley White Martin, February 3, 1863, and Bettie Penick to Rawley White Martin, May 2, 1862, both from Martin Papers, Folder 2, SHC; Larew, "Celeste Parrish," *Virginia Journal of Education* 35 (May 1942): 342–46, first and second quote from 342.

6. McClurken, *Taking Care of the Living,* 45–47, 53–54; William Sours to John Sours, October 9, 1865, and November 7, 1865, Sours Family Papers, Series I, Box 1, Folder 21, SHC; 1870 census returns for Pittsylvania County.

7. "Reminiscences of the Sixties," *War Recollections of the Confederate Veterans of Pittsylvania County, Virginia, 1861–1865,* compiled by Rawley Martin Chapter, Virginia Division, United Daughters of the Confederacy (n.p.: Randall O. Reynolds, n.d.), 12–13, 78–84, third quote from 78, fourth quote from 83; Drew Gilpin Faust, *Mothers of Invention: Women of the Slaveholding South in the American Civil War* (Chapel Hill: University of North Carolina Press, 1996). The Chatham Grays participated in Stonewall Jackson's Valley Campaign as well as Pickett's Charge at Gettysburg, as also discussed in *War Recollections of the Confederate Veterans.*

8. Mary Ann Martin to Rawley Martin, October 4 and December 16, 1862; Rebecca Tredway to Rawley Martin, November 13 and December 8, 1862, and Rawley Martin to Ladies Soldiers' Aid Society, December 25, 1863, all from Martin Papers, Folder 2, SHC; Edwin Penick to Mary Penick, March 11 and April 14, 1862, Edwin Anderson Penick Letters, VHS; Lynchburg *Daily Republican,* August 24, 1861. It is not clear whether Martin was thanking the ladies' aid society for his company still in the field, or if he received the box while in a Gettysburg hospital (before being moved to Baltimore in November) and shared it with members of his company also convalescing there.

9. "Reminiscences of the Sixties," 81; Maud Carter Clement, *History of Pittsylvania County, Virginia* (Lynchburg, Va.: J. P. Bell, 1929), 247; McFall, *Danville in the Civil War,* 19–30; Siegel, *Roots of Southern Distinctiveness,* 153, 156, 160–62.

10. Joseph T. Glatthaar, "Confederate Soldiers in Virginia," *Virginia at War: 1861,* ed. Davis and Robertson, 50–51; McFall *Danville in the Civil War,* 18; James I. Robertson Jr., "Houses of Horror: Danville's Civil War Prisons," *Virginia Magazine of History and Biography* 69 (July 1961): 329–45; Withers, *Autobiography of an Octogenarian,* 196–98; W. H. Newlin, *Narrative of Prison Escape* (Cincinnati: Western Methodist Book Concern Printers, 1887); *Lynchburg Daily Republican,* February 24 and March 12, 1862.

11. James I. Robertson Jr., "Danville Under Military Occupation, 1865," *Virginia Magazine of History and Biography* 75 (July 1967): 331–48; Withers, *Autobiography of an Octogenarian,* 218–25; I. G. Bradwell, "Making Our Way Home from Appomattox," *Confederate Veteran* 29 (March 1921): 102.

12. Quotes from Celeste Parrish, "My Experiences in Self-Culture."

13. Parrish, "My Experience in Self-Culture"; quote from Betty Parrish Morehouse, "'Georgia's Greatest Woman' buried in Clayton," *Clayton* (Ga.) *Tribune*, September 6, 1990; Virginia Cary, *Letters on Female Character, Addressed to A Young Lady on the Death of Her Mother* (Richmond, Va.: Ariel Works, 1830); Scott Stephan, *Evangelical Women and Domestic Devotion in the Antebellum South* (Athens: University of Georgia Press, 2008), 99–104. On the writings and family background of Cary, see Cynthia A. Kierner, *Beyond the Household: Women's Place in the Early South, 1700–1835* (Ithaca, N.Y.: Cornell University Press, 1998), 203–11.

14. Joseph Walker will, Pittsylvania County Clerk Wills Book 2, p. 216; James B. Stone to Katherine Spiller Moses, February 2, 1869, Katherine Spiller (Graves) Moses Papers, Section One, VHS; Jane Bankhead Madison to Phebe H. Bailey, November 23, 1861, and Mrs. William M. Howerton to Phebe H. Bailey, December 11, 1862, in Bailey Family Papers, Section B, Folder 5, VHS; *Intimate Reconstructions*, 89–92; Larew, "Celestia Parrish," *Virginia Journal of Education* 35 (May 1942): 342–46; Parrish, "My Experience in Self-Culture."

15. Anne Firor Scott, *The Southern Lady: From Pedestal to Politics, 1830–1930* (Chicago: University of Chicago Press, 1970), 110–18, 129–32; Mayo, *Southern Women in the Recent Educational Movement*, 164–67; Maria Louisa Carrington to John and Elizabeth Dabney, December 8, 1867, and John Dabney to George Dabney, December 30, 1867, from Saunders Family Papers, Section 21, VHS.

16. Beverley, "Tribute to a Great Leader," 14, 23; quotes from Parrish, "My Experience in Self-Culture." There is a biographical sketch of Page in *Theory and Practice of Teaching, or the Motives and Methods of Good School-Keeping*, ed. W. H. Payne (New York: 1847; rpt. New York: American Book Co., 1885).

17. *Fifth Semi-Annual Report on Schools for Freedmen, January 1, 1868*, War Department, Bureau of Refugees, Freedmen, and Abandoned Lands (hereafter BRFAL) (Washington, D.C.: Government Printing Office, 1868), 3–9; Alrutheus Ambush Taylor, *The Negro in the Reconstruction of Virginia* (1926; rpt. New York: Russell & Russell, 1969), 137–44; William Preston Vaughn, *Schools for All: The Blacks and Public Education in the South, 1865–1877* (Lexington: University Press of Kentucky, 1974), 9–11.

18. *First Semi-Annual Report on Schools and Finances of Freedmen, January 1, 1866* (Washington, D.C.: Government Printing Office, 1868), 2–3. BRFAL; *Third Semi-Annual Report on Schools for Freedmen, January 1, 1867* (Washington, D.C.: Government Printing Office, 1867), 10, BRFAL; *Fourth Semi-Annual Report on Schools for Freedmen, July 1, 1867* (Washington, D.C.: Government Printing Office, 1867), 18, BRFAL; *Eighth Semi-Annual Report on Schools for Freedmen, July 1, 1869* (Washington, D.C.: Government Printing Office, 1869), 20, BRFAL; William T. Anderson Jr., "The Freedmen's Bureau and Negro Education in Virginia," *North Carolina Historical Review* 29 (January 1952), 64–90; Butchart, *Schooling the Freedpeople*, 26–29; Fairclough, *A Class of Their Own*, 137–38; Heather Andrea Williams, *Self-Taught: African American Education in Slavery and Freedom* (Chapel Hill: University of North Carolina Press, 2005), 185–87.

19. *Fifth Semi-Annual Report on Schools for Freedmen*, 22; Anderson, *Education of Blacks in the South*, 7–16, BRFAL; Herbert G. Gutman, "Schools for Freedmen: The Post-Emancipation Origins of Afro-American Education," in *Power and Culture: Essays on the American Working Class*, ed. Ira Berlin (New York: Pantheon, 1987), 260–77; Morgan, *Emancipation in Virginia's Tobacco Belt*, 180, 182; Williams, *Self-Taught*, 51–66.

20. *Virginia School Report, 1880: Tenth Annual Report of the Superintendent of Public Instruction for the Year Ending July 31, 1880* (Richmond, Va.: R. F. Walker, Superintendent of Public Printing, 1880), 129–30; Alvord, *Tenth Semi-Annual Report on Schools for Freedmen, July 1, 1870* (Washington, D.C.: Government Printing Office, 1870), 12, BRFAL; Morgan, *Emancipation in Virginia's Tobacco Belt,* 182–83; John Thomas O'Brien, Jr., "From Bondage to Citizenship: The Richmond Black Community, 1865–1867," PhD diss., University of Rochester, 1975, 76–77; Taylor, *The Negro in the Reconstruction of Virginia,* 142,

21. *First Semi-Annual Report on Schools and Finances of Freedmen, January 1, 1866,* 6, BRFAL; *Third Semi-Annual Report on Schools for Freedmen, January 1, 1867,* 37, BRFAL; *Fourth Semi-Annual Report on Schools for Freedmen, July 1, 1867,* 18, 83, BRFAL; *Seventh Semi-Annual Report on Schools for Freedmen, January 1, 1869* (Washington, D.C.: Government Printing Office, 1869), 15, BRFAL; Butchart, *Schooling the Freedpeople,* xii, 13, 56–61, 65–69, 74–76; quotes from Parrish, "Problems and Progress of Universal Education," 57.

22. Dailey, *Before Jim Crow,* 16–19; Lowe, *Republicans and Reconstruction in Virginia,* 74–75.

23. Michael Hucles, "Many Voices, Similar Concerns: Traditional Methods of African-American Political Activity in Norfolk, Virginia, 1865–1875," *Virginia Magazine of History and Biography* 100 (October 1992): 543–66; Richard L. Hume, "The Membership of the Virginia Constitutional Convention of 1867–1868: A Study of the Beginnings of Congressional Reconstruction in the Upper South," *Virginia Magazine of History and Biography* 86 (October 1978): 461–84; Edward K. Knight, *Reconstruction and Education in Virginia,* pamphlet, rpt. from *South Atlantic Quarterly* 15 (January and April 1916): 5–12, quote from 10; Lowe, *Republicans and Reconstruction in Virginia,* 129–32, 138–39.

24. J. L. Blair Buck, *The Development of Public Schools in Virginia, 1607–1952* (Richmond: Virginia State Board of Education, 1952), 65–69; Knight, *Reconstruction and Education in Virginia,* 13; Manly's report on Virginia, *Sixth Semi-Annual Report on Schools for Freedmen, July 1, 1868* (Washington, D.C.: Government Printing Office, 1868), 16–18, quotes from 18, BRFAL.

25. Parrish, "My Experiences in Self-Culture"; Beverley, "Tribute to a Great Leader"; Pittsylvania County Land Books and Chancery Court Records; Walker Records; *Virginia School Report, 1871: First Annual Report,* 166.

26. Entries for Claude Augustus Swanson and William G. Swanson, *Encyclopedia of Virginia Biography* (New York: Lewis Historical Publishing Co., 1915), vol. 3: 10–11, vol. 4: 937; quote from Parrish, "My Experiences in Self-Culture"; Beverley, "Tribute to a Great Leader"; Jack Irby Hayes Jr., *The Lamp and the Cross: A History of Averett College, 1859–2001* (Macon, Ga.: Mercer University Press, 2004), 21–32. College catalogs show that Mentora Parrish attended Roanoke College in 1872–73 and 1874–75 but never graduated. George W. Dame to Katherine Moses, July 25, 1875; July 20, 1877; and July 20, 1878, Katherine Spiller (Graves) Moses Papers, Section 2, VHS.

27. William ("Willie") Hankins to Virginia Hankins, July 10, 1878; Virginia Hankins to Louis Hankins, October 17, 1877; Virginia Hankins to Louis Hankins, September 8, 1880; Virginia Hankins to Louis Hankins, April 21, 1881; quote from Virginia Hankins to Louis Hankins, November 18, 1881, all from Hankins Family Papers, Section 18, VHS.

28. Maria Louisa Carrington to John and Elizabeth Dabney, December 8, 1867, Saunders Family Papers, Section 21, VHS; Virginia Hankins to Louis Hankins, August 27, 1880, and September 8, 1880, both from Hankins Family Papers, Section 18, VHS.

29. Quotes from Parrish, "My Experience in Self-Culture."

30. *Virginia School Report, 1871, First Annual Report,* 14–15, 132–42, quotes from 14. Statistics on the number of teachers by sex are from the state superintendents' summaries contained in the annual *Virginia School Report.*

31. Isabella M. E. Blandin, *History of Higher Education of Women in the South Prior to 1860* (New York: Neale Publishing, 1909); Heatwole, *History of Education in Virginia,* 127; "Education in Virginia," typed manuscript, Mary Cooke Branch Munford Papers, Box 13, Folder 8, Library of Virginia.

32. Jane Turner Censer, *North Carolina Planters and Their Children, 1800–1860* (Baton Rouge: Louisiana State University Press, 1984), 42–53; Farnham, *Education of the Southern Belle;* Fox-Genovese, *Within the Plantation Household,* 46–47, 255–59; Anya Jabour, "'Grown Girls, Highly Cultivated': Female Education in an Antebellum Southern Family," *Journal of Southern History* 64 (February 1998): 23–64, and "Albums of Affection: Female Friendship and Coming of Age in Antebellum Virginia," *Virginia Magazine of History and Biography* 107 (Spring 1999): 128–58; Steven M. Stowe, "'The Thing Is Not Its Vision': A Woman's Courtship and Her Sphere in the Southern Planter Class," *Feminist Studies* 9 (Spring 1983): 113–30, and "The Not-So-Cloistered Academy: Elite Women's Education and Family Feeling in the Old South," in *The Web of Southern Social Relations: Women, Family, and Education,* ed. Walter J. Fraser Jr. et al. (Athens: University of Georgia Press, 1985), 90–106.

33. *Virginia School Report, 1880, Tenth Annual Report,* 101–5; Heatwole, *History of Education in Virginia,* 235–38; Christine A. Ogren, *The American State Normal School: "An Instrument of Great Good"* (New York: Palgrave Macmillan, 2005), 20–21; *Virginia School Report, 1874: Fourth Annual Report of the Superintendent of Public Instruction* (Richmond, Va.: Superintendent of Public Printing, 1874), 39, 130.

34. Dailey, *Before Jim Crow,* 36–37; Lowe, *Republicans and Reconstruction in Virginia,* 160–81; Raymond H. Pulley, *Old Virginia Restored: An Interpretation of the Progressive Impulse, 1870–1930* (Charlottesville: University Press of Virginia, 1968), 32–34.

35. *Virginia School Report, 1872: Second Annual Report,* x; *Virginia School Report, 1874: Fourth Annual Report,* 117; *Virginia School Report, 1878: Eighth Annual Report of the Superintendent of Public Instruction* (Richmond, Va.: Superintendent of Public Printing, 1878), 1, 4–6; *Virginia School Report, 1879: Ninth Annual Report of the Superintendent of Public Instruction* (Richmond, Va.: Superintendent of Public Printing, 1879), 4, 10; Dailey, *Before Jim Crow,* 28–31; Charles Chilton Pearson, *The Readjuster Movement in Virginia* (Gloucester, Mass.: Peter Smith, 1969), 26–31.

36. *Journal of the House of Delegates of the State of Virginia for the Session of 1877–78* (Richmond, Va.: Superintendent of Public Printing, 1877), 428; Robert L. Dabney, "The Negro and the Common School" and "The State Free School System Imposed Upon Virginia by the Underwood Constitution," rpt. in *Discussions* (Presbyterian Committee of Publication, 1890), vol. 4: *Secular,* 176–90, 191–99, first quote from 176, second quote from 185; Barnas Sears, *Objections to Public Schools Considered: Remarks of the Trustees of the Peabody Education Fund* (Boston: John Wilson & Son, 1875), William Henry Ruffner Circulars, Special Collections, Library of Virginia.

37. James T. Moore, *Two Paths to the New South: The Virginia Debt Controversy, 1870–1883* (1974; rpt. Lexington: University Press of Kentucky, 2014), 58–64; Moore, "Black Militancy in Readjuster Virginia," 167–86; Peter J. Rachleff, *Black Labor in Richmond, 1865–1890* (Urbana: University of Illinois Press, 1989), 86–103; Jane Dailey, "Deference and Violence in the Postbellum Urban South: Manners and Massacres in Danville, Virginia," *Journal of Southern History* 63 (August 1997): 553–90.

38. *Virginia School Report, 1884: Fourteenth Annual Report,* 158; *Virginia School Report, 1886: Sixteenth Annual Report of the Superintendent of Public Instruction for the Year Ending July 31, 1886*

(Richmond, Va.: Superintendent of Public Printing, 1886), 192; "Reminiscences for the Twenty-Fifth Anniversary at Farmville," *The Virginian*, State Normal School Yearbook for 1909, 37; *Report Concerning the State Normal School at Farmville, December 10, 1885*, House Document II, 4, Longwood University Archives, Farmville, Va.; Taylor, *The Negro in the Reconstruction of Virginia*, 160–63. In the 1870 census, only 4 of 145 women from veteran families in Pittsylvania County who had formal occupations were listed as teachers, suggesting that most financially strapped women initially lacked the education necessary to teach, as noted by McClurken in *Taking Care of the Living*, 62.

39. *Report Concerning the State Normal School at Farmville*; quotes from Parrish, "My Experience in Self-Culture."

40. *Virginia School Report, 1882: Twelfth Annual Report*, 59, 64–65; *Virginia School Report, 1884, Fourteenth Annual Report*, 140–42; Lowe, *Republicans and Reconstruction in Virginia*, 184; Moore, "Black Militancy in Readjuster Virginia," 179; Rachleff, *Black Labor in Richmond*, 103–4. In "Black Militancy in Readjuster Virginia," Moore overestimated the real increase in black schools by using the 1878–79 term, when roughly half of schools were closed, as the beginning point.

41. *Virginia School Report, 1878: Eighth Annual Report*, 2–3; *Virginia School Report, 1885: Fifteenth Annual Report*, pt. 1: 238; *Virginia School Report, 1900 and 1901: Biennial Report of the Superintendent of Public Instruction* (Richmond, Va.: Superintendent of Public Printing, 1901), xiv; Writers Program of the Work Projects Administration in the State of Virginia, *The Negro in Virginia* (1940; rpt. Winston-Salem, N.C.: John F. Blair, 1994), 297–98; Fairclough, *A Class of Their Own*, 63–66.

42. *Coalition Rule in Danville*, broadside, Special Collections, Library of Virginia. Jane Daily explains the exaggerations and inaccuracies of *Coalition Rule in Danville*, many of which have been repeated as fact by historians of the Readjuster movement, in *Before Jim Crow*, 114–116.

43. "Report of the Committee on Privileges and Elections," *Reports of Committees of the Senate of the United States for the First Session of the Forty-Eighth Congress, 1883–84* (Washington, D.C.: Government Printing Office, 1884), vol. 6, report no. 579: iii–vi, quote from vi; Walter T. Calhoun, "The Danville Riot and Its Repercussions on the Virginia Election of 1883," *Publications in History* (Greenville, N.C.: East Carolina College, 1966), vol. 3: 25–51; Allen W. Moger, *Virginia, Bourbonism to Byrd, 1870–1925* (Charlottesville: University Press of Virginia, 1968), 51–54.

44. *Coalition Rule in Danville*; quote from *The Democratic Campaign*, October 29, 1883, as cited in Calhoun, "The Danville Riot," 37.

45. "Report of the Committee on Privileges and Elections," xi–xv, xxi–xxii, xxv–xxvi, xl–xli; quotes from Parrish, "My Experience in Self-Culture," 3; Dailey, "Deference and Violence in the Postbellum Urban South"; Moger, *Virginia, Bourbonism to Byrd*, 55; Moore, *Two Paths to the New South*, 116–17.

46. Moore, *Two Paths to the New South*, 99–103. Pittsylvania County Superintendent George W. Dame thought that white teachers could help the black race "to know its place and to occupy its true position in society," *Virginia School Report, 1880: Tenth Annual Report*, 71.

47. Dailey, *Before Jim Crow*, 92–102.

48. James B. McKee, *Sociology and the Race Problem: The Failure of a Perspective* (Urbana: University of Illinois Press, 1993), 22–27; Williamson, *Crucible of Race*, 119–24.

49. William Ruffner, "The Negro," in *The Free Public School System*, 6–11, booklet, Library of Virginia; "The Co-Education of the Races Improper, as Well as Impossible," *Virginia School Report, 1874: Fourth Annual Report*, 146–55, first quote from 147, second quote from 151; "Superintendent Ruffner's Address," *Educational Journal of Virginia* XI (March 1880): 90–100, clipping from

William Henry Ruffner Papers, Folder 4, Library of Virginia; *Virginia School Report, 1882: Twelfth Annual Report*, third quote from 65. Ruffner's opinions on hereditary racial traits drew upon the research of Dr. William B. Carpenter, *Principles of Mental Physiology* (London: Henry S. King & Co., 1874).

50. "Co-Education of the Races," *Virginia School Report, 1874: Fourth Annual Report*; Samuel C. Armstrong, "Labor as a Moral Force," *Virginia School Report, 1884*, 125–26; Anderson, *Education of Blacks in the South*, 35–42. In 1876, Ruffner nonsensically observed that education made black children "more industrious, as well as more capable, more honest and more virtuous; whilst socially they are not brought any nearer to the whites than they were before," in "The Negro," 10.

51. Parrish, "Problems and Progress of Universal Education," 52–53, quotes from 52; George W. Dame to William H. Ruffner, January 23, 1882, Folder 5, William Henry Ruffner Papers, Library of Virginia; James T. Moore, "The University and the Readjusters," *Virginia Magazine of History and Biography* 78 (January 1970): 87–101.

CHAPTER TWO

1. Karen J. Blair, *The Clubwoman as Feminist: True Womanhood Redefined, 1868–1914* (New York: Homes & Meier, 1980), 15–29, 45–51; Ruth Bordin, *Women at Michigan: The "Dangerous Experiment," 1870s to the Present* (Ann Arbor: University of Michigan Press, 1999), 2–13; James Orton, ed., *The Liberal Education of Women: The Demand and the Method, Current Thoughts in America and England* (New York: A. S. Barnes & Co., 1873); Solomon, *In the Company of Educated Women*, 41–45, 52–53; Elizabeth Cady Stanton, "The Solitude of Self," *Selected Papers of Elizabeth Cady Stanton and Susan B. Anthony*, vol. 5: *Their Place Inside the Body-Politic, 1887–1895*, ed. Ann D. Gordon (New Brunswick, N.J.: Rutgers University Press, 2009), ed. Ann D. Gordon, 423–36; Rosenberg, *Beyond Separate Spheres*, 5–11; W. Le Conte Stevens, *The Admission of Women to Universities* (New York: Association for Promoting the Higher Education of Women in New York, 1883), 15.

2. William A. Hammond, "Brain-Forcing in Childhood," *Popular Science Monthly* 30 (April 1887): 721–32, first quote from 731, and "Men's and Women's Brains," *Popular Science Monthly* 31 (August 1887): 554–58, second quote from 554; Kathi L. Kern, "Gray Matters: Brains, Identities, and Natural Rights," *The Social and Political Body* (New York: Guilford Press, 1996), ed. Theodore R. Schatski and Wolfgang Natter, 103–21.

3. Carl N. Degler, *In Search of Human Nature: The Decline and Revival of Darwinism in American Social Thought* (New York: Oxford University Press, 1991), 16–30; Gregory Michael Door, *Segregation's Science: Eugenics and Society in Virginia* (Charlottesville: University of Virginia Press, 2008), 21–24, 50; Jeanne L. Noble, *The Negro Woman's College Education* (New York: Columbia University Teachers College Press, 1950), 18–22.

4. James H. Fairchild, "The Experience of Oberlin College," 238–56; Jonathan Blanchard, "The Experience at Knox College," 261–65; James Orton, "Vassar College," 272–85; John Raymond, "The Demand of the Age for a Liberal Education for Women, and How It Should Be Met," 47–57, second quote from 49, all rpt. in Orton, ed., *Liberal Education of Women*. Stevens, *Admission of Women to Universities*, first quote from 17.

5. *Virginia School Report, 1873: Third Annual Report of the Superintendent of Public Instruction, for the Year Ending August 31, 1873* (Richmond, Va.: Superintendent of Public Printing, 1873), first quote from 14; *Virginia School Report, 1879: Ninth Annual Report*, 29–43, remaining quotes from

39. After stepping down as superintendent, Ruffin continued to push for a female university comparable to the University of Virginia, as seen in his speech to county superintendents, *Virginia School Report, 1885: Fifteenth Annual Report*, pt. 3: 38.

6. Quotes from Parrish, "My Experience in Self-Culture"; *Virginia School Report, 1880: Tenth Annual Report*, 102–7; *Educational Journal of Virginia* 2 (August 1880): 290.

7. William Arthur Maddox, *The Free School Idea in Virginia Before the Civil War: A Phase of Political and Social Evolution* (New York: Columbia University Teachers College, 1918), first quote from 139; first report of the State Normal School, *Virginia School Report, 1885: Fifteenth Annual Report*, appendix, 9–15, second quote from 15; *Acts and Joint Resolutions Passed by the General Assembly of the State of Virginia during the Session of 1883–1884* (Richmond, Va.: Superintendent of Public Printing, 1884), 417–18; letter, W. H. Ruffner to Grover Cleveland, November 27, 1885, Folder 5, William Henry Ruffner Papers, Library of Virginia. *Virginia School Report, 1879: Ninth Annual Report*, 41–43; Mary E. Whitney, *Women and the University* (Charlottesville: University of Virginia, 1969), 10–12.

8. "Reminiscences for the Twenty-Fifth Anniversary at Farmville," quotes from 29; *Catalog of the State Female Normal School, at Farmville, Virginia, Second Session, 1885–1886* (Richmond, Va.: Haughman Bros., 1886), 10–11.

9. Whitney, *Women and the University*, 6–8, 12–17, quote from faculty-meeting minutes as cited on 14.

10. First report of the State Normal School, 5; W. H. Ruffner, *What Are the Normal Schools in Fact?* booklet, Library of Virginia; "Report of the Principal," handwritten manuscript of Ruffin's report to the SFNS Board of Trustees, Longwood University Archives; "What a Normal Is," *Staunton Vindicator*, April 15, 1886. Since Parrish received free tuition as a public schoolteacher, she must have needed part-time employment to pay room and board.

11. *Catalog of SFNS, 1885–'86* (Richmond, Va.: Haughman Bros., 1886); handwritten ledger, *Minutes of the Board of Trustees, April 9, 1884–April 21, 1896*, entry for June 22, 1887, 80–82, quote from 81, Longwood University Archives.

12. *Minutes of the Board of Trustees*, entry for June 4, 1886, 61; letter, Celeste E. Bush to her parents, December 21, 1884, both in Longwood University Archives. Rosemary Sprague, *Longwood College: A History* (Farmville, Va.: Longwood College, 1989), 60–61.

13. *Minutes of the Board of Trustees*, entries for June 22, 1887, 82–91, Longwood University Archives.

14. Jurgen Herbst, *And Sadly Teach: Teacher Education and Professionalization in American Culture* (Madison: University of Wisconsin Press, 1989); Ogren, *American State Normal School*, 25–29; Shirley Kreason Strout, *The History of Zeta Tau Alpha, 1898–1948* (Menasha, Wis.: Collegiate Press, for the Fraternity, 1956), 23; Carter G. Woodson, *The Mis-Education of the Negro* (1933; rpt. Mineola, N.Y.: Dover, 2005), 72–74.

15. "Reminiscences for the Twenty-Fifth Anniversary at Farmville," quote from 32; *Virginia School Report, 1887: Seventeenth Annual Report of the Superintendent of Public Instruction of the State of Virginia, with Accompanying Documents* (Richmond, Va.: Superintendent of Public Printing, 1887), pt. 2: 81–82; *Virginia School Report, 1888: Eighteenth Annual Report of the Superintendent of Public Instruction of the Commonwealth of Virginia, with Accompanying Documents* (Richmond, Va.: E. T. Walthall, 1888), pt. 2: 41–42; Sprague, *Longwood College*, 64–67; E. L. Fox, "Dr. W. H. Ruffner," *John P. Branch Historical Papers of Randolph-Macon College* 3 (June 1910): 143–44.

16. U.S. Census returns for Richmond, 1870 and 1880; list of former graduates, *Catalogue of the University of Nashville: State Normal College, Session of 1887–1888* (Nashville: Wheeler Publishing, 1888), 43.

17. Annual Report of the State Normal School, *Annual Reports of Officers, Boards, and Institutions of the Commonwealth of Virginia for the Year Ending September 30, 1886* (Richmond, Va.: Superintendent of Public Printing, 1886), 5. *Educational Journal of Virginia* 17 (February 1886): 74–81, vol. 17 (April 1886): 268–69, vol. 19 (June 1888): 272–73, vol. 20 (June 1889): 272–73. *Virginia School Report, 1886: Sixteenth Annual Report,* quote from 25, emphasis in original. *Virginia School Report, 1887: Seventeenth Annual Report,* 39–41. Of the southern states. Virginia received the second-largest appropriations from the Peabody Education Fund, in part because its general agent, J. L. M. Curry, was a former professor of Richmond College and married to a Richmond woman. Curry also briefly served as the first president of the SFNS Board of Trustees.

18. Parrish, "My Experience in Self-Culture"; C. S. Parrish, "The Grading of Country Schools," *Educational Journal of Virginia* 19 (January 1888): 1–4; *Virginia School Report, 1886: Sixteenth Annual Report,* 37–39, quote from 38.

19. *Catalog of SFNS, 1885–'86,* quote from 12; Ogren, *American State Normal School,* 91. Lists and descriptions of institute instructors for each year can be found in the state school superintendents' annual reports and in the *Educational Journal of Virginia,* which became the *Virginia School Journal* in 1892.

20. *Virginia School Journal* 8 (October 1899): 260–62.

21. *Educational Journal of Virginia* 22 (January 1891): 43–45, 22 (December 1891): 529–537; Dabney, *Universal Education in the South* 1: 139n9.

22. *Educational Journal of Virginia* 21 (March 1891): 101–4, first three quotes from 102, remaining quotes from 103.

23. Program of the State Educational Association and Conference of Superintendents of Schools of Virginia, *Virginia School Report, 1891: Twenty-First Annual Report of the Superintendent of Public Instruction of the Commonwealth of Virginia, with Accompanying Documents* (Richmond, Va.: Superintendent of Public Printing, 1891), 216–18, quote from 217; U.S. Census records from Virginia show that R. C. Saunders was born in 1827 and George Blick in 1843.

24. Ibid., quotes from 218.

25. All the officers and members of the executive committee for 1891–92 were men (*Virginia School Report, 1891,* 240); *Educational Journal of Virginia* 22 (December 1891): 535–37, quotes from 537; William Henry Stewart, *History of Norfolk County, Virginia, and Representative Citizens* (Chicago: Biographical Publishing Co., 1902), 1031–32.

26. *Virginia School Report, 1892 and 1893: Biennial Report of the Superintendent of Public Instruction of the Commonwealth of Virginia, with Accompanying Documents* (Richmond, Va.: Superintendent of Public Printing, 1893), first quote from xxxviii, second quote xxxviii–xxxix; *Virginia School Journal* 1 (September 1892): 213; *Virginia School Journal* 2 (December 1893): 330.

27. Lucy Irvine, "Memories of the Days Spent in Farmville," typed manuscript, Longwood University Archives; Jurgen Herbst, "Nineteenth-Century Normal Schools in the United States: A Fresh Look," *History of Education* 9 (July 2006): 219–27; *Virginia School Report, 1892–1893, Biennial Report,* xiv; *Virginia School Journal* 2 (February 1893): 45–46, quote from 45.

28. U.S. Census returns for Virginia, 1870 and 1880; Morehouse, "'Georgia's Greatest Woman' Buried in Clayton."

29. *Minutes of the SFNS Board of Trustees, April 9, 1884–April 21, 1896*, 81, Longwood University Archives; *Report of the Commissioner of Education for the Year 1891–'92*, (Washington, D.C.: Government Printing Office, 1894), vol. 2: 945–50; Parrish, "My Experience in Self-Culture," quote from 3; Bordin, *Women at Michigan*, 5–6, 9–13, 19–20.

30. Cornelius, *History of RMWC*, 10–11, 31, 46–47; quote from Creswell, "Personal Recollections of Celeste Parrish."

31. Report of the University of Virginia for 1892, *Virginia School Report, 1892 and 1893, Biennial Report*, 97–99; *Minutes of the General Faculty* 13: 411–12, Albert and Shirley Small Special Collections Library, University of Virginia; letter, Fannie Littleton Kline to Roberta Hollingsworth, University of Virginia Library Online Exhibits, accessed September 2, 2015, explore.lib.virginia .edu/items/show/2657; Whitney, *Women and the University*, 18–22; Mary R. S. Creese, *Ladies in the Laboratory: American and British Women in Science, 1800–1900* (Lanham, Md.: Scarecrow Press, 1998), 260.

32. Parrish, "Women in the University of Virginia," *Virginia School Journal* 2 (January 1893): 7–8, quotes from 7.

33. Ibid., first three quotes from 8; *Virginia School Journal* 2 (November 1893): 294–95, second two quotes from 295; Report of the Peabody Institutes for 1893, *Virginia School Report, 1892 and 1893, Biennial Report*, 351–52.

34. Report of the University of Virginia for 1893, *Virginia School Report, 1892 and 1893, Biennial Report*, 395–97, first quote from 396; Whitney, *Women and the University*, 27–29, second quote from 29.

35. *Minutes of the General Faculty* 13: 408–20, all quotes from 417; letter, William H. Payne to J. L. M. Curry, *Educational Journal of Virginia* 22 (November 1891): 484–85. Davis argued that proponents of coeducation were biased in their assessments of its effectiveness, while its opponents were disinterested and objective parties.

36. *Minutes of the General Faculty*, second quote from 416, first and third quotes from 417.

37. Charles W. Kent, *Address by Prof. Charles W. Kent of the University of Va., at Hollins Institute, June 6th, 1894, 51st Commencement Day*, Special Collections, University of Virginia Libraries, Charlottesville, first two quotes from 3, third quote from 5, fourth and fifth quotes from 9; Whitney, *Women and the University*, 28–29.

38. *University of Virginia Faculty Minutes* 13, June 4, 1894, quote from 418; Robert Williamson, "Co-Education of the Sexes," *Virginia School Journal* 2 (February 1893): 45–46.

39. Kent, *Address*, 5, first quote from 9; second quote from Orra Langhorne, "Coeducation in Virginia," [Boston] *Woman's Journal*, July 21, 1894, 229; *Virginia School Report, 1894 and 1895: Biennial Report of the Superintendent of Public Instruction of the Commonwealth of Virginia, with Accompanying Documents* (Richmond, Va.: Superintendent of Public Printing, 1895), 97.

40. Langhorne, "Coeducation in Virginia"; Orra Langhorne, "Virginia," *The Woman's Journal*, August 8, 1896, quote from 256; Langhorne's report on Virginia in *Proceedings of the Twenty-Seventh Annual Convention of the National-American Woman Suffrage Association held in Atlanta, GA, January 31st to February 5th, 1895* (Warren, Ohio: W. M. Ritezel & Co., 1895), 94–95; Susan B. Anthony and Ida Husted Harper, eds., *The History of Woman Suffrage* (Indianapolis: Hollenbeck Press, 1900), vol. 4: 964.

41. *Virginia School Journal* 3 (February 1894): 62; *Virginia School Journal* 3 (May 1894): 151–52, quotes from 152; "William A. Fentress," in *Report of the Eleventh Annual Meeting of the Virginia*

State Bar Association, Held at the Hot Springs of Virginia, August 1, 2, & 3rd, 1899 (Richmond, Va.: Everett Waddey Co., 1899), ed. Eugene C. Massie, 110. Fentress died in 1898 one day before his thirty-second birthday and shortly before he was to be married.

42. Quote from Parrish, "My Experience in Self-Culture," 3; Robert W. Proctor and Rand Evans, "E. B. Titchener, Women Psychologists, and the Experimentalists," *American Journal of Psychology* 127 (Winter 2014): 501–26; Parrish, "Cutaneous Estimation of Open and Filled Space," 514–22; C. S. Parrish, "The Localisation of Cutaneous Impressions by Arm Movement Without Pressure Upon the Skin," *American Journal of Psychology* 8 (January 1897): 250–67.

43. Geoffrey O'Shea and Theodore R. Bashore Jr., "The Vital Role of *The American Journal of Psychology* in the Early and Continuing History of Mental Chronometry," *American Journal of Psychology* 125 (Winter 2012): 435–48; Green, "Scientific Objectivity and E. B. Titchener's Experimental Psychology," 697–721.

44. Quote from Parrish, "My Experience in Self-Culture"; letter, G. D. Haupin to Helen Peak, March 1, 1939, Randolph-Macon Women's College Archives, Lynchburg, Va.

45. Ludy T. Benjamin Jr., "The Psychology Laboratory at the Turn of the 20th Century," *American Psychologist* 55 (March 2000): 318–21; Murray and Rowe, "Psychology Laboratories in the United States Prior to 1900," 19–21, and "A Note on the Titchener Influence on the First Psychology Laboratory in the South," *Journal of the History of the Behavioral Sciences* 15 (July 1979): 282–84; Peak, "The Parrish Laboratories of Psychology at Randolph-Macon Woman's College," 551–53.

46. A. Tolman Smith, "The Psychological Revival," in *Report of the Commissioner of Education for the Year 1893–1894* (Washington, D.C.: Government Printing Office, 1896), vol. 1: 429–30; "Report of the [NEA] Subcommittee on the Training of Teachers," in *Report of the Commissioner of Education, 1893–94* 1: 472–87; *Report of the Commissioner of Education, 1893–94* 2: 2035; *Randolph-Macon Woman's College Catalog, 1893–94, Announcements, 1894–95* (Lynchburg, Va.: J. P. Bell Co., 1894), 21–23; Cornelius, *History of RMWC*, quote from 47.

47. Emily S. Davidson and Ludy T. Benjamin Jr., "A History of the Child Study Movement in America," in *Historical Foundations of Educational Psychology* (New York: Plenum Press, 1987), ed. John A Glover and Royce R. Ronning, 41–60; Smith, "Psychological Revival," 431; G. Stanley Hall, "The New Psychology as a Basis of Education," *The Forum* 17 (August 1894): 710–20, quote from 716.

48. James Mark Baldwin, "Child Study," *Psychological Review* 5 (March 1898): 218–20; Nicholas Murray Butler, Editorial, *Educational Review* 12 (November 1896): 411–13; G. Stanley Hall, "Child-Study and Its Relation to Education," *The Forum* 29 (August 1900): 688–702, quote from 700; Dorothy Ross, *G. Stanley Hall: The Psychologist as Prophet* (Chicago: University of Chicago Press, 1972), 286–87.

49. Hugo Münsterberg, "The Danger from Experimental Psychology," *Atlantic Monthly* 81 (February 1898): 159–67, first two quotes from 165; Hugo Münsterberg, "Psychology and Education," *Educational Review* 16 (September 1898): 105–19; Erwin V. Johanningmeier, "William Chandler Bagley's Changing Views on the Relationship between Psychology and Education," *History of Education Quarterly* 9 (Spring 1969): 3–27; Celeste Parrish, "Child Study," *Southern Educational Journal* 12 (February 1899): 121–32, third and fourth quotes from 125 and 126.

50. Quote from Maria Louisa Carrington to Elizabeth Dabney, October 11, 1868, Saunders Family Papers, Section 21, VHS.

CHAPTER THREE

1. Wendy J. Deichmann Edwards and Carolyn De Swarte Gifford, "Restoring Women and Reclaiming Gender in Social Gospel Studies," in *Gender and the Social Gospel* (Urbana: University of Illinois Press, 2003), ed. Edwards and Gifford, 1–17; Carolyn De Swarte Gifford, "'The Woman's Cause is Man's': Frances Willard and the Social Gospel," in *Gender and the Social Gospel*, 21–34; Ronald C. White Jr. and C. Howard Hopkins, *The Social Gospel: Religion and Reform in Changing America* (Philadelphia: Temple University Press, 1976), 132–38; Higginbotham, *Righteous Discontent*, 31–46; Elna C. Green, *Southern Strategies: Southern Women and the Woman Suffrage Question* (Chapel Hill: University of North Carolina Press, 1997), 19–22; Wheeler, *New Women of the New South*, 53–54.

2. Wayne Flynt, "Southern Methodists and Social Reform, 1900–1940," *International Social Science Review* 74, nos. 3 and 4 (1999): 104–14, and *Alabama Baptists: Southern Baptists in the Heart of Dixie* (Tuscaloosa: University of Alabama Press, 1998), 172–77, 267–68; Elizabeth Hayes Turner, *Women, Culture, and Community: Religion and Reform in Galveston, 1880–1920* (New York: Oxford University Press, 1997); Mary Martha Thomas, *The New Woman in Alabama: Social Reforms and Suffrage, 1890–1920* (Tuscaloosa: University of Alabama Press, 1992); John Patrick McDowell, *The Social Gospel in the South: The Woman's Home Mission Movement in the Methodist Episcopal Church, South, 1886–1939* (Baton Rouge: Louisiana State University Press, 1982), 21–38; Anne Firor Scott, "Women, Religion, and Social Change in the South, 1830–1930," in *Religion and the Solid South*, ed. Samuel S. Hill Jr. et al. (New York: Abingdon Press, 1972), 92–121.

3. Samuel S. Hill Jr., "The South's Two Cultures," in *Religion and the Solid South*, ed. Hill et al., 36–49; Bill T. Leonard, *Baptists in America* (New York: Columbia University Press, 2005), 205–12; Mary Beth Mathews, "'To Educate, Agitate, and Legislate': Baptists, Methodists, and the Anti-Saloon League of Virginia, 1901–1910," *Virginia Magazine of History and Biography* 17 (2009): 254–55; Higginbotham, *Righteous Discontent*, 58–78.

4. "Women's Missionary Society," *Baltimore Sun*, October 26, 1898; Juliette Mather, *Light Three Candles: History of Woman's Missionary Union of Virginia, 1874–1973* (Richmond, Va.: Woman's Missionary Union of Virginia, Baptist General Association of Virginia, 1972), 27–59, quote from 35; *Religious Herald*, October 8, 1970, 17.

5. Celestia S. Parrish, "Address of Welcome," *Publications of the Association of Collegiate Alumnae*, ser. 3, no. 13: 7–9, quotes from 8.

6. *Maconiana, 1899* (Lynchburg, Va.: Randolph Macon Woman's College, 1899), 21, 27; Mary Fitzhugh Eggleston and Maud Pollard Turman, "History, Fifty Years of the June Class 1894 of State Female Normal School, now State Teachers College of Farmville, Virginia," typed manuscript, Longwood University Archives, 4–5; Cornelius, *History of RMWC*, first quote from 53, second quote from 34.

7. Eggleston and Turman, "History, Fifty Years of the June Class 1894," quote from 5; letter, Jean Carruther to family, December 24, 1885, Longwood University Archives; Hayes, *The Lamp and the Cross*, 21–29; Munford, "Education in Virginia," 34–39.

8. Larew, "Celestia Parrish," *Virginia Journal of Education* 35 (May 1942): 342–46, quote from 346.

9. Virginia State Teachers College *Bulletin* 28 (February 1942): 7–8, first and second quotes from 7; Nellie Virginia Powell, "Our Master Builders," Randolph-Macon Woman's College *Alumnae Bulletin* 36 (September 1943): 20–21, third and fourth quotes from 21.

10. John W. Boyer, *"Broad and Christian in the Fullest Sense": William Rainey Harper and the University of Chicago* (Chicago: College of the University of Chicago, 2005), first quote as cited on 129; Nicholas Murray Butler, "Democracy and Education," *Educational Review* 12 (September 1896): 120–32; Thomas Wakefield Goodspeed, *A History of the University of Chicago: The First Quarter-Century* (Chicago: University of Chicago Press, 1916), 12–30, 101–3; William Rainey Harper, "The University and Democracy," [University of California] *University Chronicle* 2 (April 1899): 65–88, second and third quotes from 66; Richard J. Storr, *Harper's University: The Beginnings* (Chicago: University of Chicago Press, 1966), 31–35, 40–43.

11. Deegan, *Jane Addams and the Men of the Chicago School*, 1–5, and *Annie Marion MacLean and the Chicago Schools of Sociology*, 65–70; Fitzpatrick, *Endless Crusade*, 32–33, 54–60, 78–79; Goodspeed, *History of the University of Chicago*, 136–37.

12. Deegan, *Jane Addams and the Men of the Chicago School*, 55–67, 247–56; Deegan, *Annie Marion MacLean*, 58–61, 73–97; Caroline M. Hill, ed., *Mary E. McDowell and Municipal Housekeeping: A Symposium* (Chicago: Millar Publishing, 1938); Mary Jo Deegan, Michael R. Hill, and Susan L. Wortmann, "Annie Marion MacLean, Feminist Pragmatist and Methodologist," *Journal of Contemporary Ethnography* 38 (December 2009): 655–65.

13. Rosenberg, *Beyond Separate Spheres*, xvi–xviii; Rossiter, *Women Scientists in America*, 64–65; Marion Talbot, *More Than Lore: Reminiscences of Marion Talbot* (1936; rpt. Chicago: University of Chicago Press, 2015), foreword by Hanna Holborn Gray, 85–86; "An Historical Sketch," *President's Report, July 1897–July 1898, with Summaries for 1891–1897* (Chicago: University of Chicago Press, 1899), quote from 7.

14. Alice Lloyd diary, first quote from entry for November 5, 1901, Alice Lloyd Papers, Folder 3, Special Collections Research Center, University of Chicago Library (hereafter Lloyd Papers); University of Chicago *University Record* 2, no. 32 (November 5, 1897): 256; *University of Chicago Weekly* 6, no. 43 (August 18, 1898), second and third quotes from 447; Goodspeed, *History of the University of Chicago*, 141, 156, 391.

15. *University of Chicago Weekly*, July 7, 1898, p. 388; July 14, 1898, p. 400; July 28, 1898, p. 420; August 4, 1898, p. 430; and August 11, 1898, p. 438. In the summer of 1898 female enrollment included 33 southern women and 176 non-southerners, as documented in "The Women of the University," University of Chicago *President's Report, July 1897–July 1898*, 118.

16. Ellen Fitzpatrick, "For the 'Women of the University': Marion Talbot, 1858–1948," in *Lone Voyagers: Academic Women in Coeducational Universities, 1870–1937* (New York: Feminist Press of CUNY, 1989), ed. Geraldine JonÐich Clifford, 87–97; Marion Talbot, "The Duty and the Opportunity of the Association of Collegiate Alumnae," *Michigan Alumnus* (November 1897): 3–14; Marion Talbot, *The Education of Women* (Chicago: University of Chicago Press, 1910), 225–27, quote from 226; Talbot and Rosenberry, *History of the American Association of University Women*, 6–14.

17. "The University of Chicago Settlement League," *President's Annual Report, July 1897–July 1898*, 217–19; *University Record* 4, no. 43 (January 26, 1900): 298–99; Deegan, *Annie Marion MacLean*, 74–76; Maureen Flanagan, "Gender and Urban Political Reform: The City Club and the Woman's City Club of Chicago in the Progressive Era," *American Historical Review* 95 (October 1990): 1032–50; Goodspeed, *History of the University of Chicago*, 447–48; Gordon, *Gender and Higher Education in the Progressive Era*, 1–4, 88–89; Marion Talbot, *History of the Chicago Association of Collegiate Alumnae, 1882–1917* (Chicago: The Association, 1917).

18. Jane Addams, "A New Impulse to an Old Gospel," *Forum* (November 1892): 345–58, and "The College Woman and Christianity," *The Independent*, August 8, 1901, 1852–55; "The University

Settlement," *Annual Register, July 1899–July 1900* (Chicago: University of Chicago Press, 1900), first quote from 143; Susan Curtis, *A Consuming Faith: The Social Gospel and Modern American Culture* (1991; rpt. Columbia: University of Missouri Press, 2001), 24–31, 156–62, second quote from 158, third quote from 161.

19. Letter, Madeline Wallin to Keyes Wallin, December 12, 1892, Madeline Wallin Papers, Special Collections Research Center, University of Chicago Library, Folder 3 (hereafter Wallin Papers); letter, Madeline Wallin to Keyes Wallin, January 15, 1893, Folder 4, Wallin Papers; quotes from clipping, "Social Settlements: A New Philanthropy," Folder 17, Wallin Papers; Westbrook, *John Dewey and American Democracy*, 79–82.

20. Rosenberg, *Beyond Separate Spheres*, 68–80. Parrish's Baptist loyalties presented no obstacle to accepting this integration of scientific and religious goals, since nineteenth-century Baptist educational institutions commonly combined a modern curriculum with Christian moral instruction. See John M. Heffron, "'To Form a More Perfect Union': The Moral Example of Southern Baptist Thought and Education, 1890–1920," *Religion and American Culture: A Journal of Interpretation* 8 (Summer 1998): 179–204.

21. Celeste S. Parrish, "The Education of Girls: First Paper," *Religious Herald* 73, no. 5: 2.

22. First quote from Celeste S. Parrish, "The Education of Girls: Sixth Paper," *Religious Herald* 73, no. 12: 2; second quote from Parrish, "The Education of Girls: Second Paper," *Religious Herald* 73, no. 6: 2; Parrish, "The Education of Girls: Fourth Paper," *Religious Herald* 73, no. 10: 3; Parrish, "The Education of Girls: Fifth Paper," *Religious Herald* 73, no. 11: 3.

23. All quotes from Parrish, "The Education of Girls: Third Paper," *Religious Herald* 73, no. 9: 2.

24. First two quotes from Parrish, "The Education of Girls: Third Paper"; remaining quotes from Parrish, "The Education of Girls: Sixth Paper," 2.

25. All quotes from Parrish, "The Education of Girls: Sixth Paper."

26. John Dewey, "Ethical Principles Underlying Education," *Third Yearbook of the National Herbart Society* (Chicago: The Society, 1897), 7–33, first quote from 24; Dewey, "My Pedagogic Creed," 3–18, second and third quotes from 18.

27. Daniel M. Savage, *John Dewey's Liberalism: Individual, Community, and Self-Development* (Carbondale: Southern Illinois University Press, 2002); Seigfried, *Pragmatism and Feminism*; Jane Addams, *Democracy and Social Ethics* (New York: Macmillan Co., 1902). Jane Addams discussed the family claim in "A New Impulse to an Old Gospel."

28. M. Carey Thomas, "The Association of Collegiate Alumnae and Its Relation to Women's Education," *Publications of the Association of Collegiate Alumnae*, ser. 3, no. 1 (December 1898): 40–46, quote from 41.

29. Parrish, "Problems and Progress of Universal Education," 48–61, first three quotes from 53, remaining quotes from 59.

30. Ibid., first two quotes from 55, remaining quotes from 56.

31. Parrish, "Some Defects in the Education of Women in the South," 45–55; Parrish, "Education of Women in the South," 45–56. On the southern universities open to women and the restrictions that limited female enrollment, see McCandless, *The Past in the Present*, 83–100.

32. Richard J. Tighe, "The Southern Educational Association," in *National Educational Association Fiftieth Anniversary Volume, 1857–1906* (Winona, Minn.: The Association, 1907), 499–504; "Report of the Southern Educational Association," *Southern Educational Journal* 12 (January 1899): 81–98; *Southern Educational Association Journal of Proceedings and Addresses of the Ninth Annual Meeting, Held at Memphis, Tenn., December 27–29, 1899* (n.p.: The Association, 1899), 10–11; "To

Earnest Teachers in the Southern States and Elsewhere," *School and Home* 17 (December 1899): 90–91, first quote from 90; "Memphis Meeting," *Arkansas Democrat*, December 15, 1899; Parrish, "Problems and Progress of Universal Education," 55, second quote from 58; Dabney, *Universal Education in the South* 2: 3–12; Dennis, *Lessons in Progress*, 91–94.

33. Parrish, "Education of Women in the South," 47–49, 53–56, second quote from 55, remaining quotes from 56.

34. Ibid., first quote from 45; Parrish, "Some Defects in the Education of Women in the South," second and third quotes from 69, fourth quote from 70.

35. Parrish, "Some Defects in the Education of Women in the South," 70–72, 76, first three quotes from 71, remaining quotes from 72; Parrish, "Education of Women in the South," 53.

36. Parrish, "Some Defects in the Education of Women in the South," 71–76, first quote from 71, second quote from 72, remaining quotes from 76; Parrish, "Education of Women in the South," 52–53.

37. Henry T. Finck, "Are Womanly Women Doomed?" *The Independent* 53 (January 1901): 267–71, first quote f269, second quote 271; Parrish, "Womanly Woman," 775–78, third quote 777.

38. Parrish, "Womanly Woman," first and second quotes from 777, third quote from 778.

39. Parrish, "Woman's Problems," 2582–85, first quote 2584; second, third. and fourth quotes from 2582; fifth quote from 2585.

40. G. Stanley Hall, "Coeducation in the High School," *National Educational Association Journal of Proceedings and Addresses, 1903* (Winona, Minn.: The Association, 1903), 446–60, second quote 451; G. Stanley Hall, "Feminization in School and Home: The Undue Influence of Women Teachers—The Need of Different Training for the Sexes," *World's Work* 16 (1908): 10237–44, first quote 10240; G. Stanley Hall, *Adolescence: Its Psychology and Its Relation to Physiology, Anthropology, Sociology, Sex, Crime, Religion and Education* (1904; rpt. New York: Appleton & Co., 1921), vol. 2: 590–92, 602–6.

41. Hall, "Feminization in School and Home," 10238; Shaun Johnson, "The Woman Peril and Male Teachers in the Early Twentieth Century," *American Educational History Journal* 35 (2008): 149–67; David Tyack and Elisabeth Hansot, *Learning Together: A History of Coeducation in American Public Schools* (New Haven, Conn.: Yale University Press, 1990), 154–59, 163–64, 207. Male educators were alarmed at the growing militancy of female schoolteachers, who were forming unions and confronting the male leadership of the National Education Association to force officials to address issues of gender discrimination. Jill Bystydzienski, "Women's Participation in Teachers' Unions in England and the United States," in *Women Educators: Employees of Schools in Western Countries* (Albany: State University of New York Press, 1987), ed. Patricia A. Schmuck, 151–72; David B. Tyack, *The One Best System: A History of American Urban Education* (Cambridge, Mass.: Harvard University Press, 1974), 64–65, 255–68.

42. Solomon, *In the Company of Educated Women*, 58–60; Rosalind Rosenberg, "The Limits of Access: The History of Coeducation in America," in *Women and Higher Education in American History*, ed. John Mack Faragher and Florence Howe (New York: W. W. Norton, 1988), 107–29; Linda Perkins, "The Impact of the 'Cult of True Womanhood' on the Education of Black Women," *Journal of Social Issues* 39 (October 1983): 17–28.

43. Gordon, *Gender and Higher Education*, 43–44, 112–17, quote as cited on 114; Talbot, *More Than Lore*, 115–19.

44. John Dewey, "Is Coeducation Injurious to Girls," *Ladies Home Journal* 28 (June 1911): 22, 60–61; J. H. Tufts, "Feminization," *School Review* 17 (January 1909): 55–58; Deegan, *Jane Addams*

and the Men of the Chicago School, 2–3, 36–37; Talbot, *More Than Lore,* 85–89; White and Hopkins, *Social Gospel,* 132–38.

45. *Publications of the Association of Collegiate Alumnae,* ser. 3, no. 5 (February 1902): 34–38, quotes from 34; Laurel Furumoto and Elizabeth Scarborough, "Placing Women in the History of Psychology: The First American Women Psychologists," *American Psychologist* 41 (January 1986): 35–42; Ellen Kimmel, "Contributions to the History of Psychology: XXIV. Role of Women Psychologists in the History of Psychology in the South," *Psychological Reports* 38 (1976): 611–18; Maxine Seller, "G. Stanley Hall and Edward Thorndike on the Education of Women: Theory and Policy in the Progressive Era," *Educational Studies* 11 (1981): 365–74; Abigail J. Stewart and Andrea L. Dottolo, "Feminist Psychology," *Signs* 31 (Winter 2006): 493–509; Sue Wilkinson et al., *"Feminism & Psychology*: From Critique to Reconstruction," *Feminism & Psychology* 1: no. 1 (1991): 5–18.

46. Gail Bederman, *Manliness and Civilization: A Cultural History of Gender and Race in the United State, 1880–1917* (Chicago: University of Chicago Press, 1995), 10–30, 185–206; Kristin L. Hoganson, *Fighting for American Manhood: How Gender Politics Provoked the Spanish-American and Philippine-American Wars* (New Haven, Conn.: Yale University Press, 1998), 36–39, 124–54; Matthew Frye Jacobson, *Barbarian Virtues: The United States Encounters Foreign Peoples at Home and Abroad, 1876–1917* (New York: Hill and Wang, 2000), 140–70.

47. J. D. Zahniser and Amelia R. Fry, *Alice Paul: Claiming Power* (New York: Oxford University Press, 2014), 137–44, 217–18.

48. *Annual Register, July 1898–July, 1899,* first quote from 215, second quote from 216. W. I. Thomas, "The Psychology of Race Prejudice," *American Journal of Sociology* 9 (March 1904): 593–611; "The Mind of Woman and the Lower Races," *American Journal of Sociology* 12 (January 1907): 435–69; and "Race Psychology: Standpoint and Questionnaire," *American Journal of Sociology* 17 (May 1912): 725–75. W. E. B. Du Bois, *The Philadelphia Negro: A Social Study* (Philadelphia: University of Pennsylvania, 1899). McKee, *Sociology and the Race Problem,* 22–51.

49. Parrish, "Problems and Progress of Universal Education," first three quotes from 58, remaining quote from 59.

50. Williamson, *Crucible of Race,* 86–104, 415–21; Ralph E. Luker, *The Social Gospel in Black and White: American Racial Reform, 1885–1912* (Chapel Hill: University of North Carolina Press, 1991), 125–58, 282–89; Anderson, *Education of Blacks in the South,* 80–94; Wheeler, *New Women of the New South,* 104–8; Ethel Holbrook Riehm, "Dorothy Tilly and the Fellowship of the Concerned," in *Throwing Off the Cloak of Privilege: White Southern Women Activists in the Civil Rights Era,* ed. Gail S. Murray (Gainesville: University Press of Florida, 2004), 23–48; Jacqueline Dowd Hall, *Revolt Against Chivalry: Jessie Daniel Ames and the Women's Campaign Against Lynching* (New York: Columbia University Press, 1979), 89–95, 162–64.

51. Kilman, "Southern Collegiate Women," 97; "Branson Tells Board His Side," *Atlanta Constitution,* April 15, 1904; "Miss Celeste Parrish: Her Address on 'The Educational Outlook in Virginia,'" clipping, *Richmond Dispatch,* March 23, 1902, Section 8, Folder 1, Lila Meade Valentine Papers, VHS; quotes from Meta Glass, president of Sweet Briar College, in "Reminiscences of Miss Parrish," 343.

52. Celestia Susannah Parrish entry, *Woman's Who's Who of America,* ed. John W. Leonard (1914; rpt. Detroit: Gale Research Co., 1976), 623; first quote from C. S. Parrish to Wickliffe Rose, May 4, 1911, Southern Education Board Records, ser. 1.1, SHC; remaining quotes from *Southern Educational Association Journal of Proceedings and Addresses of the Eleventh Annual Meeting Held at Columbia, S.C., December 26–29, 1901* (Knoxville, Tenn.: The Association, 1902), 199.

53. Dailey, *Before Jim Crow*, 160–65; Louis R. Harlan, *Separate and Unequal: Public School Campaigns and Racism in the Southern Seaboard States, 1901–1915* (1958; rpt. New York: Atheneum, 1969), 137–44; Ralph Clipman McDaniel, *The Virginia Constitutional Convention of 1901–1902* (Baltimore: Johns Hopkins University Press, 1928), 122–29.

CHAPTER FOUR

1. Fairclough, *A Class of Their Own*, 142–47; Crystal N. Feimster, *Southern Horrors: Women and the Politics of Rape and Lynching* (Cambridge, Mass.: Harvard University Press, 2009), 188–89; Kantrowitz, *Ben Tillman and the Reconstruction of White Supremacy*, 216–20, 258–61; *Race Problems of the South: Report of the Proceedings of the First Annual Conference Held Under the Auspices of the Southern Society for the Promotion of the Study of Race Conditions and Problems in the South* (Richmond, Va.: B. F. Johnson Publishing, ca. 1900), 39–57.

2. Michael Perman, *The Struggle for Mastery: Disfranchisement in the South, 1888–1908* (Chapel Hill: University of North Carolina Press, 2001), 168–69; Williamson, *Crucible of Race*, 225–41; Jay Winston Driskell, *Schooling Jim Crow: The Fight for Atlanta's Booker T. Washington High School and the Roots of Black Protest Politics* (Charlottesville: University of Virginia Press, 2014), 40–48; Ann Field Alexander, *Race Man: The Rise and Fall of the "Fighting Editor," John Mitchell Jr.* (Charlottesville: University of Virginia Press, 2002), 111–14; Harlan, *Separate and Unequal*; J. Morgan Kousser, "Progressivism—for Middle-Class Whites Only: North Carolina Education, 1880–1910," *Journal of Southern History* 46 (May 1980): 189–94.

3. Russell Korobkin, "The Politics of Disfranchisement in Georgia," *Georgia Historical Quarterly* 74 (Spring 1990): 20–58; Dennis, *Lessons in Progress*, 50–52; Dewey W. Grantham Jr., *Hoke Smith and the Politics of the New South* (Baton Rouge: Louisiana State University Press, 1958), 118–24,

4. *Thirty-First Annual Report from the Department of Education*, 58–60; Mary E. Mabry (Mrs. Clyde F.) Anderson, *A Walk Through History: Georgia Federation of Women's Clubs* (n.p.: Georgia Federation of Women's Clubs, 1986); Mary (Mrs. E. T.) Brown, "How the Federation of Woman's Clubs May Co-operate With the Teacher," *Proceedings of the Thirty-Seventh Annual Meeting of the Georgia Educational Association, 1903* (Atlanta: Foote and Davies, 1904), 101–17; Sallie B. Hill, "Women's Clubs," Box 53, Folder 9, Sallie Barker Hill Papers, Hargrett Manuscript Collection and University Archives; Andra Mari Knecht, "The Tallulah Falls School: Female Reform and Rural Education in the New South," PhD diss., Mississippi State University, 2005; Montgomery, *Politics of Education in the New South*, 29–31, 66–82.

5. Sell, *History of the State Normal School*, 25–30; Parrish, "An Educational Development in Georgia," 131–45, quote from 132.

6. Ogren, *American State Normal School*, 60–74; Edgar W. Knight, "The Story of Teacher Training," *High School Journal* 10 (November 1927): 194–202; Sarah H. Case, *Leaders of Their Race: Educating Black and White Women in the New South* (Urbana: University of Illinois Press, 2017), 79–81; Cynthia Neverdon-Morton, *Afro-American Women of the South and the Advancement of the Race, 1895–1925* (Knoxville: University of Tennessee Press, 1989).

7. Kilman, "Southern Collegiate Women," 97; "New Teachers for Normal School," *Atlanta Constitution*, December 31, 1901; letter, Walter B. Hill to George Foster Peabody, January 28, 1904, Walter B. Hill Papers, Hargrett Manuscript Collection and University Archives (hereafter Hill Papers), Box 16, Folder 10; "The State Normal School," *Bulletin of the University of Georgia: The General Catalog* 4, no. 2: 173–76; T. W. Reed, "Invincible Southern Heroes Who Struggle to Learn:

The Georgia State Normal School," *Success* 5 (September 1902): 491–92; "Georgia's Training School for Teachers," *Pandora, 1903*, second and third quotes from 268, fourth quote from 269.

8. *Catalogue of Trinity College, North Carolina, 1878–'79* (Raleigh, N.C.: L. Branson, 1879), 16; *Catalogue of Trinity College, North Carolina, 1879–1880* (n.p., n.d.), 2, 28; *Peabody College Bulletin,* new ser., vol. 1 (April 1913): 13; Lanier Branson, *Eugene Cunningham Branson, Humanitarian* (Charlotte, N.C.: Heritage Printers, 1967), 6–8. Much of the information compiled on Branson's education and included in his papers (and repeated in various secondary sources) is inaccurate. He apparently never earned a college degree, although he was awarded two honorary ones, or attended graduate school. On his faculty information form at the University of North Carolina he wrote under graduate and professional training that "mainly his professional training has been a matter of self-tuition" (Eugene Cunningham Branson Papers, Main Series, Box 1, Folder 1, SHC).

9. *University of Georgia General Catalogue, 1900–1901* (Atlanta: Foote and Davies, 1901), 189–204; *University of Georgia General Catalogue, 1901–1902* (Atlanta: Foote and Davies, 1902), 150–55; "New Teachers for Normal School," *Atlanta Constitution,* December 31, 1901; Mary Elizabeth Outlaw, "State Normal School to State Teachers College: The Transition of an Institution," EdD diss., University of Georgia, 1990, 92–95; Sell, *History of the State Normal School,* 19–31.

10. Christine A. Ogren, "'A Large Measure of Self-Control and Personal Power': Women Students at State Normal Schools During the Late-Nineteenth and Early-Twentieth Centuries," *Women's Studies Quarterly* 28 (Winter 2000): 211–32; Z. X. Snyder, "The Practice School," *Journal of Education* 48 (July 28, 1898): 93–94; E. E. Lewis, "Practice Teaching in Model Schools," *Elementary School Teacher* 13 (May 1913): 434–44.

11. Quotes from "Miss Parrish Talks of State Practice School," *Atlanta Constitution,* June 29, 1902; "Georgia's Training School for Teachers"; Creswell, "Personal Recollections of Celeste Parrish"; May Zeigler, "Growth and Development of Psychology at the University of Georgia," *Journal of Genetic Psychology* 75 (1949): 51–59. Sell's *History of the State Normal School* is typical in completely ignoring Parrish's role in acquiring institutional funding and implementing curricular improvements.

12. Parrish, "An Educational Development in Georgia," first two quotes from 145, third quote from 133, fourth quote from 133–34; "Meaning and Purpose of the Muscogee Elementary School," 62–66.

13. Quote from *Athens Banner,* December 17, 1903; Celeste Parrish to Walter B. Hill, December 18, 1903, Hill Papers.

14. Quotes from "Trouble Brewing at the State Normal," *Macon Telegraph,* December 15, 1903; "Denial Entered by Miss Parrish," *Atlanta Constitution,* December 15, 1903; E. C. Branson to Walter B. Hill, January 5, 1904, Box 7, Folder 4, Hill Papers.

15. John Dittmer, *Black Georgia in the Progressive Era, 1900–1920* (1977; Urbana: University of Illinois Press, 1980), 90–101; Barton C. Shaw, *The Wool-Hat Boys: Georgia's Populist Party* (Baton Rouge: Louisiana State University Press, 1984), 197–200; C. Vann Woodward, *Tom Watson, Agrarian Rebel* (New York: Rinehart & Co., 1938).

16. Watson repeated these themes in numerous versions of the same speech delivered between 1902 and 1904. Quotes from Tom Watson, "The South," Folder 370; "The South: Historical Injustice to the South, What We Ought to Do," Folders 371 and 372, all from sub-series 2.1.3, Thomas E. Watson Papers, SHC.

17. John Temple Graves, "The Mob Spirit in the South," in *The Mob Spirit in America: Addresses Delivered at Chautauqua, New York* (New York: Chautauqua Press, 1903), 12–19, quote from 19,

and "The Problem of the Races," *University Record* 8 (September 1903): 121–34; W. B. Hill to Charles D. McIver, July 7, 1904, Hill Papers; Clarence A. Bacote, "Some Aspects of Negro Life in Georgia, 1880–1908," *Journal of Negro History* 43 (July 1958): 186–213, William F. Holmes, "The Georgia Alliance Legislature," *Georgia Historical Quarterly* 68 (Winter 1984): 479–515.

18. "Opposes Negro Schools," [Charleston, S.C.] *Weekly News and Courier*, July 15, 1899; Paul B. Barringer, "Negro Education in the South," *SEA Journal of Proceedings and Addresses of the Tenth Annual Meeting Held at Richmond, Virginia, December 17–20, 1900* (Richmond, Va.: The Association, 1901), 127–45, quote from 132; John R. Straton, "Will Education Solve the Race Problem?" *North American Review* 170 (June 1900): 785–801; Albert D. Kirwan, *Revolt of the Rednecks: Mississippi Politics, 1876–1925* (1951; rpt. Gloucester, Mass.: Peter Smith, 1964), 145–47; Leloudis, *Schooling the New South,* 177–83; Donald Johnson, "W. E. B. DuBois, Thomas Jesse Jones, and the Struggle for Social Education, 1900–1930," *Journal of Negro History* 85 (Summer 2000): 71–95.

19. "More Southern Education," *Manufacturers' Record*, September 3, 1903, 114; "Unique Southern Educational Methods," *Manufacturers' Record*, September 15, 1904, 205–6; "Ogdenism Begins to Squirm," *Manufacturers' Record*, February 9, 1905, 65–66; quote from "Hat-Holding in Southern Education, a Protest," *Manufacturers' Record*, March 30, 1905, 215; letter, Charles Duncan McIver to James A Hoyt, March 21, 1903, Box 13, Folder: SEB, 1903, Correspondence C–F, Charles Duncan McIver Papers, University Archives and Manuscripts, University of North Carolina at Greensboro.

20. "Union League on Negro Question," *Springfield* [Mass.] *Republican*, April 10, 1903; "Union League and the Negro," *Charlotte Observer*, April 10, 1903; Robert C. Ogden to Lila Meade Valentine, April 13, 1903, Folder 3, Richmond Education Association Papers, VHS; "Union League Meddlers," New Orleans *Times-Picayune*, December 11, 1903; quote from "Calls Club's Action a Mistake," *New York Times*, December 11, 1903; "How It Would Work," *New York Times*, December 12, 1903; Edward Ingle, *Ogdenism and the Chicago Suffrage Plank* (Baltimore: Manufacturers' Record, 1904); Perman, *Struggle for Mastery,* 224–44. Like Ogden, southern progressives regarded universities and their faculty as agents of modernization, as discussed in Dennis, *Lessons in Progress.*

21. First two quotes from Edward Ingle to William A. Courtenay, August 4, 1904, and third quote from Edward Ingle to William A. Courtenay, August 23, 1904, both from Folder 4, Edward Ingle Papers, Virginia Historical Society (hereafter Ingle Papers); fourth quote from Edward Ingle to James Calvin Hemphill, February 22, 1905, Folder 7, Ingle Papers; Ingle, *The Ogden Movement: An Educational Monopoly in the Making* (Baltimore: Manufacturers' Record, 1908); Eric Anderson and Alfred A. Moss Jr., *Dangerous Donations: Northern Philanthropy and Southern Black Education, 1902–1930* (Columbia: University of Missouri Press, 1999), 48–49. On the *Manufacturers' Record* criticisms, see also Anderson, *Education of Blacks in the South,* 94–95, and for an overview of the debate over federal aid to southern schools, see Dabney, *Universal Education in the South* 2: 12–17.

22. Edward Ingle to William A. Courtenay, February 23, 1905, Folder 4, Ingle Papers; all quotes from Thomas Dixon Jr. letter to the editor of the *Baltimore Sun*, June 8, 1905; the same letter was sent to the Columbia, S.C., *State*. Ogden was lifelong friends with Samuel Armstrong, Washington's mentor and founder of Hampton Institute, as discussed in Robert C. Ogden, *Samuel Chapman Armstrong, A Sketch* (New York: Fleming H. Revell, 1894), and he served on the board of trustees of Hampton and Tuskegee.

23. G. R. Glenn to H. B. Frissell, September 30 and October 12, 1901; E. C. Branson to H. B. Frissell, October 17, 1901, Southern Education Board Records (hereafter SEB Records), ser. 1.1, SHC; *Proceedings of the Fifth Conference for Education in the South, Held at Athens, Georgia,*

April 24, 25, and 26, 1902 (Knoxville: Southern Education Board, 1902), 5–6; "Will Campaign for Education," *Atlanta Constitution,* March 21, 1903; *Thirty-Second Annual Report from the Department of Education to the General Assembly of the State of Georgia for the School Year Ending December 31, 1903* (Atlanta: G. W. Harrison, State Printer, 1904), 27, 30–33.

24. John Spencer Bassett, "Stirring Up the Fires of Race Antipathy," *South Atlantic Quarterly* 2 (October 1903): 297–305; Andrew Sledd, "The Negro: Another View," *Atlantic Monthly* 90 (July 1902): 65–73; Ogden to Parrish, February 6, 1904, Robert C. Ogden Papers, Manuscripts Division, Library of Congress (hereafter Ogden Papers); Henry Y. Warnock, "Andrew Sledd, Southern Methodists, and the Negro: A Case History," *Journal of Southern History* 31 (August 1965): 251–71; Williamson, *Crucible of Race,* 259–71.

25. Tom Watson, "The Negro Question," *Watson's Jeffersonian Magazine* 1 (November 1907): 1032–40; Estelle Freedman, *Redefining Rape* (Cambridge, Mass.: Harvard University Press, 2013), 90–94; Kantrowitz, *Ben Tillman and the Reconstruction of White Supremacy*; Gilmore, *Gender and Jim Crow,* 82–89; Patricia A. Schechter, *Ida B. Wells-Barnett and American Reform, 1880–1930* (Chapel Hill: University of North Carolina Press, 2001); Williamson, *Crucible of Race,* 115–19.

26. Feimster, *Southern Horrors,* 28–31, 64–66, 127–28; LeeAnn Whites, "Rebecca Latimer Felton and the Problem of Protection," in *Visible Women: New Essays on American Activism,* eds. Nancy Hewitt and Suzanne Lebsock (Urbana: University of Illinois Press, 1993), 41–61; Warnock, "Andrew Sledd, Southern Methodists, and the Negro," 257–61. See also LeeAnn Whites, "The DeGraffenried Controversy: Race, Class, and Gender in the New South," *Journal of Southern History* 54 (August 1988): 449–78, and "Rebecca Latimer Felton and the Wife's Farm: The Class and Racial Politics of Gender Reform," *Georgia Historical Quarterly* 76 (Summer 1992): 354–72.

27. Celestia S. Parrish, "The Reliability of Negroes," *Southern Workman* 30, no. 9 (1901): 478–80.

28. Quote from C. S. Parrish to Walter B. Hill, December 15, 1903, Box 7, Folder 4, Hill Papers; David C. Barrow, "Mr. Hill's Relation to the University," and Rebecca Latimer (Mrs. W. H.) Felton, "Hon. Walter B. Hill as a Temperance Advocate," in *Bulletin of the University of Georgia,* Memorial Number, May 1906, 24–27 and 65–66; Harlan, *Separate and Unequal,* 215–16; Walter B. Hill, "What To Do With the Negro," *Augusta Chronicle,* November 11, 1901; Walter B. Hill, "Nationalism Not Opposed to Truest Sectionalism," *Atlanta Constitution,* April 9, 1903; Walter B. Hill, "Negro Education in the South," *Annals of the American Academy of Political and Social Science* 22 (September 1903): 320–29; Walter B. Hill, "A Plea for Tolerance," *Atlanta Constitution,* February 12, 1905; Ray Mathis, "Walter B. Hill and the Savage Ideal," *Georgia Historical Quarterly* 60 (Spring 1976): 23–34. For a fuller account of the role of faith in Hill's reform philosophy, see Mary Kathryn Mathis, "Walter Barnard Hill: Constructive Southern American," MA thesis, Georgia Southern College, 1969.

29. C. S. Parrish to Walter B. Hill, December 18, 1903, Box 7, Folder 4, Hill Papers; Robert Ogden to C. S. Parrish, October 17 and November 19, 1903, quote from February 6, 1904, Box 13, Ogden Papers; Robert C. Ogden to John Spencer Bassett, November 16, 1903, Box 13, Ogden Papers.

30. First quote from John N. Rogers to George S. Dickerman, January 12, 1902, and remaining quotes from Edward T. Ware to George S. Dickerman, May 9, 1902, SEB Records, ser. 9.1.

31. Quotes from "Branson Chosen to Head School," *Atlanta Constitution,* December 17, 1903; "Instruction of the Negroes," *Macon Telegraph,* December 17, 1903; *Thirtieth Annual Report from the Department of Education to the General Assembly of the State of Georgia for 1901* (Atlanta: G. W. Harrison, State Printer, 1902), 35–36.

32. First quote from C. S. Parrish to Walter B. Hill, December 15, 1903, Box 7, Folder 4, Hill Papers; C. S. Parrish to Walter B. Hill, December 18, 1903, Box 7, Folder 4, Hill Papers; second quote from Walter B. Hill to Georgia Foster Peabody, January 28, 1904, Box 16, Folder 10, Hill Papers; "Spicy Charges Made by Woman," *Atlanta Constitution*, April 14, 1904; "Miss Parrish Must Resign," *Macon Telegraph*, April 15, 1904.

33. Walter B. Hill to George F. Peabody, January 28, 1904, Box 16, Folder 10, and February 13, 1904, Box 5, Folder 18, Hill Papers; quote from E. C. Branson to W. B. Merritt, January 7, 1904, Box 7, Folder 4, Hill Papers; "Miss Parrish Must Resign," *Macon Telegraph*, April 15, 1904.

34. Quotes from "Branson Tells Board His Side," *Atlanta Constitution*, April 15, 1904.

35. W. B. Hill to G. F. Peabody, April 20, 1904, Box 5, Folder 18, Hill Papers; quotes from "Good of School Her Whole Idea," *Atlanta Constitution*, April 16, 1904.

36. Glass, "Reminiscences of Miss Parrish," 343; Andrew Jackson Ritchie, *Sketches of Rabun County History, 1819–1948* (Clayton, Ga.: Rabun County Historical Society, 1948), quotes from 333.

37. Branson, *Eugene Cunningham Branson*, first quote from 2; remaining quotes from W. B. Hill to G. F. Peabody, January 28, 1904, Box 16, Folder 10, Hill Papers.

38. First quote excerpted from a statement by Howard Odum, as cited in Daniel Joseph Singal, *The War Within: From Victorian to Modernist Thought in the South, 1919–1945* (Chapel Hill: University of North Carolina Press, 2014), 120; second quote from E. C. Branson to W. B. Hill, January 5, 1904, Hill Papers; H. J. Rowan to David C. Barrow, June 4, 1907, Box 2, David Crenshaw Barrow Papers (hereafter Barrow Papers), Hargrett Manuscript Collection and University Archives; "Miss Parrish Denies Charges," *Atlanta Constitution*, June 8, 1911.

39. Eugene C. Branson, "The Real Southern Question," *World's Work* 3 (March 1902): 1888–91, first three quotes from 1888, fourth quote from 1889; E. C. Branson, "The Betterment of Common School Education in Georgia," *Farmers Institutes in Georgia, Including Report of the Proceedings of The Farmers' Conference, held under the auspices of the Georgia State College of Agriculture, Univ. of Ga., Athens, Ga., January 18–21, 1910*, 127–37, Box 6, Andrew M. Soule Collection, Series Two: Reference File, Hargrett Manuscript Collection and University Archives; E. C. Branson, "Now Is the Time to Buy Land: The Tenant Farmers of the South Will Never Have a Better Time to Get a Hold on the Soil—How the Negro Is Improving His Opportunity," *Progressive Farmer*, December 16, 1911, 4; clipping, *Memphis Commercial Appeal*, February 20, 1912, Box 10, Routine Correspondence Series, Branson Papers.

40. First two quotes from W. B. Hill to G. F. Peabody, April 20, 1904, Box 5, Folder 18, Hill Papers; remaining quotes from C. S. Parrish to W. B. Hill, February 28, 1904, Box 7, Folder 4, Hill Papers (emphasis in original); flyer, *Hon. Walter B. Hill on Woman Suffrage: Women Have No Right Not to Vote* (n.p.: Georgia Woman Suffrage Association, n.d.), Folder 6, Georgia Women's Suffrage Collection, Special Collections, Georgia State Department of Archives and History.

41. "The Investigation," *Athens Banner*, April 22, 1904; W. B. Merritt to W. B. Hill, May 26, 1904, Box 1, Folder 16, Hill Papers; W. B. Hill to G. F. Peabody, June 4, 1904, Box 5, Folder 18, Hill Papers.

42. "Even the Children Demand Leave to Work on the Roads," *Augusta Chronicle*, January 19, 1911; "South Georgia State Normal School News," *Macon Telegraph*, April 4, 1915; "Georgia State Normal College," May 23, 1915; 1910 Census for Clarke County, Georgia, Athens District; Carroll Smith-Rosenberg, *Disorderly Conduct: Visions of Gender in Victorian America* (New York: A. A. Knopf, 1985), 252–57. The 1900 Census records for Decatur, DeKalb County, list Lottie Jarrell as a six-year-old pupil in the Orphans House.

43. John Collier, *From Every Zenith: A Memoir and Some Essays on Life and Thought* (Denver: Sage Books, 1963), 46–47, 97, quotes from 47.

44. "Mrs. W. B. Lowe's Committees," *Atlanta Constitution*, January 9, 1899; "Report of the Southern Educational Association," 93–94; Parna Hill to Sallie Hill, September 16, 1900, and Parna Hill to Roger Hill, September 17, 1900, Box 15, Folder 3, Hill Papers, Sallie Barker Hill Division; *Athens Woman's Club Minutes, 1899–1911*, vol. 1 (hereafter AWC Minutes), Athens Woman's Club Collection, Heritage Room, Athens–Clarke County Library, Athens; Mary I. Wood, *The History of the General Federation of Women's Clubs for the First Twenty-Two Years of Its Organization* (New York: General Federation of Women's Clubs, 1918), 112–25.

45. First quote from an announcement of a Congress of Mothers meeting, *Atlanta Constitution*, April 22, 1906; Parrish, "Child Study," 121–32, second quote from 132; Parrish, "Child Study in the School and in the Home," *Virginia School Journal* 10 (June 1901): 169–73; announcement of child-study class in *Athens Banner*, May 3, 1902, and *Atlanta Constitution*, May 5, 1902; Molly Ladd-Taylor, *Mother-Work: Women, Child Welfare, and the State, 1890–1930* (Urbana: University of Illinois Press, 1994).

46. "Woman's Congress of Georgia Holds First Session Here," *Atlanta Constitution*, April 23, 1906; "Closing Sessions of the Atlanta Meeting of the Georgia Mothers Congress," *Atlanta Constitution*, April 26, 1906; Sadie M. (Mrs. John W.) Rowlett, *History of the Georgia Congress of Mothers and Parent-Teacher Associations* (n.p.: Donaldson-Woods, 1925); Ladd-Taylor, *Mother-Work*, 45–48.

47. *Atlanta Constitution*, April 29, 1906; "Atlanta Women Prepare to Visit Practice School," *Atlanta Constitution*, May 2, 1906.

48. "Mrs. James Jackson at Head of Woman's Club," *Atlanta Constitution*, May 14, 1901; "Her Own Handiwork," *Atlanta Constitution*, December 1, 1901; "Model District Schools Fill a Long Felt Want," *Atlanta Constitution*, March 23, 1902; "State President's Address," *Atlanta Constitution*, January 27, 1903; "Woman's Clubs; Teachers' Aids," *Atlanta Constitution*, July 17, 1903; "Colonel Lindsay Johnson Dead," *Atlanta Constitution*, August 1, 1915; Obituary for Passie Fenton Ottley, *Atlanta Constitution*, August 17, 1940; Leonard, ed., *Woman's Who's Who of America*, 435; Lucien Lamar Knight, *History of Fulton County, Georgia* (Atlanta: A. H. Cawston, 1930), 251–52; *Prominent Women of Georgia* (Atlanta: National Biographical Publishers, n.d.), 69, 163–64; Anderson, *A Walk Through History*; U.S. Census records for 1880, 1900, and 1910.

49. AWC Minutes, 41, 71–76; "YWCA Convention," *Atlanta Constitution*, November 22, 1903; C. S. Parrish to W. B. Hill, August 4, 1904, Box 1, Folder 22, Hill Papers; "Athens Citizens Show Generosity," *Athens Banner*, September 24, 1905; "Daughters Will Help Rabun County School," *Athens Banner*, March 13, 1906; "Miss Parrish's Address," *Athens Banner*, November 24, 1908; "YWCA Meeting in Classic City," *Augusta Chronicle*, February 15, 1910; Marguerite B. Sheffer, *Memorabilia of the Athens Woman's Club* (Athens, Ga.: Athens Woman's Club, 1982).

50. Emily Hendree (Mrs. R. E.) Park, "Club Women in Educational Work," *Southern Educational Journal* 11 (October 1898): 803; Passie Fenton Ottley, "Club Women in Educational Work," *Southern Educational Journal* 12 (November 1898): 28–30; 1896–1901 petitions of the GFWC, Colonial Dames, Daughters of the American Revolution, United Daughters of the Confederacy, and teachers Rosa Woodberry and Susie Gerdine, in Board of Trustees Correspondence and Reports, 1866–1932, Box 4, Folder 3, Hargrett Manuscript Collection and University Archives; Rosa Woodberry to David C. Barrow, June 5, 1911, and David C. Barrow to Rosa Woodberry, June 24, 1911, Box 7, Barrow Papers; quote from Celeste Parrish, "Co-education in the South," *Southern Educational Journal* 15 (May 1902): 160; Montgomery, *Politics of Education in the New South*, 32–36.

For examples of male opposition to gender equality and coeducation, see the proceedings of the Georgia Educational Association for 1906 and 1910.

51. C. S. Parrish, "Southern College Women's New Educational Plan," *Atlanta Constitution*, September 3, 1903, and "Alumnae to Meet Here This Week," *Atlanta Constitution*, November 20, 1905; *Fourth Annual Report of the Southern Association of College Women, 1906*, Box 1, Folder 1, American Association of University Women, Georgia Division Records, Georgia Department of Archives and History; Marion and Rosenberry, *History of the American Association of University Women*, 249–60.

52. *Fourth Annual Report of the Southern Association of College Women, 1906*, 1–6, quotes as cited on 5–6, Box 1, Folder 1, American Association of University Women, Georgia Division Records, Georgia Department of Archives and History; "College Women to Meet Here," *Atlanta Constitution*, October 24, 1905.

CHAPTER FIVE

1. George Foster Peabody to C. S. Parrish, July 18, 1905, and E. C. Branson to George Foster Peabody, July 26, 1905, Box 3, George Foster Peabody Papers, Library of Congress (hereafter Peabody Papers).

2. Entry for May 22, 1906, *Faculty Minutes, 1903–1916*, Box 2, State Normal School Records, 1894–1933, Hargrett Manuscript Collection and University Archives; "Will Open: Muscogee Practice School of the State Normal School Will Open September 1st," *Athens Banner*, August 12, 1906; quote from *Athens Banner*, November 15, 1907; "Mothers' and Teachers' Cooperative Club," *Athens Banner*, November 15, 1908; Harry Hodgson to George Foster Peabody, March 14, 1906, Box 3, Peabody Papers; Eugene C. Branson to George Foster Peabody, May 30, 1906, Box 4, Peabody Papers.

3. "Mrs. Hill Re-Elected President of the Georgia School Improvement Club," *Athens Banner*, July 26, 1907; quote from "Athens Educators Present," *Athens Banner*, March 30, 1909; Farmers' Wives Conference pamphlet, Box 22, Folder 8, Hill Papers, Sallie Barker Hill Division; Mary Creswell, "Home Economics in Extension," Home Extension Service Programs and Essays Folder, Leila R. Mize Papers, Hargrett Manuscript Collection and University Archives; *Proceedings of the Tenth Conference for Education in the South, with an Appendix in Review of Five Years* (Richmond, Va.: CES Executive Committee, n.d.), 108–15.

4. *Atlanta Constitution*, August 21, 1910; "Miss Parrish Denies Charges," *Atlanta Constitution*, June 8, 1911; *Yearbook and List of Active Members of the National Education Association* (Washington, D.C.: NEA, 1917), 131; Sell, *History of the State Normal School*, 97–98.

5. Outlaw, "State Normal School to Georgia State Teachers College," 105–6; quotes from Celeste Parrish to E. C. Branson, May 31, 1910, Box 5, Barrow Papers; Parrish, "Statement of Hours of Work for Department of Psychology and Pedagogy for 1910–1911," Box 3, Folder 7, State Normal School Records, 1894–1933, Hargrett Manuscript Collection and University Archives.

6. C. S. Parrish to E. C. Branson, May 31 and June 1, 1910, and E. C. Branson to C. S. Parrish, June 2, 1910, Box 5, Barrow Papers.

7. Quote from Laura M. Smith, Mary E. Creswell, Mamie Mitchell, Bessie Miller, Elise Gibbs, Kate Hicks, and Carlotta Alexander to E. C. Branson, May 31, 1910, Box 5, Barrow Papers; C. S. Parrish to E. C. Branson, May 31, 1910, Box 5, Barrow Papers.

8. *Bulletin of the University of Georgia* 10, no. 12: 278–79; H. B. Frissell to C. S. Parrish, February 24, March 10, and April 10, 1911, and Emily K. Herron to C. S. Parrish, February 24 and April 19, 1911, all from Hollis Burke Frissell Letterbooks, Hampton University Archives; C. S.

Parrish to D. C. Barrow, May 5, 1911, quote from D. C. Barrow to C. S. Parrish, May 23, 1911, both from Box 7, Barrow Papers.

9. D. C. Barrow to A. P. Bourland, April 8, 1911; A. P. Bourland to D. C. Barrow, May 3, 1911; and C. S. Parrish to A. P. Bourland, May 4, 1911, all from SEB Records, ser. 1.1. George Foster Peabody to D. C. Barrow, April 18, 1911, Box 7, Barrow Papers. *Report of the Commissioner of Education for the Year Ended June 30, 1912* (Washington, D.C.: Government Printing Office, 1913), vol. 1: 189–92, 196–97. The General Education Board assumed responsibility for funding rural-school supervisors when the Peabody Education Fund shut down in 1914, as discussed in *The General Education Board: An Account of its Activities, 1902–1914* (New York: GEB, 1915), 179–89.

10. C. S. Parrish to Wickliffe Rose, May 4, 1911, and Wickliffe Rose to C. S. Parrish, May 6, 1911, quotes from the former, SEB Records.

11. Quotes from C. S. Parrish to Wickliffe Rose, May 4, 1911, SEB Records; South Georgia State Normal College *Catalogue and Announcement of the Courses of Instruction, 1913–1914* (Valdosta, Ga.: Southern Stationary & Printing, n.d.), 9–10, 19–20; *Catalogue and Announcement, 1915–1916*, South Georgia State Normal College *Bulletin*, vol. 3 (March 1915): 19–28, 80; "South Georgia State Normal College," *Macon Telegraph*, May 23, 1915. U.S. Census records show that Lottie Jarrell Stump was teaching in Valdosta public schools in 1930, and she later retired from her teaching position at Valdosta High School.

12. Quotes from C. S. Parrish to Wickliffe Rose, May 4, 1911.

13. Quotes from C. S. Parrish to A. P. Bourland, May 4, 1911, SEB Records; C. S. Parrish to Wickliffe Rose, May 4, 1911, SEB Records; A. P. Bourland to Sallie B. Hill, January 4, 1911, and M. L. Brittain to Sallie B. Hill, January 6, 1911, Box 23, Folder 9, Sallie Barker Hill Papers, Hargrett Manuscript Collection and University Archives; Dabney, *Universal Education in the South* 2. Also see the annual proceedings of the Conference for Education in the South, 1906–1914.

14. "Significant Prominence of South's Club Women at Little Rock Conference," *Atlanta Constitution*, April 17, 1910.

15. "State Normal Faculty Vacancies Are Filled," *Macon Telegraph*, May 28, 1911; quote from "Teachers Resent Action of Board," *Macon Telegraph*, May 30, 1911; "Teachers Resign from GA. Normal," *Atlanta Constitution*, May 31, 1911.

16. First quote from "Women Backing Miss Parrish," *Atlanta Constitution*, June 1, 1911; "Club Women Ask Investigation," *Atlanta Constitution*, June 4, 1911; second quote from "Miss Parrish Is Lauded by Athens Club Women," *Atlanta Constitution*, June 9, 1911; "Georgia Sorosis Regrets Loss of Miss Parrish," *Atlanta Constitution*, June 10, 1911.

17. Quotes from "Women Ask Pay Equal to Men," *Atlanta Constitution*, April 28, 1911; "High School Must Go on Brown Lot," *Atlanta Constitution*, May 26, 1911; "Daley Succeeds Eugene Mitchell," *Atlanta Constitution*, October 27, 1911; "Women Teachers Ask More Pay," *Atlanta Constitution*, November 24, 1911; "Atlanta Schools After Teachers," *Atlanta Constitution*, February 4, 1912.

18. First quote from "Teachers Resent Action of Board," *Macon Telegraph*, May 30, 1911; second quote from "Mrs. Bryan Defends Miss Celeste Parrish," *Atlanta Constitution*, June 2, 1911; third quote from "Club Women Ask Investigation," *Atlanta Constitution*, June 4, 1911; "Branson Wins in School Fight," *Atlanta Constitution*, September 14, 1911.

19. "Teachers Resent Action of Board," *Macon Telegraph*, May 30, 1911; quote from "Guinn Defends Normal Teacher," *Atlanta Constitution*, June 1, 1911.

20. C. S. Parrish, "Much Needed Changes in the School System," *Atlanta Constitution*, June 25, 1911; "Miss Par[r]ish Now in State Work," *Athens Banner*, June 29, 1911; C. S. Parrish, "Unity of

Plan Essential For Educational Work," *Atlanta Constitution,* July 2, 1911; "Rural Schools," *Athens Banner,* July 14, 1911; "Prof. Brittain Explains the Educational Bill," *Atlanta Constitution,* August 19, 1911; "Athens Man on the State Board of Education Which Met Yesterday," *Athens Banner,* September 29, 1911; *Fortieth Annual Report of the Department of Education to the General Assembly of the State of Georgia for the School Year Ending December 31, 1911* (Atlanta: State Printer, 1912), quotes from 26–27; *Georgia State Board of Education Minutes and Correspondence, 1870–1923,* 263–64, Georgia Department of Archives and History.

21. *General Education Board: An Account of Its Activities, 1902–1914; Forty-First AR,* 56; *Report of the Commissioner of Education for the Year Ended June 30, 1912* (Washington, D.C.: Government Printing Office, 1913), vol. 1: 189; *Forty-Second Annual Report of the Department of Education to the General Assembly of the State of Georgia for the School Year Ending December 31, 1913* (Atlanta: State Printer, 1914) (hereafter *Forty-Second AR*), 73.

22. *Fortieth Annual Report of the Department of Education to the General Assembly of the State of Georgia for the School Year Ending December 31, 1911* (Atlanta: State Printer, 1912), 26–29; *Report of the Commissioner of Education for the Year Ended June 30, 1912* (Washington, D.C.: Government Printing Office, 1913), vol. 1: 190–92. For a discussion regarding the rural-school supervisor's place within larger structural educational reforms, see Spencer J. Maxcy, "Progressivism and Rural Education in the Deep South, 1900–1950," in *Education and the Rise of the New South,* ed. Goodenow and White, 47–71.

23. *Fortieth Annual Report of the Department of Education to the General Assembly of the State of Georgia for the School Year Ending December 31, 1911* (Atlanta: State Printer, 1912), 31; first quote from Celeste Parrish, "Federation Does Great Work for State Education," *Atlanta Constitution,* May 26, 1912; second quote from *Forty-First AR,* 45; Creswell, "Personal Recollections of Celeste Parrish." Creswell provides what is likely a first-hand account of the flooding incident, as she accompanied Parrish on school visits to assist in teaching home economics.

24. *Fortieth Annual Report of the Department of Education to the General Assembly of the State of Georgia for the School Year Ending December 31, 1911* (Atlanta: State Printer, 1912), 31–33; *Forty-First AR,* 42–43, quote from 43; *Forty-Second AR,* 43, 45; *Forty-Third Annual Report of the Department of Education to the General Assembly of the State of Georgia for the School Year Ending December 31, 1914* (Atlanta: State Printer, 1915) (hereafter *Forty-Third AR*), 28–29; "Miss Parrish to Hold Week-Long Institutes," *Atlanta Constitution,* April 25, 1912; Celeste Parrish, "Federation Does Great Work for State Education," *Atlanta Constitution,* May 26, 1912; "Rural Home and School Clubs," *Atlanta Constitution,* June 4, 1913.

25. Ann Short Chirhart, *Torches of Light: Georgia Teachers and the Coming of the Modern South* (Athens: University of Georgia Press, 2005), 98–101; *The General Education Board: An Account of its Activities, 1902–1914,* 196–97, 201–3; *Forty-First AR,* 58; *Forty-Second AR,* 57–59; Lance G. E. Jones, *The Jeanes Teacher in the United States, 1908–1933* (Chapel Hill: University of North Carolina Press, 1937); Henry Allen Bullock, *A History of Negro Education in the South from 1619 to the Present* (Cambridge, Mass.: Harvard University Press, 1967), 134–38; Mary S. Hoffschwelle, "A Black Woman 'in Orthority': Claiming Professional Status in Jim Crow Alabama," *Journal of Southern History* 81 (November 2015): 843–86.

26. *Forty-Second AR,* 43, 45–46; *Forty-Third AR,* 31–36.

27. *Forty-Fourth Annual Report of the Department of Education to the General Assembly of the State of Georgia for the School Year Ending December 31, 1915* (Atlanta: State Printer, 1916) (hereafter *Forty-Fourth AR*), 21–22; *Forty-Fifth Annual Report of the Department of Education to the General*

Assembly of the State of Georgia for the School Year Ending December 31, 1916 (Atlanta: Johnson-Dallis Co., 1917) (hereafter *Forty-Fifth AR*), 20–21; *Forty-Sixth Annual Report of the Department of Education to the General Assembly of the State of Georgia for the School Year Ending December 31, 1917* (Atlanta: State Printer, 1918) (hereafter *Forty-Sixth AR*), quote from 23–24.

28. *Forty-Second AR*, 46; *Forty-Third AR*, 28, 36; *Forty-Fourth AR*, 22–23; "For State Organizer Plans Are Made by Georgia Congress," *Atlanta Constitution*, August 24, 1913; "Much Business Conducted at Executive Board Meeting," *Atlanta Constitution*, January 31, 1915; "Holt Organizing Parent-Teacher Clubs," *Atlanta Constitution*, April 14, 1915.

29. Quotes from Parrish, "Federation Does Great Work for State Education," *Atlanta Constitution*, May 26, 1912; *Forty-First AR*, 43.

30. *Fortieth AR*, 32; *Forty-First AR*, 43, 45; *Forty-Second AR*, 46–47; quote from Nellie Peters Black, "The Need of County Federations," *Atlanta Constitution*, August 26, 1917; "Some Pointers From Mrs. Ottley," *Atlanta Constitution*, June 18, 1911; "Teachers Institute Work Means Better Schools," *Rome Tribune-Herald*, December 22, 1911; "Rural Home and School Clubs," *Atlanta Constitution*, June 4, 1913. The 1914 Ellis Health Law made county boards of health responsible for addressing public health issues, but the boards could be established only if two successive county grand juries requested it. The GFWC supported the law but knew that local support must be mobilized to render it effective. Anderson, *A Walk Through History*; Kenneth Coleman et al., *A History of Georgia* (Athens: University of Georgia Press, 1977), 331.

31. Quotes from Parrish, "Federation Does Great Work for State Education," *Atlanta Constitution*, May 26, 1912; *Official Register and Directory of Women's Clubs in America* 14 (1912): 63; "Old Officers Re-elected by Georgia Federation," *Atlanta Constitution*, October 30, 1913; *Forty-Third AR*, 14–15; M. L. Duggan, *Educational Survey of Rabun County Georgia* (Atlanta: State Department of Education, 1914), 44–46; "A Visit to Our School," *Atlanta Constitution*, December 13, 1914; "New Teachers for Tallulah School," *Atlanta Constitution*, August 15, 1915; "Important Meeting Held by Federation Executive Board," *Atlanta Constitution*, October 3, 1915; "The Tallulah Falls School," *Atlanta Constitution*, September 17, 1916.

32. "Brittain's Good Work for County School Tax," *Atlanta Constitution*, April 14, 1914; "A Banner School County," *Atlanta Constitution*, July 19, 1914; "Committee Chairmen Named for Atlanta Woman's Club," *Atlanta Constitution*, October 11, 1915; "Clemency for Frank Urged by Atlantans," *Atlanta Constitution*, May 21, 1915; "Attacks Watson in Frank Case," *New York Times*, September 13, 1915; *Forty-Third AR*, 14–15; M. L. Brittain, *The Story of Georgia Tech* (Chapel Hill: University of North Carolina Press, 1948), 275–77; Woodward, *Tom Watson*, 384–415; quote as cited in Steve Oney, *And the Dead Shall Rise: The Murder of Mary Phagan and the Lynching of Leo Frank* (New York: Vintage Books, 2003), 596.

33. Social items in the *Atlanta Constitution*, March 15, 1908; "Piano Recital," *Atlanta Constitution*, October 10, 1909; *Forty-Third AR*, 34. While the 1910 census shows that the Hutchinsons were residing at Woodberry's school, the 1920 census for Fulton County shows that they had established a separate residence with Minnie Bell's mother, a thirteen-year-old daughter, and three boarders, all of whom were single, women teachers.

34. C. S. Parrish, "The Teaching of Arithmetic" and "The Teaching of Reading," in *Manual for Georgia Teachers* (Atlanta: Department of Education, ca. 1912), 37–51, 77–85; C. S. Parrish, "Correlation of Agriculture and Home Economics with the Common School Subjects of Georgia" and "Arithmetic Problems Based on Club Work," in *Girls' and Boys' Club Work—A Manual for Rural Teachers*, ed. Mary E. Creswell, Georgia State College of Agriculture Bulletin 101 (February 1916):

12–23, 45–46; "Miss Celeste Parrish Wanted as Surveyor," *Atlanta Constitution,* March 31, 1914; "Miss Parrish to Survey City School Systems," *Atlanta Constitution,* April 26, 1914; C. S. Parrish, *Survey of the Atlanta Public Schools* (Atlanta: City Board of Education, 1914); Driskell, *Schooling Jim Crow,* 141–46.

35. Tyack, *The One Best System,* 191–96; Wayne J. Urban, "Educational Reform in a New South City: Atlanta, 1890–1925," in *Education and the Rise of the New South,* ed. Goodenow and White, 126; "Reflection Upon Atlanta," *Atlanta Constitution,* August 18, 1912; Parrish, *Survey of the Atlanta Public Schools,* 14, 16, 19–20, 28–29, first three quotes from 14, fourth quote from 23.

36. Barry M. Franklin, "Progressivism and Curricular Differentiation: Special Classes in the Atlanta Public Schools, 1898–1923," *History of Education Quarterly* 29 (Winter 1989): 571–93; Urban, "Educational Reform in a New South City," 117–22.

37. Melvin W. Ecke, *From Ivy Street to Kennedy Center: Centennial History of the Atlanta Public Schools* (Atlanta: Atlanta Board of Education, 1972); "G.H.S. Building Unfit for School Says Daley Following Charge That It Caused Girl's Death," *Atlanta Constitution,* August 16, 1912; "A Reflection Upon Atlanta," *Atlanta Constitution,* August 18, 1912; "Local School Tax Needed in Atlanta Asserts R. J. Guinn," *Atlanta Constitution,* May 29, 1914; Parrish, *Survey of Atlanta Public Schools,* 21–22, 32.

38. Parrish, *Survey of Atlanta Public Schools,* first three quotes from 7–8; remaining quotes from C. S. Parrish, "A Week in the Atlanta Schools," *Atlanta Constitution,* June 3, 1917.

39. Parrish, *Survey of Atlanta Public Schools,* 22; quote from Parrish, "Federation Does Great Work for State Education," *Atlanta Constitution,* May 26, 1912. Wayne J. Urban provides an account of Atlanta school reform as an elite-controlled, undemocratic process in "Progressive Education in the Urban South: The Reform of the Atlanta Schools, 1914–1918," in *The Age of Urban Reform: New Perspectives on the Progressive Era* (Port Washington, N.Y.: Kennikat Press, 1977), ed. Michael H. Ebner and Eugene M. Tobin, 131–41.

40. J. O. Martin address, "Presentation of the Celeste Parrish Gavel to the Georgia Education Association," Celeste Parrish Memorials, Hargrett Manuscript Collection and University Archives; quotes from Creswell, "Personal Recollections of Celeste Parrish," 3; *Forty-Third AR,* 28–29.

41. Tracy L. Steffes, *School, Society, and State: A New Education to Govern Modern American, 1890–1940* (Chicago: University of Chicago Press, 2012), 52–57; David Nasaw, *Schooled to Order: A Social History of Public Schooling in the United States* (New York: Oxford University Press, 1979), 126–39; John Dewey, "An Undemocratic Proposal," *Vocational Education* 2 (May 1913): 374; John Dewey, "Industrial Education—A Wrong Kind," *New Republic* 2 (February 20, 1915): 71–73; Link, *A Hard Country and a Lonely Place,* 177–81; Anderson, *Education of Blacks in the South.*

42. "Educate Youth Coweta's Slogan," *Atlanta Constitution,* August 27, 1911; "Meeting Held in Seventh District," *Atlanta Constitution,* April 21, 1912; quotes from Celeste Parrish, "Training People to Make a Living," *Atlanta Constitution,* June 4, 1913.

43. Thomas G. Dyer, *The University of Georgia: A Bicentennial History, 1785–1985* (Athens: University of Georgia Press, 1985), 144–45; Ann M. Keppel, "The Myth of Agrarianism in Rural Educational Reform, 1890–1914," *History of Education Quarterly* 2 (June 1962): 100–112; Steffes, *School, Society, and State,* 52–53; C. S. Parrish, "Unity of Plan Essential for Educational Work," *Atlanta Constitution,* July 2, 1911; "Industrial Schools Are Fast Becoming Philanthropic Fad, Says Miss Parrish," *Atlanta Constitution,* March 23, 1913; "Colleges Need Practical Work," *Richmond Times Dispatch,* April 16, 1913; Ritchie, *Sketches of Rabun County History,* 333–34.

44. Solomon, *In the Company of Educated Women,* 85–87; Sarah Stage, "Ellen Richards and the Social Significance of the Home Economics Movement," in *Rethinking Home Economics: Women*

and the History of a Profession (Ithaca, N.Y.: Cornell University Press, 1997), ed. Sarah Stage and Virginia B. Vincenti, 17–33; Rossiter, *Women Scientists in America*, 65–70; Fitzpatrick, *Endless Crusade*, 83–86; Palmieri, *In Adamless Eden*, 176.

45. M. Carey Thomas, "Should the Higher Education of Women Differ from That of Men?" *Educational Review* 21 (January 1901): 1–10; Celestia S. Parrish, "Shall the Higher Education of Women Be the Same as That of Men? *Educational Review* 22 (November 1901): 383–96, quotes from 387.

46. Parrish, *Survey of the Atlanta Public Schools*, 24; Ecke, *From Ivy Street to Kennedy Center*, 41–43, 75, 106; Urban, "Educational Reform in a New South City"; John L. Rury, *Education and Women's Work: Female Schooling and the Division of Labor in Urban America, 1870–1930* (Albany: State University of New York Press, 1991), 163–72. The Girls' High School business courses, and later the English-Commercial and Commercial high schools, attracted the daughters of skilled and semiskilled workers (Timothy James Crimmins, "The Crystal Stair: A Study of the Effects of Class, Race, and Ethnicity on Secondary Education in Atlanta, 1872–1925," PhD diss., Emory University, 1972, 116–17, 152–62).

47. Georgia Federation of Women's Clubs *Yearbook, 1910–1911* (n.p., ca. 1911), 41, Georgia Federation of Women's Clubs Records, Georgia Department of Archives and History; *Forty-Third AR*, 37; *Forty-Fourth AR*, 23–24, first quote from 24; *Forty-Fifth AR*, 20–22, second quote from 22; Montgomery, *Politics of Education in the New South*, 109–10.

48. Quote from Creswell, "Personal Recollections of Celeste Parrish"; Rabun County deed records, entries for August 4, 1914, Recorded Book Z, 37, for May 25, 1917, Recorded Book AA, 323, and for July 1, 1919, Recorded Book A–Z, 340, Rabun County Courthouse, Clayton.

49. First quote from Wier L. Boyd, "Miss Parrish at Young Harris," *School and Home* 6 (December 1914): 16–18; second quote from Creswell, "Personal Recollections of Celeste Parrish," 4; *Forty-First AR*, 396–98; *Forty-Second AR*, 466–68; *Forty-Third AR*, 362–73; *Forty-Fifth AR*, 370–81; *Forty-Sixth AR*, 342–53; *Forty-Seventh Annual Report of the Department of Education to the General Assembly of the State of Georgia for the School Year Ending December 31, 1918* (Atlanta, Ga.: Byrd Printing Co.), 444–55.

50. Quote from *Forty-First AR*, 43.

51. Quote from Lizzie Shed, "The Teacher's Cottage," *School and Home* 8 (June 1916): 10–11.

52. *Forty-Seventh AR*, 19–20.

53. Quote from Creswell, "Personal Recollections of Celeste Parrish"; Isma Dooley, "Celeste Parrish, Noted Georgia Educator, Is Dead," *Atlanta Constitution*, September 9, 1918; "The Death of Miss Parrish," *Atlanta Constitution*, September 18, 1918.

CONCLUSION

1. Quotes from Creswell, "Personal Recollections of Celeste Parrish," 4–5; "Educators Down to Work at Macon," *Augusta Chronicle*, May 3, 1919; "Memorial Meeting Held Saturday in Honor of Miss Celeste Parrish," *Atlanta Constitution*, September 22, 1918; "I. S. Smith Succeeds Miss C. S. Parrish," *Atlanta Constitution*, October 8, 1918.

2. Amy Thompson McCandless, "Maintaining the Spirit and Tone of Robust Manliness: The Battle Against Coeducation at Southern Colleges and Universities, 1890–1940," *NWSA Journal* 2 (Spring 1990): 199–216; Sara Bertha Townsend, "The Admission of Women to the University of Georgia," *Georgia Historical Quarterly* 43 (June 1959): 156–69; "Report of the President of the

Board of Trustees, Georgia State College of Agriculture, June 14, 1918," in *Reports, Board of Trustees, Georgia State College of Agriculture* 4, box 4, Andrew M. Soule Collection, Hargrett Manuscript Collection and University Archives; Mary Creswell, "The Celeste Parrish Memorial," *Atlanta Constitution*, May 9, 1920.

3. "Memorial Meeting Held Saturday in Honor of Miss Celeste Parrish," *Atlanta Constitution*, September 22, 1918; "First Scholarship for Women at the University of Georgia," *Atlanta Constitution*, September 23, 1918; "Women in the University of Georgia," *High School Quarterly* 7 (October 1918): 9–10; "Georgia's Educators and Students Plan Memorial to Celeste S. Parrish," *Atlanta Constitution*, November 3, 1918; Georgia Federation of Women's Clubs *Yearbook, 1919–1920* (n.p., n.d.), 67; Dyer, *University of Georgia*, 172–73.

4. McCandless, *The Past in the Present*, 86–100; Robert C. McMath Jr. et al., *Engineering the New South: Georgia Tech, 1885–1985* (Athens: University of Georgia Press, 1985), 270–75; Orie Lathan Hatcher, "The New Virginia Man and the New Era for Women," *The Nation* 106 (June 1, 1918): 650–52, quotes from 652; Anne Hobson Freeman, "Mary Munford's Fight for a College for Women Co-ordinate with the University of Virginia," *Virginia Magazine of History and Biography* 78 (October 1970): 481–91.

5. Elizabeth Colton, *Various Types of Southern Colleges for Women* (Raleigh, N.C.: Edwards & Broughton, 1916); Colton, "Past and Future Work of the Southern Association of College Women," 224–30; Elizabeth Colton, "How Southern Colleges for Women Might More Effectively Fit Women for Their Life Work," *High School Quarterly* 4 (October 1915): 45–48; Mary Lynch Johnson, *Elizabeth Avery Colton: An Educational Pioneer in the South* (n.p.: North Carolina Division of the South Atlantic Section of the American Association of College Women, n.d.); Elizabeth Colton, "The Approximate Value of Recent Degrees of Southern Colleges," *SACW Bulletin*, January 1914, 1–15; DeMoss, "'A Fearless Stand,'" 249–60.

6. Mary Ann Dzuback, "Gender and the Politics of Knowledge," *History of Education Quarterly* 43 (Summer 2003): 171–95; Madeleine Arnot and Jo Anne Dillabough, "Feminist Politics and Democratic Values in Education," *Curriculum Inquiry* 29 (Summer 1999): 159–89.

7. "School Campaign Gets Good Start at Mass Meeting," *Atlanta Constitution*, February 7, 1915; "Unusual Interest Shown in Schools," *Atlanta Constitution*, February 8, 1915; "Mothers to Make Probe of Schools," *Atlanta Constitution*, March 5, 1915; "Atlanta Mothers Score Conditions in Public Schools," *Atlanta Constitution*, March 19, 1915; "School Conditions Scored in Report to Education Board," *Atlanta Constitution*, March 26, 1915; "One of the Liveliest Clubs in the World," *The Rotarian* 6 (March 1915): 11; "The Machinery in Motion," *Atlanta Constitution*, April 11, 1915; "Ad Men to Get Behind Better Schools Fight," *Atlanta Constitution*, April 18, 1915; "School Reforms in Atlanta Urged," *Atlanta Constitution*, April 23, 1915; "Prospects Bright for City Schools," *Atlanta Constitution*, May 28, 1915; Driskell, *Schooling Jim Crow*, 139–47; Jacqueline Anne Rouse, *Lugenia Burns Hope: Black Southern Reformer* (Athens: University of Georgia Press, 1989), 73–78.

8. Quote from "Mayor Confident Money Sheet Veto Will be Sustained," *Atlanta Constitution*, February 7, 1915; "Council Adopts Amended Sheet; Signed by Mayor," *Atlanta Constitution*, February 10, 1915; "Pay of Teachers May Cause Fight," *Atlanta Constitution*, February 15, 1915; "Board to Take Action on Salary Increases," *Atlanta Constitution*, March 25, 1915.

9. Quotes from "Professor Dykes Made Head of High Schools," *Atlanta Constitution*, July 9, 1915.

10. "Probe of Schools by Council Urged by Board Chairman," *Atlanta Constitution*, May 29, 1918; "Charges of Trial by Mob Law Made at First Meeting for School Probe," *Atlanta Constitution*, June 13, 1918. For other interpretations of the politics of municipal educational policy in Atlanta,

see David N. Plank and Paul E. Peterson, "Does Urban Reform Imply Class Conflict? The Case of Atlanta's Schools," *History of Education Quarterly* 23 (Summer 1983): 151–73; Urban, "Progressive Education in the Urban South," 131–41; Wayne Urban, "Organized Teachers and Educational Reform during the Progressive Era, 1890–1920," *History of Education Quarterly* 16 (Spring 1976): 35–52.

11. Urban, "Progressive Education in the Urban South"; "Urges Separation of City's Schools from the Council," *Atlanta Constitution*, June 14, 1918; "Guinn Takes Stand to Defend Himself and School Board," *Atlanta Constitution*, June 19, 1918; "School Board Fixes Salaries in City Schools," *Atlanta Constitution*, July 31, 1915.

12. First two quotes from "Urges Separation of City's Schools from the Council," *Atlanta Constitution*, June 14, 1918; third quote from "Miss Laura Smith Declares Finance Committee at Fault," *Atlanta Constitution*, June 21, 1918.

13. Miss Laura Smith Declares Finance Committee at Fault," *Atlanta Constitution*, June 21, 1918.

14. Quote from "Council Amends Report of the School Probers Striking Two Sections," *Atlanta Constitution*, July 16, 1918; "Fight for School Reform Won in One Day," *Atlanta Constitution*, August 1, 1918; "Plan Launched to Divorce Atlanta's School System from the Mire of Politics," *Atlanta Constitution*, August 2, 1918; "Entire Delegation from Fulton Back School Change," *Atlanta Constitution*, August 4, 1918; "Measure Giving School Reforms Passed by House," *Atlanta Constitution*, August 7, 1918; "Expect Vote Today on School Changes," *Atlanta Constitution*, August 9, 1918.

15. "Board of Education Plans for Heating of New School," *Atlanta Constitution*, August 17, 1918; "Money Is Denied for New Schools," *Atlanta Constitution*, August 20, 1918; "New School Board Candidate Announces," *Atlanta Constitution*, September 19, 1918; "Great Interest Is Now Being Shown in Election of New School Board," *Atlanta Constitution*, September 20, 1918; "Meeting Called on City Schools," *Atlanta Constitution*, September 21, 1918; "Citizens Organize to Name Best Men for School Board," *Atlanta Constitution*, September 25, 1918.

16. "Patrons to Name Board Candidates," *Atlanta Constitution*, October 6, 1918; "Series of Meetings on School Situation Held During Week," *Atlanta Constitution*, October 16, 1918; "School Campaign Gains Momentum," *Atlanta Constitution*, October 17, 1918; "Big School Meeting to be Held Tonight," *Atlanta Constitution*, October 18, 1918.

17. "Ban on Public Gatherings in Atlanta Repealed Friday by Action of City Council," and "Terrell is Named for School Board," *Atlanta Constitution*, October 26, 1918; "Turman Is Named for School Board," *Atlanta Constitution*, October 30, 1918; "Fifth and Eighth Ward School Meeting Called," *Atlanta Constitution*, October 31, 1918; "School Campaign to Be Discussed," *Atlanta Constitution*, November 24, 1918; "Education Board Candidates Tell of School Plans," *Atlanta Constitution*, November 26, 1918; "School Campaign Activity Grows," *Atlanta Constitution*, November 27, 1918; first quote from "School Campaign Interest Grows," *Atlanta Constitution*, November 30, 1918; second quote from "Board Nominees Pledge Support," *Atlanta Constitution*, December 1, 1918.

18. School election returns, *Atlanta Constitution*, December 5, 1918; quotes from "School Election Pleases Atlanta," *Atlanta Constitution*, December 6, 1918.

BIBLIOGRAPHY

ARCHIVES

Athens–Clarke County Library
   Athens Woman's Club Minutes, 1899–1911.

Georgia Department of Archives and History
   American Association of University Women, Georgia Division Records.
   Georgia State Board of Education Minutes and Correspondence, 1870–1923.
   Georgia Women's Suffrage Collection.

Hampton University Archives
   Hollis Burke Frissell Letterbooks.

Hargrett Manuscript Collection and University Archives, University of Georgia
Libraries, Athens
   David Crenshaw Barrow Papers.
   Sallie Barker Hill Papers.
   Walter B. Hill Papers.
   Leila R. Mize Papers.
   Celeste Parrish Memorials.
   Andrew M. Soule Collection.
   State Normal School Records.
   University Board of Trustees Correspondence and Reports.

Library of Congress
   Robert C. Ogden Papers.
   George Foster Peabody Papers.

Library of Virginia
    Mary Cooke Branch Munford Papers.
    William Henry Ruffner Circulars.
    William Henry Ruffner Papers.

Longwood University
    Minutes of the Board of Trustees.
    State Female Normal School *Catalog.*
    Virginia State Teachers College *Bulletin.*

Pittsylvania County Courthouse, Chatham, Va.
    Chancery Court Records.
    County Land Books, 1861–1865.

Southern Historical Collection, University of North Carolina, Chapel Hill
    Eugene Cunningham Branson Papers.
    Rawley White Martin Papers.
    Sours Family Papers.
    Southern Education Board Records.
    Thomas E. Watson Papers.

University of Chicago
    Annual Register.
    Alice Lloyd Papers.
    President's Report.
    University of Chicago Weekly.
    University Record.
    Madeline Wallin Papers.

Virginia Historical Society
    Bailey Family Papers.
    Hankins Family Papers.
    Edward Ingle Papers.
    Edwin Anderson Penick Letters.
    Richmond Education Association Papers.
    Saunders Family Papers.
    Katherine Spiller (Graves) Moses Papers.
    Lila Meade Valentine Papers.

NEWSPAPERS AND JOURNALS

Augusta Chronicle.
Athens Banner.
Atlanta Constitution.
Educational Journal of Virginia.
High School Quarterly.
Lynchburg Daily Republican.
Macon Telegraph.
Manufacturers' Record.
Rome Tribune-Herald.
School and Home.
Southern Educational Journal.
Virginia School Journal.

GOVERNMENT AND INSTITUTIONAL RECORDS

Annual Report of Officers, Boards, and Institutions of the Commonwealth of Virginia.
Annual Report of the Department of Education to the General Assembly of the State of Georgia.
Bulletin of the University of Georgia.
Journal of the House of Delegates of the State of Virginia.
Journal of the Senate of the Commonwealth of Virginia.
Report of the U.S. Commissioner of Education.
Semi-Annual Report on Schools and Finances of Freedmen.
Semi-Annual Report on Schools for Freedmen.
Virginia School Report.

OTHER PRIMARY SOURCES

Addams, Jane. "The College Woman and Christianity." *The Independent,* August 8, 1901.
———. *Democracy and Social Ethics.* New York: Macmillan, 1902.
———. "A New Impulse to an Old Gospel." *Forum* (November 1892): 345–58.
Anthony, Susan B., and Ida Husted Harper, eds. *The History of Woman Suffrage.* Vol. 4. Indianapolis: Hollenbeck Press, 1900.
Baldwin, James Mark. "Child Study." *Psychological Review* 5 (March 1898): 218–20.
Barringer, Paul B. "Negro Education in the South." In *Southern Educational Association Journal of Addresses and Proceedings of the Tenth Annual Meeting Held at Richmond, Virginia, December 17–20, 1900,* 127–45. Richmond: The Association, 1901.
Bassett, John Spencer. "Stirring Up the Fires of Race Antipathy." *South Atlantic Quarterly* 2 (October 1903): 297–305.

Beverley, Archie Swanson. "A Tribute to a Great Leader." *Religious Herald*, February 24, 1949, 14, 23.

Blandin, Isabella M. E. *History of Higher Education of Women in the South Prior to 1860.* New York: Neale Publishing, 1909.

Bradwell, I. G. "Making Our Way Home from Appomattox." *Confederate Veteran* 29 (March 1921): 102.

Branson, Eugene C. "Now Is the Time to Buy Land: The Tenant Farmers of the South Will Never Have a Better Time to Get a Hold on the Soil—How the Negro Is Improving His Opportunity." *Progressive Farmer,* December 16, 1911, 4.

———. "The Real Southern Question." *World's Work* 3 (March 1902): 1888–91.

Brittain, M. L. *The Story of Georgia Tech.* Chapel Hill: University of North Carolina Press, 1948.

Brown, Mary. "How the Federation of Woman's Clubs May Co-operate with the Teacher." In *Proceedings of the Thirty-Seventh Annual Meeting of the Georgia Educational Association, 1903,* 101–17. Atlanta: Foote and Davies, 1904.

Butler, Nicholas Murray. "Democracy and Education." *Educational Review* 12 (September 1896): 120–32.

———. Editorial. *Educational Review* 12 (November 1896): 411–16.

Campbell, Alexander. *Popular Lectures and Addresses.* Philadelphia: James Challen & Son, 1863.

Carpenter, William B. *Principles of Mental Physiology.* London: Henry S. King & Co., 1874.

Cary, Virginia. *Letters on Female Character, Addressed to a Young Lady on the Death of Her Mother.* Richmond, Va.: Ariel Works, 1830.

Catalog of SFNS, 1885–'86. Richmond, Va.: Haughman Bros., 1886.

Catalogue of Trinity College, North Carolina, 1878–'79. Raleigh, N.C.: L. Branson, 1879.

Catalogue of Trinity College, North Carolina, 1879–1880. N.p., n.d.

Coalition Rule in Danville. Broadside. Special Collections, Library of Virginia.

Collier, John. *From Every Zenith: A Memoir and Some Essays on Life and Thought.* Denver: Sage Books, 1963.

Colton, Elizabeth Avery. "The Approximate Value of Recent Degrees of Southern Colleges." *SACW Bulletin,* January 1914, 1–15.

———. "How Southern Colleges for Women Might More Effectively Fit Women for Their Life Work." *High School Quarterly* 4 (October 1915): 45–48.

———. "The Past and Future Work of the Southern Association of College Women." *High School Quarterly* 6 (July 1918): 224–30.

———. *Various Types of Southern Colleges for Women.* Raleigh, N.C.: Edwards & Broughton, 1916.

Creswell, Mary. "Personal Recollections of Celeste Parrish." Typed manuscript. Celeste Parrish Memorials, Hargrett Rare Book and Manuscript Library, University of Georgia, Athens.

Dabney, Robert L. "The Negro and the Common School." In *Discussions 4: Secular,* 176–90. Richmond, Va.: Presbyterian Committee of Publication, 1890.

———. "The State Free School System Imposed Upon Virginia by the Underwood Constitution." In *Discussions 4: Secular,* 191–99. Richmond, Va.: Presbyterian Committee of Publication, 1890.

De Tocqueville, Alexis. *Democracy in America.* Rpt. New York: Vintage Books, 1945.

Dew, Thomas R. *Review of the Debate in the Virginia Legislature, 1831–'32.* Rpt. in *The Pro-Slavery Argument, as Maintained by the Most Distinguished Writers of the Southern States.* Philadelphia: Lippincott, Grambo, & Co., 1853.

Dewey, John. "Democracy in Education." *The Elementary School Teacher* 4 (December 1903): 193–204.

———. "Ethical Principles Underlying Education." In *Third Yearbook of the National Herbart Society.* Chicago: The Society, 1897.

———. "Industrial Education—A Wrong Kind." *New Republic* 2 (February 20, 1915): 71–73.

———. "Is Coeducation Injurious to Girls." *Ladies Home Journal* 28 (June 1911): 22, 60–61.

———. "My Pedagogic Creed." In *My Pedagogic Creed by Prof. John Dewey, also The Demands of Sociology upon Pedagogy by Prof. Albion W. Small,* ed. John Dewey and Albion Small, 3–18. New York: E. L. Kellogg & Co., 1897.

———. *The School and Society* and *The Child and the Curriculum.* 1900. Rpt. Chicago: University of Chicago Press, 1990.

———. "The School as Social Center." *The Elementary School Teacher* 3 (October 1902): 73–86.

———. "An Undemocratic Proposal." *Vocational Education* 2 (May 1913): 374.

Du Bois, W. E. B. *The Philadelphia Negro: A Social Study.* Philadelphia: University of Pennsylvania, 1899.

Duggan, M. L. *Educational Survey of Rabun County Georgia.* Atlanta: State Department of Education, 1914.

Eggleston, Mary Fitzhugh, and Maud Pollard Turman. "History, Fifty Years of the June Class 1894 of State Female Normal School, now State Teachers College of Farmville, Virginia." Typed manuscript. Longwood University Archives.

Encyclopedia of Virginia Biography. Vols. 3 and 4. New York: Lewis Historical Publishing Co., 1915.

"Epidemic of Lynching in Georgia." *Colored American Magazine* 14 (February–March 1908): 88.

Finck, Henry T. "Are Womanly Women Doomed?" *The Independent* 53 (January 1901): 267–71.

Fitzhugh, George. *Sociology for the South, or the Failure of Free Society.* Richmond, Va.: A. Morris, 1854.

The General Education Board: An Account of its Activities, 1902–1914. New York: GEB, 1915.

"Georgia's Training School for Teachers." In *Pandora, 1903,* 267–69. Athens: University of Georgia, 1903.

Glass, Meta. "Reminiscences of Miss Parrish." *Virginia Journal of Education* 35 (May 1942): 343.

Goodspeed, Thomas Wakefield. *A History of the University of Chicago: The First Quarter-Century.* Chicago: University of Chicago Press, 1916.

Graves, John Temple. "The Mob Spirit in the South." In *The Mob Spirit in America; Addresses Delivered at Chautauqua, New York,* 12–19. New York: Chautauqua Press, 1903.

———. "The Problem of the Races." *University Record* 8 (September 1903): 121–34.

Hall, G. Stanley. *Adolescence: Its Psychology and Its Relation to Physiology, Anthropology, Sociology, Sex, Crime, Religion and Education.* 1904; Rpt. New York: Appleton & Co., 1921.

———. "Child-Study and Its Relation to Education." *The Forum* 29 (August 1900): 688–702.

———. "Coeducation in the High School." In *National Educational Association Journal of Proceedings and Addresses, 1903,* 446–60. Winona, Minn.: The Association, 1903.

———. "Feminization in School and Home: The Undue Influence of Women Teachers—The Need of Different Training for the Sexes." *World's Work* 16 (1908): 10237–44.

———. "The New Psychology as a Basis of Education." *The Forum* 17 (August 1894): 710–20.

Hammond, William A. "Brain-Forcing in Childhood." *Popular Science Monthly* 30 (April 1887): 721–32.

———. "Men's and Women's Brains." *Popular Science Monthly* 31 (August 1887): 554–58.

Harper, William Rainey. "The University and Democracy." [University of California] *University Chronicle* 2 (April 1899): 65–88.

Hatcher, Orie Latham. "The New Virginia Man and the New Era for Women." *The Nation* 106 (June 1, 1918): 650–52.

Heatwole, Cornelius Jacob. *A History of Education in Virginia.* New York: Macmillan, 1916.

Hersey, John. *An Appeal to Christians, on the Subject of Slavery.* 2nd ed. Baltimore: Armstrong & Plaskitt, 1833.

Hill, Caroline M., ed. *Mary E. McDowell and Municipal Housekeeping: A Symposium.* Chicago: Millar Publishing, 1938.

Hill, Walter B. "Negro Education in the South." *Annals of the American Academy of Political and Social Science* 22 (September 1903): 320–29.

Holmes, George Frederick. "Ancient Slavery." *De Bow's Review* 19 (December 1855): 617–37.

———. "Ancient Slavery." *De Bow's Review* 19 (November 1855): 559–78.

———. "Failure of Free Societies." *Southern Literary Messenger* 21 (March 1855): 129–41.

———. "Uncle Tom's Cabin." *Southern Literary Messenger* 18 (October 1852): 630–38.

Hundley, Daniel Robinson. *Social Relations in Our Southern States.* New York: Henry B. Price, 1860.

Ingle, Edward. *The Ogden Movement: An Educational Monopoly in the Making.* Baltimore: Manufacturers' Record, 1908.

———. *Ogdenism and the Chicago Suffrage Plank.* Baltimore: Manufacturers' Record, 1904.

Irvine, Lucy. "Memories of the Days Spent in Farmville." Typed manuscript, Longwood University Archives.

Jefferson, Thomas. "A Bill for the More General Diffusion of Knowledge." In *Crusade Against Ignorance: Thomas Jefferson on Education,* 83–92. New York: Teachers College, Columbia University, 1961.

———. *Notes on the State of Virginia.* London: John Stockdale, 1787.

Johnson, Mary Lynch. *Elizabeth Avery Colton: An Educational Pioneer in the South.* N.p.: North Carolina Division of the South Atlantic Section of the American Association of College Women, n.d.

Kent, Charles W. *Address by Prof. Charles W. Kent of the University of Va., at Hollins Institute, June 6, 1894, 51st Commencement Day.* Special Collections, University of Virginia Libraries, Charlottesville.

Kline, Fannie Littleton. Letter to Roberta Hollingworth. University of Virginia Library Online Exhibits, explore.lib.virginia.edu/items/show/2657. Accessed September 2, 2015.

Knight, Edgar W. *Public Education in the South.* Boston: Ginn and Co., 1922.

———. *Reconstruction and Education in Virginia.* Pamphlet. Rpt. from *South Atlantic Quarterly* 15 (January and April 1916): 25–40, 157–74.

———. "The Story of Teacher Training." *High School Journal* 10 (November 1927): 194–202.

Knight, Lucian Lamar. *History of Fulton County, Georgia.* Atlanta: A. H. Cawston, 1930.

Langhorne, Orra. "Coeducation in Virginia." [Boston] *Woman's Journal,* July 21, 1894, 229.

———. Report on Virginia. In *Proceedings of the Twenty-Seventh Annual Convention of the National-American Woman Suffrage Association held in Atlanta, GA, January 31st to February 5th, 1895,* 94–95. Warren, Ohio: W. M. Ritezel & Co., 1895.

———. "Virginia." *The Woman's Journal,* August 8, 1896, 256.

Larew, Gillie A. "Celestia Parrish." *Virginia Journal of Education* 35 (May 1942): 342–46.

Lewis, E. E. "Practice Teaching in Model Schools." *Elementary School Teacher* 13 (May 1913): 434–44.

Maddox, William Arthur. *The Free School Idea in Virginia Before the Civil War: A Phase of Political and Social Evolution.* New York: Columbia University Teachers College, 1918.

Mayo, A. D. *Southern Women in the Recent Educational Movement in the South.* Ed. Dan T. Carter and Amy Friedlander. 1892. Rpt. Baton Rouge: Louisiana State University Press, 1978.

"Meaning and Purpose of the Muscogee Elementary School." In *Georgia State Normal School Bulletin, 1909–1910,* 62–66. Box 8, State Normal School Records, 1894–1933, Hargrett Manuscript Collection and University Archives.

Mercer, Charles Fenton. *A Discourse on Popular Education.* N.p.: Princeton, 1826.

Minutes of the General Faculty. Vol. 13. Albert and Shirley Small Special Collections Library, University of Virginia.

"The Mob Is Not Yet Dead." *Colored American Magazine* 9 (August 1905): 404.

Munford, Mary Cooke Branch. "Education in Virginia." Library of Virginia.

Münsterberg, Hugo. "The Danger from Experimental Psychology." *Atlantic Monthly* 81 (February 1898): 159–67.

——. "Psychology and Education." *Educational Review* 16 (September 1898): 105–19.

The Negro in Virginia. Writers Program of the Work Projects Administration in the State of Virginia. 1940. Rpt. Winston-Salem, N.C.: John F. Blair, 1994.

Newlin, W. H. *Narratives of Prison Escape.* Cincinnati: Western Methodist Book Concern Printers, 1887.

Ogden, Robert C. *Samuel Chapman Armstrong, A Sketch.* New York: Fleming H. Revell, 1894.

Olmstead, Frederick Law. *A Journey in the Seaboard Slave States; With Remarks on Their Economy.* London: Sampson Low, Son, & Co., 1856.

Orton, James, ed. *The Liberal Education of Women: The Demand and the Method, Current Thoughts in America and England.* New York: A. S. Barnes & Co., 1873.

Ottley, Passie Fenton. "Club Women in Educational Work." *Southern Educational Journal* 12 (November 1898): 28–30.

Page, David Perkins. *Theory and Practice of Teaching, or the Motives and Methods of Good School-Keeping.* Ed. W. H. Payne. 1847. Rpt. New York: American Book Co., 1885.

Park, Emily Hendree. "Club Women in Educational Work." *Southern Educational Journal* 11 (October 1898): 803.

Parrish, Celeste [C. S., Celestia S.]. "Address of Welcome." *Publications of the Association of Collegiate Alumnae,* ser. 3, no. 13: 7–9.

——. "Arithmetic Problems Based on Club Work." In *Girls' and Boys' Club Work—A Manual for Rural Teachers,* ed. Mary E. Creswell, 45–46. Georgia State College of Agriculture *Bulletin* 101 (February 1916).

——. "Child Study." *Southern Educational Journal* 12 (February 1899): 121–32.

——. "Child Study in the School and in the Home." *Virginia School Journal* 10 (June 1901): 169–73.

——. "Co-education in the South." *Southern Educational Journal* 15 (May 1902): 160.

——. "Correlation of Agriculture and Home Economics with the Common School Subjects of Georgia." In *Girls' and Boys' Club Work—A Manual for Rural Teachers,* ed. Mary E. Creswell, 12–23. Georgia State College of Agriculture *Bulletin* 101 (February 1916).

——. "The Cutaneous Estimation of Open and Filled Space." *American Journal of Psychology* 6 (January 1895): 514–22.

——. "The Education of Girls: Fifth Paper." *Religious Herald* 73, no. 11: 3.

——. "The Education of Girls: First Paper." *Religious Herald* 73, no. 5: 2

——. "The Education of Girls: Fourth Paper." *Religious Herald* 73, no. 10: 3.

——. "The Education of Girls: Second Paper." *Religious Herald* 73, no. 6: 2.

——. "The Education of Girls: Sixth Paper." *Religious Herald* 73, no. 12: 2.

——. "The Education of Girls: Third Paper." *Religious Herald* 73, no. 9: 2.

———. "The Education of Women in the South." In *Southern Educational Association Journal of Proceedings and Addresses of the Tenth Annual Meeting, 1900*, 45–56. Richmond: The Association, 1901.

———. "An Educational Development in Georgia." *The Elementary School Teacher* 6 (1905): 131–45.

———. "My Experiences in Self-Culture." In *The Early Life Story of Miss Celeste Parrish, Noted Georgia Educator*. Pamphlet. Atlanta: State Department of Education, 1925.

———. "The Grading of Country Schools." *Educational Journal of Virginia* 19 (January 1888): 1–4.

———. "The Localisation of Cutaneous Impressions by Arm Movement Without Pressure Upon the Skin." *American Journal of Psychology* 8 (January 1897): 250–67.

———. "Problems and Progress of Universal Education in the South." *Publications of the Association of Collegiate Alumnae*, ser. 3 (February 1900): 57.

———. "The Reliability of Negroes." *Southern Workman* 30, no. 9 (1901): 478–80.

———. "Shall the Higher Education of Women Be the Same as That of Men?" *Educational Review* 22 (November 1901): 383–96.

———. "Some Defects in the Education of Women in the South." *Proceedings of the Second Capon Springs Conference for Christian Education in the South, 1899*. Raleigh: Edwards and Broughton, 1899.

———. *Survey of the Atlanta Public Schools*. Atlanta: City Board of Education, 1914.

———. "The Teaching of Arithmetic." In *Manual for Georgia Teachers*, 37–51. Atlanta: Department of Education, ca. 1912.

———. "The Teaching of Reading." In *Manual for Georgia Teachers*, 77–85. Atlanta: Department of Education, ca. 1912.

———. "The Womanly Woman." *The Independent* 53 (April 1901): 775–78.

———. "Woman's Problems." *The Independent* 53 (October 1901): 2582–85.

———. "Women in the University of Virginia." *Virginia School Journal* 2 (January 1893): 7–8.

Paxton, John D. *Letters on Slavery: Addressed to the Cumberland Congregation, Virginia.* Lexington, Ky.: Abraham T. Skillman, 1833.

Peabody College Bulletin. New ser., vol. 1 (April 1913).

Perdue, Charles L., Jr., Thomas E. Barden, and Robert K. Phillips, eds. *Weevils in the Wheat: Interviews with Virginia Ex-Slaves.* Charlottesville: University Press of Virginia, 1976.

Proceedings and Debates of the Virginia State Convention of 1829–1830. Richmond, Va.: Ritchie & Cook, 1830.

Proceedings of the Fifth Conference for Education in the South, Held at Athens, Georgia, April 24, 25, and 26, 1902. Knoxville, Tenn.: Southern Education Board, 1902.

Proceedings of the Tenth Conference for Education in the South, with an Appendix in Review of Five Years. Richmond, Va.: CES Executive Committee, n.d.

Prominent Women of Georgia. Atlanta: National Biographical Publishers, n.d.

Pulliam, David Loyd. *The Constitutional Conventions of Virginia from the Foundations of the Commonwealth to the Present Time.* Richmond: John T. West, 1901.

Race Problems of the South: Report of the Proceedings of the First Annual Conference Held Under the Auspices of the Southern Society for the Promotion of the Study of Race Conditions and Problems in the South. Richmond, Va.: B. F. Johnson Publishing, ca. 1900.

Reed, T. W. "Invincible Southern Heroes Who Struggle to Learn: The Georgia State Normal School." *Success* 5 (September 1902): 491–92.

"Reminiscences for the Twenty-Fifth Anniversary at Farmville." *The Virginian,* 1909.

"Reminiscences of the Sixties." In *War Recollections of the Confederate Veterans of Pittsylvania County, Virginia, 1861–1865.* Compiled by Rawley Martin Chapter, Virginia Division, United Daughters of the Confederacy. N.p.: Randall O. Reynolds, n.d.

Report Concerning the State Normal School at Farmville, December 10, 1885. House Document II, 4. Longwood College Archives, Farmville, Va.

"Report of the Committee on Privileges and Elections." *Reports of Committees of the Senate of the United States for the First Session of the Forty-Eighth Congress, 1883–84.* Vol. 6, Report no. 579. Washington, D.C.: Government Printing Office, 1884.

"Report of the [NEA] Subcommittee on the Training of Teachers." In *Report of the Commissioner of Education for the Year 1893–1894.* Vol. 1: 472–87. Washington, D.C.: Government Printing Office, 1896.

"Report of the Southern Educational Association." *Southern Educational Journal* 12 (January 1899): 81–98.

Ritchie, Andrew Jackson. *Sketches of Rabun County History, 1819–1948.* Clayton, Ga.: Rabun County Historical Society, 1948.

Rowlett, Sadie M. *History of the Georgia Congress of Mothers and Parent-Teacher Associations.* N.p.: Donaldson-Woods, 1925.

Ruffin, Edmund. *Address to the Virginia State Agricultural Society, on the Effects of Domestic Slavery on the Manners, Habits and Welfare of the Agricultural Population of the Southern States; And the Slavery of Class to Class in the Northern States.* Richmond: Virginia State Agricultural Society, 1853.

———. *African Colonization Unveiled.* Washington, D.C.: Lemuel Towers, 1859.

———. *The Political Economy of Slavery; or the Institution Considered in Regard to Its Influence on Public Wealth and the General Welfare.* Washington, D.C.: Lemuel Towers, 1857.

———. "Slavery and Free Labor Described and Compared." *Southern Planter* 19 (1859): 726–27, 731–32.

Ruffner, Henry. *Address to the People of West Virginia Shewing that Slavery is Injurious to the Public Welfare, and that it May be Gradually Abolished Without Detriment to the Rights and Interests of Slaveholders.* Lexington: R. C. Noel, 1847.

———. "Proposed Plan for the Organization and Support of Common Schools in Virginia." In *Report of the Commissioner of Education for the Year 1899–1900.* Vol. 1: 381–97. Washington, D.C.: Government Printing Office, 1901.

Ruffner, William. "The Negro." In *The Free Public School System*, 6–11. Booklet. Library of Virginia.

———. "Report of the Principal." Handwritten manuscript. Longwood University Archives.

———. *What Are the Normal Schools in Fact?* Booklet. Library of Virginia.

Sears, Barnas. *Objections to Public Schools Reconsidered; Remarks of the Trustees of the Peabody Education Fund*. Boston: John Wilson & Son, 1875.

Sell, E. S. *History of the State Normal School, Athens, Georgia*. N.p., 1923.

Sledd, Andrew. "The Negro: Another View." *Atlantic Monthly* 90 (July 1902): 65–73.

Smith, A. Tolman. "The Psychological Revival." In *Report of the Commissioner of Education for the Year 1893–1894*. Vol. 1: 429–30. Washington, D.C.: Government Printing Office, 1896.

Snyder, Z. X. "The Practice School." *Journal of Education* 48 (July 28, 1898): 93–94.

Southern Educational Association Journal of Proceedings and Addresses of the Eleventh Annual Meeting Held at Columbia, S.C., December 26–29, 1901. Knoxville, Tenn.: The Association, 1902.

Southern Educational Association Journal of Proceedings and Addresses of the Ninth Annual Meeting, Held at Memphis, Tenn., December 27–29, 1899. N.p.: The Association, 1899.

Stanton, Elizabeth Cady. "The Solitude of Self." In *Selected Papers of Elizabeth Cady Stanton and Susan B. Anthony*. Vol. 5: *Their Place Inside the Body-Politic, 1887–1895*, ed. Ann D. Gordon, 423–36. New Brunswick, N.J.: Rutgers University Press, 2009.

Stevens, W. Le Conte. *The Admission of Women to Universities*. New York: Association for Promoting the Higher Education of Women in New York, 1883.

Stewart, William Henry. *History of Norfolk County, Virginia, and Representative Citizens*. Chicago: Biographical Publishing Co., 1902.

Straton, John R. "Will Education Solve the Race Problem?" *North American Review* 170 (June 1900): 785–801.

"Superintendent Ruffner's Address." *Educational Journal of Virginia* 11 (March 1880): 90–100.

Talbot, Marion. "The Duty and the Opportunity of the Association of Collegiate Alumnae." *Michigan Alumnus* (November 1897): 3–14.

———. *The Education of Women*. Chicago: University of Chicago Press, 1910.

———. *History of the Chicago Association of Collegiate Alumnae, 1882–1917*. Chicago: The Association, 1917.

———. *More Than Lore: Reminiscences of Marion Talbot*. With Foreword by Hanna Holborn Gray. 1936. Rpt. Chicago: University of Chicago Press, 2015.

———, and Lois Kimball Mathews Rosenberry. *The History of the American Association of University Women, 1881–1931*. Boston: Houghton Mifflin Co., 1931.

Thomas, M. Carey. "The Association of Collegiate Alumnae and Its Relation to Women's Education." *Publications of the Association of Collegiate Alumnae*, ser. 3 (December 1898): 40–46.

————."Should the Higher Education of Women Differ from That of Men?" *Educational Review* 21 (January 1901): 1–10.

Thomas, W. I. "The Mind of Woman and the Lower Races." *American Journal of Sociology* 12 (January 1907): 435–69.

————. "The Psychology of Race Prejudice." *American Journal of Sociology* 9 (March 1904): 593–611.

————. "Race Psychology: Standpoint and Questionnaire." *American Journal of Psychology* 17 (May 1912): 725–75.

Tighe, Richard J. "The Southern Educational Association." In *National Educational Association Fiftieth Anniversary Volume, 1857–1906*, 499–504. Winona, Minn.: The Association, 1907.

"To Earnest Teachers in the Southern States and Elsewhere." *School and Home* 17 (December 1899): 90–91.

Tribute to a Pioneer Teacher: Celeste Parrish. Danville, Va.: Delta Kappa Gamma Society, Iota State Organization, 1941.

Tufts, James H. "Feminization." *School Review* 17 (January 1909): 55–58.

University of Georgia General Catalogue, 1900–1901. Atlanta: Foote and Davies, 1901.

University of Georgia General Catalogue, 1901–1902. Atlanta: Foote and Davies, 1902.

"Virginia: Educational Conventions." *American Journal of Education* 16 (March 1866): 173–76.

Watson, Tom. "The Negro Question." *Watson's Jeffersonian Magazine* 1 (November 1907): 1032–40.

"William A. Fentress." In *Report of the Eleventh Annual Meeting of the Virginia State Bar Association, Held at the Hot Springs, Virginia, August 1, 2, & 3rd, 1899*, ed. Eugene C. Massie, 110. Richmond, Va.: Everett Waddey Co., 1899.

Williamson, Robert. "Co-Education of the Sexes." *Virginia School Journal* 2 (February 1893): 45–46.

Withers, Robert Enoch. *Autobiography of an Octogenarian*. Roanoke, Va.: Stone Printing, 1907.

Wood, Mary I. *The History of the General Federation of Women's Clubs for the First Twenty-Two Years of Its Organization*. New York: General Federation of Women's Clubs, 1918.

SECONDARY SOURCES

Alexander, Ann Field. *Race Man: The Rise and Fall of the "Fighting Editor," John Mitchell Jr.* Charlottesville: University of Virginia Press, 2002.

Allen, Louise Anderson. "Silenced Sisters: Dewey's Disciples in a Conservative New South, 1900–1940." *Journal of the Gilded Age and Progressive Era* 5 (April 2006): 119–37.

Anderson, Eric, and Alfred A. Moss Jr. *Dangerous Donations: Northern Philanthropy and Southern Black Education, 1902–1930*. Columbia: University of Missouri Press, 1999.

Anderson, James D. *The Education of Blacks in the South, 1860–1935.* Chapel Hill: University of North Carolina Press, 1988.

Anderson, Mary Elizabeth Mabry. *A Walk Through History: Georgia Federation of Women's Clubs.* N.p.: Georgia Federation of Women's Clubs, 1986.

Anderson, William T., Jr. "The Freedmen's Bureau and Negro Education in Virginia." *North Carolina Historical Review* 29 (January 1952): 64–90.

Angulo, A. J. "William Barton Rogers and the Southern Sieve: Revisiting Science, Slavery, and Higher Learning in the South." *History of Education Quarterly* 45 (Spring 2005): 18–37.

Antler, Joyce. *The Educated Woman and Professionalization: The Struggle for a New Feminine Identity, 1890–1920.* New York: Garland, 1987.

Arnot, Madeleine, and Jo Anne Dillabough. "Feminist Politics and Democratic Values in Education." *Curriculum Inquiry* 29 (Summer 1999): 159–89.

Ayers, Edward L. *In the Presence of Mine Enemies: The Civil War in the Heart of America, 1859–1863.* New York: W. W. Norton, 2003.

———. *Vengeance and Justice: Crime and Punishment in the Nineteenth-Century American South.* New York: Oxford University Press, 1984.

Bacote, Clarence A. "Some Aspects of Negro Life in Georgia, 1880–1908." *Journal of Negro History* 43 (July 1958): 186–213.

Bederman, Gail. *Manliness and Civilization: A Cultural History of Gender and Race in the United States, 1880–1917.* Chicago: University of Chicago Press, 1995.

Benjamin, Ludy T., Jr. "The Psychology Laboratory at the Turn of the 20th Century." *American Psychologist* 55 (March 2000): 318–21.

Blair, Karen J. *The Clubwoman as Feminist: True Womanhood Redefined, 1868–1914.* New York: Homes & Meier, 1980.

Blair, William. *Virginia's Private War: Feeding Body and Soul in the Confederacy, 1861–1865.* New York: Oxford University Press, 1998.

Bogger, Tommy L. *Free Blacks in Norfolk, Virginia, 1790–1860: The Darker Side of Freedom.* Charlottesville: University Press of Virginia, 1997.

Bordin, Ruth. *Woman at Michigan: The "Dangerous Experiment," 1870s to the Present.* Ann Arbor: University of Michigan Press, 1999.

Boring, Edwin G. "Edward Bradford Titchener, 1867–1927." *American Journal of Psychology* 100 (Autumn-Winter 1987): 376–94.

Boyer, John W. *"Broad and Christian in the Fullest Sense": William Rainey Harper and the University of Chicago.* Chicago: College of the University of Chicago, 2005.

Branson, Lanier. *Eugene Cunningham Branson, Humanitarian.* Charlotte, N.C.: Heritage Printers, 1967.

Breen, Patrick H. "Contested Communion: The Limits of White Solidarity in Nat Turner's Virginia." *Journal of the Early American Republic* 27 (Winter 2007): 685–703.

Brown, Elsa Barkley. "To Catch the Vision of Freedom: Reconstructing Southern Black Women's Political History." In *African American Women and the Vote, 1837–1965,* ed.

Ann D. Gorden, with Bettye Collier-Thomas, John H. Bracey, Arlene Voski Avakian, and Joyce Avrech Berkman, 19–31. Amherst: University of Massachusetts Press, 1997.

Brown, W. H. *The Education and Economic Development of the Negro in Virginia.* Publications of the University of Virginia. Phelps-Stokes Fellowship Papers, no. 6.

Bruce, Dickson D., Jr. *The Rhetoric of Conservatism: The Virginia Convention of 1829–1830 and the Conservative Tradition in the South.* San Marino, Calif.: Huntington Library, 1982.

———. *Violence and Culture in the Antebellum South.* Austin: University of Texas Press, 1979.

Brundage, W. Fitzhugh. *Lynching in the New South: Georgia and Virginia, 1880–1930.* Urbana: University of Illinois Press, 1993.

Bullock, Henry Allen. *A History of Negro Education in the South from 1619 to the Present.* Cambridge, Mass.: Harvard University Press, 1967.

Butchart, Ronald E. *Schooling the Freedpeople: Teaching, Learning, and the Struggle for Black Freedom, 1861–1876.* Chapel Hill: University of North Carolina Press, 2010.

Bystydzienski, Jill. "Women's Participation in Teachers' Unions in England and the United States." In *Women Educators: Employees of Schools in Western Countries,* ed. Patricia A. Schmuck, 151–72. Albany: State University of New York Press, 1987.

Calhoun, Walter T. "The Danville Riot and Its Repercussions on the Virginia Election of 1883." *Publications in History* 3 (1966): 25–51.

Carter, Susan B. "Incentives and Rewards to Teaching." In *American Teachers: Histories of a Profession at Work,* ed. Donald Warren, 49–62. New York: Macmillan, 1989.

Case, Sarah H. *Leaders of Their Race: Educating Black and White Women in the New South.* Urbana: University of Illinois Press, 2017.

Censer, Jane Turner. *North Carolina Planters and Their Children, 1800–1860.* Baton Rouge: Louisiana State University Press, 1984.

———. *The Reconstruction of White Southern Womanhood, 1865–1895.* Baton Rouge: Louisiana State University Press, 2003.

Chirhart, Ann Short. *Torches of Light: Georgia Teachers and the Coming of the Modern South.* Athens: University of Georgia Press, 2005.

Clement, Maud Carter. *History of Pittsylvania County, Virginia.* Lynchburg, Va.: J. P. Bell, 1929.

Cornelius, Janet Duitsman. *Slave Missions and the Black Church in the Antebellum South.* Columbia: University of South Carolina Press, 1999.

Cornelius, Roberta D. *The History of Randolph-Macon Woman's College from the Founding in 1891 through the Year of 1949–1950.* Chapel Hill: University of North Carolina Press, 1951.

Coulter, E. Merton. *College Life in the Old South.* Athens: University of Georgia Press, 1928.

Creese, Mary R. S. *Ladies in the Laboratory: American and British Women in Science, 1800–1900.* Lanham, Md.: Scarecrow Press, 1998.

Crimmins, Timothy James. "The Crystal Stair: A Study of the Effects of Class, Race, and Ethnicity on Secondary Education in Atlanta, 1872–1925." PhD diss., Emory University, 1972.

Cromwell, John W. "The Aftermath of Nat Turner's Insurrection." *Journal of Negro History* 5 (April 1920): 208–34.

Curtis, Christopher M. "Reconsidering Suffrage Reform in the 1829–1830 Virginia Constitutional Convention." *Journal of Southern History* 74 (February 2008): 89–124.

Curtis, Susan. *A Consuming Faith: The Social Gospel and Modern American Culture.* 1991. Rpt. Columbia: University of Missouri Press, 2001.

Dabney, Charles William. *Universal Education in the South.* Chapel Hill: University of North Carolina Press, 1936.

Dailey, Jane. *Before Jim Crow: The Politics of Race in Postemancipation Virginia.* Chapel Hill: University of North Carolina Press, 2000.

———. "Deference and Violence in the Postbellum Urban South: Manners and Massacres in Danville, Virginia." *Journal of Southern History* 63 (August 1997): 553–90.

Davidson, Emily S., and Ludy T. Benjamin Jr. "A History of the Child Study Movement in America." In *Historical Foundations of Educational Psychology,* ed. John A. Glover and Royce R. Ronning, 41–60. New York: Plenum Press, 1987.

Davis, William C., and James I. Robertson Jr., eds. *Virginia at War: 1861.* Lexington: University Press of Kentucky, 2003.

Deegan, Mary Jo. *Annie Marion MacLean and the Chicago Schools of Sociology, 1894–1934.* New Brunswick, N.J.: Transaction Publishers, 2014.

———. *Jane Addams and the Men of the Chicago School, 1892–1918.* New Brunswick, N.J.: Transaction Publishers, 1988.

———, Michael R. Hill, and Susan L. Wortmann. "Annie Marion MacLean, Feminist Pragmatist and Methodologist." *Journal of Contemporary Ethnography* 38 (December 2009): 655–65.

Degler, Carl N. *In Search of Human Nature: The Decline and Revival of Darwinism in American Social Thought.* New York: Oxford University Press, 1991.

DeMoss, Dorothy D. "'A Fearless Stand': The Southern Association of College Women, 1903–1921." *Southern Studies* 26 (Winter 1987): 249–60.

Dennis, Michael. *Lessons in Progress: State Universities and Progressivism in the New South, 1880–1920.* Urbana: University of Illinois Press, 2001.

Dittmer, John. *Black Georgia in the Progressive Era, 1900–1920.* 1977. Urbana: University of Illinois Press, 1980.

Driskell, Jay Winston. *Schooling Jim Crow: The Fight for Atlanta's Booker T. Washington High School and the Roots of Black Protest Politics.* Charlottesville: University Press of Virginia, 2014.

Dorr, Gregory Michael. *Segregation's Science: Eugenics and Society in Virginia.* Charlottesville: University Press of Virginia, 2008.

Dyer, Thomas G. *The University of Georgia: A Bicentennial History, 1785–1985.* Athens: University of Georgia Press, 1985.

Dzuback, Mary Ann. "Gender and the Politics of Knowledge." *History of Education Quarterly* 43 (Summer 2003): 171–95.

Eaton, Clement. *The Mind of the South*. Baton Rouge: Louisiana State University Press, 1967, revised edition.

Ecke, Melvin W. *From Ivy Street to Kennedy Center: Centennial History of the Atlanta Public Schools*. Atlanta: Atlanta Board of Education, 1972.

Edwards, Wendy J. Deichmann and Carolyn De Swarte Gifford. "Restoring Women and Reclaiming Gender in Social Gospel Studies." In *Gender and the Social Gospel*, ed. Wendy J. Deichmann Edwards and Carolyn De Swarte Gifford, 1–17. Urbana: University of Illinois Press, 2003.

Egerton, Douglas R. "To the Tombs of the Capulets: Charles Fenton Mercer and Public Education in Virginia, 1816–1817." *Virginia Magazine of History and Biography* 93 (April 1985): 155–74.

Eschbach, Elizabeth Seymour. *The Higher Education of Women in England and America, 1865–1920*. New York: Garland, 1993.

Fairclough, Adam. *A Class of Their Own: Black Teachers in the Segregated South*. Cambridge, Mass.: Belknap Press, 2007.

Farnham, Christie Anne. *The Education of the Southern Belle: Higher Education and Student Socialization in the Antebellum South*. New York: New York University Press, 1994.

Faust, Drew Gilpin. *Mothers of Invention: Women of the Slaveholding South in the American Civil War*. Chapel Hill: University of North Carolina Press, 1996.

———. *A Sacred Circle: The Dilemma of the Intellectual in the Old South, 1840–1860*. Philadelphia: University of Philadelphia Press, 1977.

Feimster, Crystal N. *Southern Horrors: Women and the Politics of Race and Lynching*. Cambridge, Mass.: Harvard University Press, 2009.

Feuer, Louis S. "America's First Jewish Professor: James Joseph Sylvester at the University of Virginia." *American Jewish Archives* 36 (November 1984): 152–201.

Fitzpatrick, Ellen. *Endless Crusade: Women Social Scientists and Progressive Reform*. New York: Oxford University Press, 1990.

———. "For the 'Women of the University': Marion Talbot, 1858–1948." In *Lone Voyagers: Academic Women in Coeducational Universities, 1870–1937*, ed. Gerldine Jonçich Clifford, 87–97. New York: Feminist Press of City University of New York, 1989.

Flanagan, Maureen. "Gender and Urban Political Reform: The City Club and the Woman's City Club of Chicago in the Progressive Era." *American Historical Review* 95 (October 1990): 1032–50.

Flynt, Wayne. *Alabama Baptists: Southern Baptists in the Heart of Dixie*. Tuscaloosa: University of Alabama Press, 1998.

———. "Southern Methodists and Social Reform, 1900–1940." *International Social Science Review* 74 (1999): 104–14.

Fox, E. L. "Dr. W. H. Ruffner." *John P. Branch Historical Papers of Randolph Macon College* 3 (June 1910): 143–44.

Fox-Genovese, Elizabeth. *Within the Plantation Household: Black and White Women of the Old South*. Chapel Hill: University of North Carolina Press, 1988.

Franklin, Barry M. "Progressivism and Curricular Differentiation: Special Classes in the Atlanta Public Schools, 1898–1923." *History of Education Quarterly* 29 (Winter 1989): 571–93.

Franklin, John Hope. *The Militant South, 1800–1861*. Cambridge, Mass.: Belknap Press, 1956.

Freehling, Alison Goodyear. *Drift Toward Dissolution: The Virginia Slavery Debate of 1831–1832*. Baton Rouge: Louisiana State University Press, 1982.

Freehling, William W. *The Road to Disunion: Secessionists at Bay, 1776–1854*. New York: Oxford University Press, 1990.

Friedlander, Amy. "A More Perfect Christian Womanhood: Higher Learning for a New South." In *Education and the Rise of the New South*, ed. Goodenow and White, 72–91.

Friend, Craig Thompson. "Belles, Benefactors, and the Blacksmith's Son: Cyrus Stuart and the Enigma of Southern Gentlemanliness." In *Southern Manhood: Perspectives on Masculinity in the Old South*, eds. Craig Thompson Friend and Lorri Glover, 92–112. Athens: University of Georgia Press, 2004.

Freedman, Estelle. *Redefining Rape*. Cambridge, Mass.: Harvard University Press, 2013.

Freeman, Anne Hobson. "Mary Munford's Fight for a College for Women Co-ordinate with the University of Virginia." *Virginia Magazine of History and Biography* 78 (October 1970): 481–91.

Furumoto, Laurel, and Elizabeth Scarborough. "Placing Women in the History of Psychology: The First American Women Psychologists." *American Psychologist* 41 (January 1986): 35–42.

Gifford, Carolyn De Swarte. "'The Woman's Cause is Man's': Frances Willard and the Social Gospel." In *Gender and the Social Gospel*, ed. Wendy J. Deichmann Edwards and Carolyn De Swarte Gifford, 21–34. Urbana: University of Illinois Press, 2003.

Gilmore, Glenda. *Gender and Jim Crow: Women and the Politics of White Supremacy in North Carolina, 1896–1920*. Chapel Hill: University of North Carolina Press, 1996.

Glatthaar, Joseph T. "Confederate Soldiers." In *Virginia at War: 1861*, ed. Davis and Robertson, 50–51.

Glazer, Penina Migdal, and Miriam Slater. *Unequal Colleagues: The Entrance of Women into the Professions, 1890–1940*. New Brunswick, N.J.: Rutgers University Press, 1987.

Godshalk, David Fort. *Veiled Visions: The Atlanta Race Riot and the Reshaping of American Race Relations*. Chapel Hill: University of North Carolina Press, 2005.

Goodenow, Ronald K., and Arthur O. White, eds. *Education and the Rise of the New South*. Boston: G. K. Hall, 1981.

Gordon, Lynn D. *Gender and Higher Education in the Progressive Era*. New Haven, Conn.: Yale University Press, 1990.

Graham, Patricia Albjerg. "Expansion and Exclusion: A History of Women in American Higher Education." *Signs* 3 (Summer 1978): 759–73.

Grant, Susan-Mary C. "Representative Mann: Horace Mann, the Republican Experiment and the South." *Journal of American Studies* 32 (April 1998): 105–23.

Grantham, Dewey W., Jr. *Hoke Smith and the Politics of the New South.* Baton Rouge: Louisiana State University Press, 1958.

Green, Christopher D. "Scientific Objectivity and E. B. Titchener's Experimental Psychology." *Isis* 101 (December 2010): 697–721.

Green, Elna C. *Southern Strategies: Southern Women and the Woman Suffrage Question.* Chapel Hill: University of North Carolina Press, 1997.

Green, Hilary. *Educational Reconstruction: African American Schools in the Urban South, 1865–1890.* New York: Fordham University Press, 2016.

Gutman, Herbert G. "Schools for Freedmen: The Post-Emancipation Origins of Afro-American Education." In *Power and Culture: Essays on the American Working Class,* ed. Ira Berlin, 260–77. New York: Pantheon, 1987.

Hall, Jacqueline Dowd. *Revolt Against Chivalry: Jesse Daniel Ames and the Women's Campaign Against Lynching.* New York: Columbia University Press, 1979.

Harlan, Louis R. *Separate and Unequal: Public School Campaigns and Racism in the Southern Seaboard States, 1901–1915.* 1958. Rpt. New York: Atheneum, 1969.

Hayes, Jack Irby, Jr. *The Lamp and the Cross: The History of Averett College.* Macon, Ga.: Mercer University Press, 2004.

Heffron, John M. "'To Form a More Perfect Union': The Moral Example of Southern Baptist Thought and Education, 1890–1920." *Religion and American Culture: A Journal of Interpretation* 8 (Summer 1998): 179–204.

Herbst, Jurgen. *And Sadly Teach: Teacher Education and the Professionalization of American Culture.* Madison: University of Wisconsin Press, 1989.

———. "Nineteenth-Century Normal Schools in the United States: A Fresh Look." *History of Education* 9 (July 2006): 219–27.

Hickin, Patricia. "Gentle Agitator: Samuel M. Janney and the Anti-Slavery Movement in Virginia, 1842–1851." *Journal of Southern History* 37 (May 1971): 159–190.

Higginbotham, Evelyn Brooks. *Righteous Discontent: The Women's Movement in the Black Baptist Church, 1880–1920.* Cambridge, Mass.: Harvard University Press, 1993.

Hill, Samuel S., Jr. "The South's Two Cultures." In *Religion and the Solid South,* ed. Samuel S. Hill Jr., with Edgar T. Thompson, Anne Firor Scott, Charles Hudson, and Edwin S. Gaustad, 36–49. New York: Abingdon Press, 1972.

Hoffschwelle, Mary S. "A Woman 'in Orthority': Claiming Professional Status in Jim Crow Alabama." *Journal of Southern History* 81 (November 2015): 843–86.

Hoganson, Kristin L. *Fighting for American Manhood: How Gender Politics Provoked the Spanish-American and Philippine-American Wars.* New Haven, Conn.: Yale University Press, 1998.

Holland, Lorraine Eva. "Rise and Fall of the Ante-Bellum Virginia Aristocracy: A Generational Analysis." PhD diss., University of California-Irvine, 1980.

Holmes, William F. "The Georgia Alliance Legislature." *Georgia Historical Quarterly* 68 (Winter 1984): 479–515.

Hucles, Michael. "Many Voices, Similar Concerns: Traditional Methods of African-American Political Activity in Norfolk, Virginia, 1865–1875." *Virginia Magazine of History and Biography* 100 (October 1992): 543–66.

Hume, Richard L. "The Membership of the Virginia Constitutional Convention of 1867–1868: A Study of the Beginnings of Congressional Reconstruction in the Upper South." *Virginia Magazine of History and Biography* 86 (October 1978): 461–84.

Hunt, Thomas C. "Henry Ruffner and the Struggle for Public Schools in Antebellum Virginia." *American Presbyterians* 64 (Spring 1986): 18–26.

Hyde, Sarah L. *Schooling in the Antebellum South: The Rise of Public and Private Education in Louisiana, Mississippi, and Alabama.* Baton Rouge: Louisiana State University Press, 2016.

Jacobson, Matthew Frye. *Barbarian Virtues: The United States Encounters Foreign Peoples at Home and Abroad, 1876–1917.* New York: Hill and Wang, 2000.

Johanningmeier, Erwin V. "William Chandler Bagley's Changing Views on the Relationship between Psychology and Education." *History of Education Quarterly* 9 (Spring 1969): 3–27.

Johnson, Donald. "W. E. B. DuBois, Thomas Jesse Jones, and the Struggle for Social Education, 1900–1930." *Journal of Negro History* 85 (Summer 2000): 71–95.

Johnson, Joan Marie. *Southern Women at the Seven Sister Colleges: Feminist Values and Social Activism, 1875–1915.* Athens: University of Georgia Press, 2008.

Johnson, Shaun. "The Woman Peril and Male Teachers in the Early Twentieth Century." *American Educational History Journal* 35 (2008): 149–67.

Jones, Catherine A. *Intimate Reconstructions: Children in Postemancipation Virginia.* Charlottesville: University of Virginia Press, 2015.

Jones, Lance G. E. *The Jeanes Teacher in the United States, 1908–1933.* Chapel Hill: University of North Carolina Press, 1937.

Kantrowitz, Steven. *Ben Tillman and the Reconstruction of White Supremacy.* Chapel Hill: University of North Carolina Press, 2000.

Keppel, Ann M. "The Myth of Agrarianism in Rural Educational Reform, 1890–1914." *History of Education Quarterly* 2 (June 1962): 100–112.

Kern, Kathi L. "Gray Matters: Brains, Identities, and Natural Rights." In *The Social and Political Body,* ed. Theodore R. Schatski and Wolfgang Natter, 103–21. New York: Guilford Press, 1996.

Kierner, Cynthia A. *Beyond the Household: Women's Place in the Early South, 1700–1835.* Ithaca, N.Y.: Cornell University Press, 1998.

Kilman, Gail Apperson. "Southern Collegiate Women: Higher Education at Wesleyan Female College and Randolph-Macon Woman's College, 1893–1907." PhD diss., University of Delaware, 1984.

Kimmel, Ellen. "Contributions to the History of Psychology: XXIV. Role of Women Psychologists in the History of Psychology in the South." *Psychological Reports* 38 (1976): 611–18.

Kirwan, Albert D. *Revolt of the Rednecks: Mississippi Politics, 1876–1925.* 1951. Rpt. Gloucester, Mass.: Peter Smith, 1964.

Korobkin, Russell. "The Politics of Disfranchisement in Georgia." *Georgia Historical Quarterly* 74 (Spring 1990): 20–58.

Kousser, J. Morgan. "Progressivism—for Middle-Class Whites Only: North Carolina Education, 1880–1910." *Journal of Southern History* 46 (May 1980): 189–94.

Knecht, Andra Mari. "The Tallulah Falls School: Female Reform and Rural Education in the New South." PhD diss., Mississippi State University, 2005.

Knight, Edgar W. *Public Education in the South.* Boston: Ginn and Co., 1922.

Knight, J. Stephen, Jr. "Discontent, Disunity, and Dissent in the Antebellum South: Virginia as a Test Case, 1844–1846." *Virginia Magazine of History and Biography* 81 (October 1973): 437–456.

Ladd-Taylor, Molly. *Mother-Work: Women, Child Welfare, and the State, 1890–1930.* Urbana: University of Illinois Press, 1994.

Leloudis, James L. *Schooling the New South: Pedagogy, Self, and Society in North Carolina, 1880–1920.* Chapel Hill: University of North Carolina Press, 1996.

Leonard, Bill T. *Baptists in America.* New York: Columbia University Press, 2005.

Leonard, John W., ed. *Woman's Who's Who of America.* 1914. Rpt. Detroit: Gale Research Co., 1976.

Levin, Miriam R. *Defining Women's Scientific Enterprise: Mount Holyoke Faculty and the Rise of American Science.* Hanover, N.H.: University Press of New England, 2005.

Link, William A. *A Hard Country and a Lonely Place: Schooling, Society, and Reform in Rural Virginia, 1870–1920.* Chapel Hill: University of North Carolina Press, 1986.

Lowe, Richard. *Republicans and Reconstruction in Virginia, 1856–1870.* Charlottesville: University Press of Virginia, 1991.

Luker, Ralph E. *The Social Gospel in Black and White: American Racial Reform, 1885–1912.* Chapel Hill: University of North Carolina Press, 1991.

Martin, Jay. *The Education of John Dewey.* New York: Columbia University Press, 2002.

Mather, Juliette. *Light Three Candles: History of Woman's Missionary Union of Virginia, 1874–1973.* Richmond: Woman's Missionary Union of Virginia, Baptist General Association of Virginia, 1972.

Mathew, William M. *Edmund Ruffin and the Crisis of Slavery in the Old South: The Failure of Agricultural Reform.* Athens: University of Georgia Press, 1988.

Mathews, Donald G. *Religion in the Old South.* Chicago: University of Chicago Press, 1977.

Mathews, Mary Beth. "'To Educate, Agitate, and Legislate': Baptists, Methodists, and the Anti-Saloon League of Virginia, 1901–1910." *Virginia Magazine of History and Biography* 17 (2009): 250–87.

Mathis, Mary Kathryn. "Walter Barnard Hill: Constructive Southern American." MA thesis, Georgia Southern College, 1969.

Mathis, Ray. "Walter B. Hill and the Savage Ideal." *Georgia Historical Quarterly* 60 (Spring 1976): 23–24.

Maxcy, Spencer J. "Progressivism and Rural Education in the Deep South, 1900–1950." In *Education and the Rise of the New South*, ed. Goodenow and White, 47–71.

McCandless, Amy Thompson. "Maintaining the Spirit and Tone of Robust Manliness: The Battle Against Coeducation at Southern Colleges and Universities, 1890–1940." *NWSA Journal* 2 (Spring 1990): 199–216.

———.*The Past in the Present: Women's Higher Education in the Twentieth-Century South.* Tuscaloosa: University of Alabama Press, 1999.

McClurken, Jeffrey W. *Taking Care of the Living: Reconstructing Confederate Veteran Families in Virginia.* Charlottesville: University Press of Virginia, 2009.

McDaniel, Ralph Clipman. *The Virginia Constitutional Convention of 1901–1902.* Baltimore: Johns Hopkins University Press, 1928.

McDowell, John Patrick. *The Social Gospel in the South: The Women's Home Mission Movement in the Methodist Episcopal Church, South, 1886–1939.* Baton Rouge: Louisiana State University Press, 1982.

McFall, F. Lawrence, Jr. *Danville in the Civil War.* Lynchburg, Va.: H. E. Howard, 2001.

McKee, James B. *Sociology and the Race Problem: The Failure of a Perspective.* Urbana: University of Illinois Press, 1993.

McMath, Robert C., Jr., Ronald H. Bayor, James E. Brittain, Lawrence Foster, August W. Giebelhaus, and Germaine M. Reed. *Engineering the New South: Georgia Tech, 1885–1985.* Athens: University of Georgia Press, 1985.

Mitchell, Norma Taylor. "The Political Career of Governor David Campbell of Virginia." PhD diss., Duke University, 1967.

Moger, Allen W. *Virginia, Bourbonism to Byrd, 1870–1925.* Charlottesville: University Press of Virginia, 1968.

Moldow, Gloria. *Women Doctors in Gilded-Age Washington: Race, Gender, and Professionalization.* Urbana: University of Illinois Press, 1987.

Montgomery, Rebecca S. *The Politics of Education in the New South: Women and Reform in Georgia, 1890–1930.* Baton Rouge: Louisiana State University Press, 2006.

Moore, James T. "Black Militancy in Readjuster Virginia, 1879–1883." *Journal of Southern History* 41 (May 1975): 167–86.

———. *Two Paths to the New South: The Virginia Debt Controversy, 1870–1883.* 1974. Rpt. Lexington: University Press of Kentucky, 2014.

———. "The University and the Readjusters." *Virginia Magazine of History and Biography* 78 (January 1970): 87–101.

Morehouse, Betty Parrish. "'Georgia's Greatest Woman' Buried at Clayton." *Clayton (Ga.) Tribune*, September 6, 1990.

Morgan, Lynda J. *Emancipation in Virginia's Tobacco Belt, 1850–1870.* Athens: University of Georgia Press, 1992.

Moss, Hilary J. *Schooling Citizens: The Struggle for African American Education in Antebellum America.* Chicago: University of Chicago Press, 2009.

Murray, Frank S., and Frederick B. Rowe. "A Note on the Titchener Influence on the First Psychology Laboratory in the South." *Journal of the History of the Behavioral Sciences* 15 (July 1979): 282–84.

———. "Psychology Laboratories in the United States Prior to 1900." *Teaching of Psychology* 6 (February 1979): 19–21.

Nasaw, David. *Schooled to Order: A Social History of Schooling in the United States.* New York: Oxford University Press, 1979.

Neverdon-Morton, Cynthia. *Afro-American Women of the South and the Advancement of the Race, 1895–1925.* Knoxville: University of Tennessee Press, 1989.

Noble, Jeanne L. *The Negro Woman's College Education.* New York: Columbia University Teachers College Press, 1950.

O'Brien, John Thomas, Jr. "From Bondage to Citizenship: The Richmond Black Community, 1865–1867." PhD diss., University of Rochester, 1975.

Ogren, Christine A. *The American State Normal School: "An Instrument of Great Good."* New York: Palgrave Macmillan, 2005.

———. "'A Large Measure of Self-Control and Personal Power': Women Students at State Normal Schools During the Late-Nineteenth and Early-Twentieth Centuries." *Women's Studies Quarterly* 28 (Winter 2000): 211–32.

Olney, Steve. *And the Dead Shall Rise: The Murder of Mary Phagan and the Lynching of Leo Frank.* New York: Vintage Books, 2003.

O'Shea, Geoffrey, and Theodore R. Bashore, Jr. "The Vital Role of *The American Journal of Psychology* in the Early and Continuing History of Mental Chronometry." *American Journal of Psychology* 125 (Winter 2012): 435–48.

Ott, Victoria E. *Confederate Daughters: Coming of Age During the Civil War.* Carbondale: Southern Illinois University Press, 2008.

Outlaw, Mary Elizabeth. "State Normal School to State Teachers College: The Transition of an Institution." EdD diss., University of Georgia, 1990.

Pace, Robert F. *Halls of Honor: College Men in the Old South.* Baton Rouge: Louisiana State University Press, 2004.

———, and Christopher A. Bjornsen. "Adolescent Honor and College Student Behavior in the Old South." *Southern Cultures* 6 (Fall 2000): 9–28.

Palmieri, Patricia Ann. *In Adamless Eden: The Community of Women Faculty at Wellesley.* New Haven, Conn.: Yale University Press, 1995.

Peak, Helen. "The Parrish Laboratories of Psychology at Randolph-Macon Woman's College." *Journal of Experimental Psychology* 24 (May 1939): 551–53.

Pearson, Charles Chilton. *The Readjuster Movement in Virginia.* Gloucester, Mass.: Peter Smith, 1969.

Perkins, Linda. "The Impact of the 'Cult of True Womanhood' on the Education of Black Women." *Journal of Social Issues* 39 (October 1983): 17–28.

Perman, Michael. *Struggle for Mastery: Disfranchisement in the South, 1888–1908.* Chapel Hill: University of North Carolina Press, 2001.

Powell, Nellie Virginia. "Our Master Builders." Randolph-Macon Woman's College *Alumnae Bulletin* 36 (September 1943): 20–21.

Proctor, Robert W., and Rand Evans. "E. B. Titchener, Women Psychologists, and the Experimentalists." *American Journal of Psychology* 127 (Winter 2014): 501–26.

Pulley, Raymond H. *Old Virginia Restored: An Interpretation of the Progressive Impulse, 1870–1930.* Charlottesville: University Press of Virginia, 1968.

Rachleff, Peter J. *Black Labor in Richmond, 1865–1890.* Urbana: University of Illinois Press, 1989.

Riehm, Ethel Holbrook. "Dorothy Tilly and the Fellowship of the Concerned." In *Throwing Off the Cloak of Privilege: White Southern Women Activists in the Civil Rights Era,* ed. Gail S. Murray, 23–38. Gainesville: University Press of Florida, 2004.

Robertson, James I., Jr. "Danville Under Military Occupation, 1865." *Virginia Magazine of History and Biography* 75 (July 1967): 331–48.

———. "Houses of Horror: Danville's Civil War Prisons." *Virginia Magazine of History and Biography* 69 (July 1961): 329–45.

———. "The Virginia State Convention of 1861." In *Virginia at War: 1861,* ed. Davis and Robertson, 1–25.

Rosenberg, Rosalind. *Beyond Separate Spheres: Intellectual Roots of Modern Feminism.* New Haven, Conn.: Yale University Press, 1982.

———. "The Limits of Access: The History of Coeducation in America." In *Women and Higher Education in American History,* ed. John Mack Faragher and Florence Howe, 107–29. New York: W. W. Norton, 1988.

Ross, Dorothy. *G. Stanley Hall: The Psychologist as Prophet.* Chicago: University of Chicago Press, 1972.

Rossiter, Margaret W. *Women Scientists in America: Struggles and Strategies to 1940.* Baltimore: Johns Hopkins University Press, 1982.

Rothman, Joshua D. *Notorious in the Neighborhood: Sex and Families Across the Color Line in Virginia, 1787–1861.* Chapel Hill: University of North Carolina Press, 2003.

Rury, John L. *Education and Women's Work: Female Schooling and the Division of Labor in Urban America, 1870–1930.* Albany: State University of New York Press, 1991.

Russell, John Henderson. *The Free Negro in Virginia, 1619–1865.* Baltimore: Johns Hopkins University Press, 1913.

Savage, Daniel M. *John Dewey's Liberalism: Individual, Community, and Self-Development.* Carbondale: Southern Illinois University Press, 2002.

Scarborough, William Kauffman. *Masters of the Big House: Elite Slaveholders of the Mid-Nineteenth Century.* Baton Rouge: Louisiana State University Press, 2003.

Schechter, Patricia A. *Ida B. Wells-Barnett and American Reform, 1880–1930*. Chapel Hill: University of North Carolina Press, 2001.

Schweninger, Loren. "The Underside of Slavery: The Internal Economy, Self-Hire, and Quasi-Freedom in Virginia, 1780–1865." *Slavery and Abolition: A Journal of Comparative Studies* 12 (September 1991): 1–22.

Scott, Anne Firor. *The Southern Lady: From Pedestal to Politics, 1830–1930*. Chicago: University of Chicago Press, 1970.

———. "Women, Religion, and Social Change in the South, 1830–1930." In *Religion and the Solid South*, ed. Samuel S. Hill Jr., with Edgar T. Thompson, Anne Firor Scott, Charles Hudson, and Edwin S. Gaustad, 92–121. New York: Abingdon Press, 1972.

Seigfried, Charlene Haddock. *Pragmatism and Feminism: Reweaving the Social Fabric*. Chicago: University of Chicago Press, 1996.

Seller, Maxine. "G. Stanley Hall and Edward Thorndike on the Education of Women: Theory and Policy in the Progressive Era." *Educational Studies* 11 (1981): 365–74.

Shade, William G. *Democratizing the Old Dominion: Virginia and the Second Party System, 1824–1861*. Charlottesville: University Press of Virginia, 1996.

Shaw, Barton C. *The Wool-Hat Boys: Georgia's Populist Party*. Baton Rouge: Louisiana State University Press, 1984.

Sheffer, Marguerite B. *Memorabilia of the Athens Woman's Club*. Athens, Ga.: Athens Woman's Club, 1982.

Siegel, Frederick F. *The Roots of Southern Distinctiveness: Tobacco and Society in Danville, Virginia, 1780–1865*. Chapel Hill: University of North Carolina Press, 1987.

Sims, Anastasia. *The Power of Femininity in the New South: Women's Organizations and Politics in North Carolina, 1880–1930*. Columbia: University of South Carolina Press, 1997.

Singal, Daniel Joseph. *The War Within: From Victorian to Modernist Thought in the South, 1919–1945*. Chapel Hill: University of North Carolina Press, 2014.

Smith-Rosenberg, Carroll. *Disorderly Conduct: Visions of Gender in Victorian America*. New York: A. A. Knopf, 1985.

Solomon, Barbara Miller. *In the Company of Educated Women: A History of Women and Higher Education in America*. New Haven, Conn.: Yale University Press, 1985.

Sprague, Rosemary. *Longwood College: A History*. Farmville, Va.: Longwood College, 1989.

Stage, Sarah. "Ellen Richards and the Social Significance of the Home Economics Movement." In *Rethinking Home Economics: Women and the History of a Profession*, ed. Sarah Stage and Virginia B. Vincenti, 17–33. Ithaca, N.Y.: Cornell University Press, 1997.

Stamp, Kenneth M. "The Southern Refutation of the Proslavery Argument." *North Carolina Historical Review* 21 (January 1944): 35–45.

Steffes, Tracy L. *School, Society, and State: A New Education to Govern Modern America, 1890–1940*. Chicago: University of Chicago Press, 2012.

Stephan, Scott. *Evangelical Women and Domestic Devotion in the Antebellum South.* Athens: University of Georgia Press, 2008.

Stevenson, Brenda E. *Life in Black and White: Family and Community in the Slave South.* New York: Oxford University Press, 1996.

Stewart, Abigail J., and Andrea L. Dottolo. "Feminist Psychology." *Signs* 31 (Winter 2006): 493–509.

Storr, Richard J. *Harper's University: The Beginnings.* Chicago: University of Chicago Press, 1966.

Stowe, Steven M. *Intimacy and Power in the Old South: Ritual in the Lives of Planters.* Baltimore: Johns Hopkins University Press, 1987.

Strout, Shirley Kreason. *The History of Zeta Tau Alpha, 1898–1948.* Menasha, Wis.: Collegiate Press, for the Fraternity, 1956.

Taylor, Alrutheus Ambush. *The Negro in the Reconstruction of Virginia.* 1926. Rpt. New York: Russell & Russell, 1969.

Thomas, Mary Martha. *The New Woman in Alabama: Social Reforms and Suffrage, 1890–1920.* Tuscaloosa: University of Alabama Press, 1992.

Tilley, Nannie May. *The Bright-Tobacco Industry, 1860–1929.* 1948. Rpt. New York: Arno Press, 1972.

Townsend, Sara Bertha. "The Admission of Women to the University of Georgia." *Georgia Historical Quarterly* 43 (June 1959): 156–69.

Turner, Elizabeth Hayes. *Women, Culture, and Community: Religion and Reform in Galveston, 1880–1920.* New York: Oxford University Press, 1997.

Tyack, David. *The One Best System: A History of American Urban Education.* Cambridge, Mass.: Harvard University Press, 1974.

———, and Elisabeth Hansot. *Learning Together: A History of Coeducation in American Public Schools.* New Haven, Conn.: Yale University Press, 1990.

Urban, Wayne J. "Educational Reform in a New South City: Atlanta, 1890–1925." In *Education and the Rise of the New South,* ed. Goodenow and White, 114–30.

———. "Progressive Education in the Urban South: The Reform of the Atlanta Schools, 1914–1918." In *The Age of Urban Reform: New Perspectives on the Progressive Era,* ed. Michael H. Ebner and Eugene M. Tobin, 131–41. Port Washington, N.Y.: Kennikat Press, 1977.

Varon, Elizabeth R. "Tippecanoe and the Ladies, Too: White Women and Party Politics in Antebellum Virginia." *Journal of American History* 82 (September 1995): 494–521.

Vaughn, William Preston. *Schools for All: The Blacks and Public Education in the South, 1865–1877.* Lexington: University Press of Kentucky, 1974.

Vejnar, Robert J., II. "A Battle to Preserve Republican Government: Antebellum Virginia's Struggle Over Public Education." MA thesis, James Madison University, 1992.

Von Daacke, Kirt. *Freedom Has a Face: Race, Identity, and Community in Jefferson's Virginia.* Charlottesville: University Press of Virginia, 2012.

Wagoner, Jennings L., Jr. "Honor and Dishonor at Mr. Jefferson's University: The Ante-bellum Years." *History of Education Quarterly* 26 (Summer 1986): 155–79.

———. *Jefferson and Education.* With preface by William G. Bowen. Monticello, Va.: Thomas Jefferson Foundation, 2004.

Wall, Charles Coleman, Jr. "Students and Student Life at the University of Virginia, 1825–1861." PhD diss., University of Virginia, 1978.

Warnock, Henry Y. "Andrew Sledd, Southern Methodists, and the Negro: A Case History." *Journal of Southern History* 31 (August 1965): 251–71.

Watkins, William H. *The White Architects of Black Education: Ideology and Power in America, 1865–1954.* New York: Teachers College Press, 2001.

Wenger, Mark R. "Thomas Jefferson, the College of William and Mary, and the University of Virginia." *Virginia Magazine of History and Biography* 103 (July 1995): 339–374.

Westbrook, Robert B. *John Dewey and American Democracy.* Ithaca, N.Y.: Cornell University Press, 1991.

———. "Schools for Industrial Democrats: The Social Origins of John Dewey's Philosophy of Education." *American Journal of Education* 100 (August 1992): 401–19.

Wheeler, Marjorie Spruill. *New Women of the New South: The Leaders of the Woman Suffrage Movement in the Southern States.* New York: Oxford University Press, 1993.

White, Ronald C., Jr., and C. Howard Hopkins. *The Social Gospel: Religion and Reform in Changing America.* Philadelphia: Temple University Press, 1976.

Whites, LeeAnn. "The DeGraffenreid Controversy: Race, Class, and Gender in the New South." *Journal of Southern History* 54 (August 1988): 449–78.

———. "Rebecca Latimer Felton and the Problem of Protection." In *Visible Women: New Essays on American Activism,* ed. Nancy Hewitt and Suzanne Lebsock, 41–61. Urbana: University of Illinois Press, 1993.

———. "Rebecca Latimer Felton and the Wife's Farm: The Class and Racial Politics of Gender Reform." *Georgia Historical Quarterly* 76 (Summer 1992): 354–72.

Whitney, Mary E. *Women and the University.* Charlottesville: University of Virginia, 1969.

Whitt, R. Michael. "'Free Indeed!': Trials and Triumphs of Enslaved and Freedmen in Antebellum Virginia." *Virginia Baptist Register* 50 (2011).

Williams, Heather Andrea. *Self-Taught: African American Education in Slavery and Freedom.* Chapel Hill: University of North Carolina Press, 2005.

Williamson, Joel. *The Crucible of Race: Black-White Relations in the American South Since Emancipation.* New York: Oxford University Press, 1984.

Wilkinson, Sue, et al. "*Feminism & Psychology:* From Critique to Reconstruction." *Feminism & Psychology* 1 (1991): 5–18.

Woodson, Carter G. *The Mis-Education of the Negro.* 1933. Rpt. Mineola, New York: Dover, 2005.

Woodward, C. Vann. *Tom Watson, Agrarian Rebel.* New York: Rinehart & Co., 1938.

Woody, Thomas. *A History of Women's Education in the United States.* New York: Science Press, 1929. Vol. 2.

Wyatt-Brown, Bertram. *Southern Honor: Ethics and Behavior in the Old South.* New York: Oxford University Press, 1982.

Zahniser, J. D., and Amelia R. Fry. *Alice Paul: Claiming Power.* New York: Oxford University Press, 2014.

Zeigler, May. "Growth and Development of Psychology at the University of Georgia." *Journal of Genetic Psychology* 75 (1949): 51–59.

INDEX